GREEK WARFARE BEYOND THE POLIS

GREEK WARFARE BEYOND THE POLIS

DEFENSE, STRATEGY, AND THE MAKING OF ANCIENT FEDERAL STATES

DAVID A. BLOME

CORNELL UNIVERSITY PRESS

Ithaca and London

First published 2020 by Cornell University Press

Library of Congress Cataloging-in-Publication Data

Names: Blome, David A., 1981– author.
Title: Greek warfare beyond the polis : defense, strategy, and the making of ancient federal states / David A. Blome.
Description: First edition. | Ithaca : Cornell University Press, 2020. | Includes bibliographical references and index.
Identifiers: LCCN 2019019459 (print) | LCCN 2019980516 (ebook) | ISBN 9781501747526 (cloth) | ISBN 9781501747618 (epub) | ISBN 9781501747625 (pdf)
Subjects: LCSH: Greece—History, Military—To 146 B.C. | Greece—Politics and government—To 146 B.C. | Military art and science—Greece—History—To 1500. | Politics and war—Greece—History—To 1500. | War and society—Greece—History—To 1500. | Federal government—Greece—History—To 1500.
Classification: LCC DF89 .B65 2020 (print) | LCC DF89 (ebook) | DDC 355.40938—dc23
LC record available at https://lccn.loc.gov/2019019459
LC ebook record available at https://lccn.loc.gov/2019980516

For Athena, Gabriel, and Tora

CONTENTS

Preface: The Iliad *in Iraq*   ix

Introduction   1

1. The Phocian Chalk Raid of the
   Thessalian Camp Circa 490   9

2. The Aetolian Rout of the Athenians
   in 426   29

3. The Defense of Acarnania in 389   50

4. The Defense of Arcadia in 370   73

Conclusion   96

Notes   107
References   135
Index   153

PREFACE: THE *ILIAD* IN IRAQ

At its core, this book is about ancient battle. I wrote it as a combat veteran of modern warfare who learned ancient Greek and earned a PhD in ancient Greek history. The book combines my academic expertise and military experience, but in a peculiar way.

In 2004, I chanced upon the *Iliad* while serving as a US Marine in Iraq. Earlier in the year, a group of us saw Wolfgang Petersen's *Troy*, and someone who really enjoyed the film decided to read the book. He bought the Signet Classics edition, brought it with him to Iraq, but unfortunately did not make it past book 1. The *Iliad* clearly did not live up to his expectations. In contrast, I really did not enjoy the film and at the time had no interest in the *Iliad* itself. But I did know Homer's place in the Western canon, and the back cover to the Signet Classics edition said that the *Iliad* was "The World's Greatest War Novel." So with nothing to lose, and nothing better to do, I started reading.

To be honest, I was not overly impressed, nor were my eyes suddenly opened to the marvels of classical literature. Yet I was struck by the familiarity of certain themes in the text. For instance, early in book 1, I could relate to Achilles when Agamemnon stripped him of his war prize. Frustrated and furious, Achilles said to his commander, in so many words, "I run the risks, you get the rewards, and you still want more from me!" Then there was the work of "Wildfire" Rumor wreaking havoc over the Achaean army in book 2. (Anyone who has spent a day in any sort of military organization knows the power of the rumor mill.) As a young man in love, I could identify with Hector's dilemma between family and fighting in book 6. In fact, I still hear versions of this dilemma in conversations with friends. I also knew the feeling of helplessness at the loss of a dear friend. And much like Achilles at the loss of Patroclus, I felt the very real desire for revenge. I remember thinking that Homer really knew what he was talking about, and I made a note to learn more about him and the ancient Greeks should I ever have a chance.

That chance came in 2005 when I started my undergraduate studies at the University of Pennsylvania. I took introductory courses in ancient history and classical literature and did a lot of reading on my own on ancient warfare. What amazed me the most about the Greeks was that when they decided to go to war, the same people who voted for it actually went and fought it. I have since learned that the Greeks were by no means unique in this respect, but at the time my only point of comparison was the United States Congress.

Thoroughly fascinated, I declared a major in classical studies and spent an immoderate amount of time learning ancient Greek. My experience in the Marine Corps and curiosity about ancient Greek warfare ultimately led to a senior thesis on hunting and warfare in the classical Greek world and an application to the PhD program in history at Cornell University. Fortunately, I had extraordinary advisers as both an undergraduate and graduate student who seemed genuinely excited about what I was bringing to the scholarly table—namely, nearly seven years of operational experience in the US Marine Corps.

Specifically, I was a member and eventual team leader of an amphibious reconnaissance team and spent over three years in the Asia-Pacific region observing, evading, and gathering information on conventional ground forces, mostly in mountainous jungle environments. Long-range jungle patrols, clandestine observation posts, reconnaissance and surveillance, hydrographic surveys—we did it all. I left the region in 2003 as a sergeant and became a member of the 2nd Force Reconnaissance Company, now the 2nd Marine Special Operations Battalion in Camp Lejeune, North Carolina. In July 2004, we deployed to the Northern Babil Province of Iraq, where we spent the next seven months fighting a counterinsurgency, primarily by conducting direct action raids.

Over the years, I accumulated a great deal of knowledge about military operations, and in particular about the vulnerabilities of large fighting units in mountainous terrain. I also gained firsthand knowledge of the challenges of asymmetric warfare, where opposing sides adhere to different sets of fighting conventions and different notions of victory. With this book, I have combined this knowledge with my academic expertise to study a neglected realm of ancient history: warfare in the mountains of classical Greece. Yet at the heart of the book, when the analysis of warfare is most pointed, I do not refer explicitly to my operational experiences. They remain out of sight, like most support structures.

In other words, my knowledge of military operations does not fill in the blanks when the ancient evidence is lacking, nor does my experience of warfare in the twenty-first century give me special access to the intricacies of ancient warfare. Instead, my knowledge and experience provide a framework for thinking, and I use this framework to raise questions about the operational dynamics of ancient warfare. Unconventional tactics, manipulation of terrain, communication, deception, surprise—upland Greeks brought all of these factors together with great success, but how? And if upland Greeks really were skilled mountain fighters, as I am about to argue, what can these capabilities tell us about their way of life? These are questions that no one, to my knowledge, has ever asked about the unconventional military encounters studied in this book.

Make no mistake, this book is written from the perspective of a Marine combat veteran, but it is fundamentally a work of scholarship. It advances a thesis about the significance of warfare in the mountains of classical Greece, and it attempts to do so without anachronistic comparisons between the ancient and modern worlds. These two worlds certainly share a number of similarities. That is part of the reason why the Greeks continue to fascinate modern audiences, including a Marine who chanced upon the *Iliad* while in Iraq.

The basic ideas behind this book originally came to life in a seminar with Barry Strauss. Under his guidance, they matured into a book. I simply do not have the words to express my gratitude for his encouragement and engagement with my work over the years.

I would also like to thank Stanford University for a transformative year of teaching, collaboration, and research as a postdoctoral fellow in the Thinking Matters program during the 2015–2016 academic year. During that time, Lauren Hirshberg read, commented on, and discussed various chapters of the book. I thank her for that, and for being a wonderful friend. Matt Buell made all of the maps, and I cannot thank him enough. I am also appreciative of the countless ways that Jake Nabel and Tim Sorg have improved my thinking and writing.

At Cornell University Press, I thank Mahinder Kingra and Bethany Wasik for the time and energy that they have devoted to my work. I am also grateful for the comments and suggestions of the faculty board, editorial board, and the two anonymous reviewers. I remain indebted to Jeremy McInerney and Éric Rebillard for teaching me the craft of the ancient historian, and I thank Sturt Manning and Robert Travers for encouraging me to think big.

I am immensely fortunate to teach, coach, and mentor at Cristo Rey Philadelphia High School, and I am most grateful for the support of my colleagues, especially Ryan Kelley. Finally, with a heart full of gratitude, I dedicate this book to my children, who are everything to me.

GREEK WARFARE BEYOND THE POLIS

Introduction

> For the most part, I dislike the Scythians, but they did discover the cleverest solution to the most important matter of human affairs: how to prevent anyone who attacks them from escaping, and how to avoid capture unless they want to be found.
>
> —*Herodotus* 4.45

This book examines a peculiar way of war practiced by a peculiar group of Greeks who inhabited the mountainous regions of the classical Greek mainland (map 1). The book explains how, on four occasions, a Greek *ethnos*—a people or nation—collectively repelled a large-scale invasion from the surrounding lowlands. Its central argument is that the upland peoples (*ethnē*) of Phocis, Aetolia, Acarnania, and Arcadia circa 490–362 maintained defensive strategies that enabled wide-scale, sophisticated actions in response to large-scale invasions, and they did so without the direction of a central, federal government.[1]

By focusing on the defensive capabilities of upland Greeks, the book makes a series of interventions in ancient Greek military history and ancient Greek scholarship "beyond the polis." Beyond-the-polis scholarship has done much to expand and refine our understanding of the ancient Greek world, but it has overemphasized the importance of political institutions in emergent federal states and has yet to treat warfare involving ethnē systematically or in depth. In contrast, military historians have scrutinized the sociopolitical roots of warfare in the Greek city-state but have neglected warfare beyond the polis. As a result, the broader significance of warfare vis-à-vis the sociopolitical development of upland polities remains unclear.

By bringing these two schools of thought into dialogue with each other, this book shows that although the more powerful states of the classical Greek

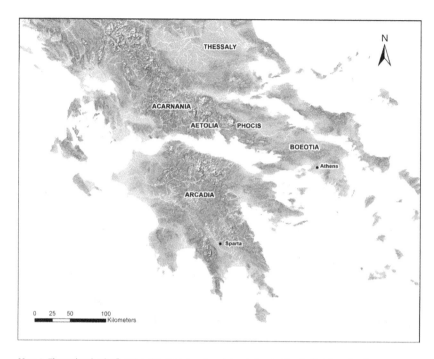

MAP 1. The upland *ethnē* of the classical Greek mainland. Created by D. Matthew Buell.

world were dismissive or ignorant of the military capabilities of upland Greeks, the reverse was not the case. The Phocians, Aetolians, Acarnanians, and Arcadians were well aware of the arrogant attitudes of their aggressive neighbors, and as highly efficient political entities, they exploited these attitudes to great effect.

The Ancient Greeks beyond the Polis

Since the mid-1980s, the classical Greek "third world" has attracted an increasing amount of scholarly interest.[2] At its broadest, third-world or beyond-the-polis scholarship encompasses all Greek polities aside from Athens and Sparta. In a more focused version, such scholarship concentrates on regions where the polis—that is, a self-governing community of citizens—coexisted with or was subsidiary to other forms of political and social organization.[3] Overall, beyond-the-polis scholars take issue with the view that the more advanced polities of the classical period were those such as Athens where a polis prevailed as the defining feature of a given region.[4] Such a view, they argue, implies that the Greeks who relied less on the city-state for social and political organization were somehow less advanced, abnormal, or even backward. Instead of viewing the Greek world through a single sociopolitical lens, these scholars seek to con-textualize the different state-forms that prevailed elsewhere in the Greek world.[5] In this way, the focus of classical Greek history can shift beyond the polis.

And when it shifts, it is usually to one of the geographical ethnē of the mainland, such as Aetolia, Thessaly, Acarnania, Phocis, or Arcadia. In these geographically distinct regions, city-states and other political communities gave shape to even broader forms of social and political organization. Thanks to this broad coherence, these regions can be assessed as sociopolitical units using a range of investigative methods.[6]

For instance, archaeological studies have illustrated the ways that sanctu-aries connected communities across an expansive geographical space.[7] In ad-dition, modern notions of ethnicity have proven to be applicable to the ancient world, especially to ethnē. Such studies have illustrated how more ethnos-oriented Greeks actively constructed ethnic identities through language, ge-nealogy, and material culture that transcended one's identification with a more localized political community.[8] Overall, these studies, among others, have pro-duced two major corrections to views of the Greek world beyond the polis.

First, beyond-the-polis scholars have overturned the Thucydidean view of classical ethnē as atavistic tribal states. According to this ancient view, ethnē consisted of dispersed village settlements and populations that depended on plunder and pastoralism for sustenance, as in "early Greece."[9] In other words, the ethnos was the negative image of the small, self-contained, agriculturally dependent polis.[10]

From a polis-centric perspective, the Greeks of the northern and western mainland were indeed peripheral vis-à-vis the major centers of power during the classical period.[11] But as beyond-the-polis scholars have shown, the Greeks from these peripheral areas had not spurned the life of the developing low-lands or failed to establish a thriving polis culture. On the contrary, they de-veloped different state-forms adapted to different geopolitical environments.[12] Interestingly, in contrast to the city-states of the polis-centric realm, these poli-ties eventually proved to be more adaptable and so were more successful in the shifting political circumstances of the Mediterranean later in the fourth and third centuries.[13]

In addition to overturning the Thucydidean view, beyond-the-polis schol-ars have revealed a great deal of variation between and within individual ethnē. For instance, the Aetolian ethnos was more tribal in its political and social organization.[14] Other ethnos-oriented Greeks formed a network of city-states associated with a specific geographical space, as in Phocis and Boeotia, while the Acarnanians, Achaeans, and Arcadians developed a mix of both. A few ethnē formed dynasties that represented a range of tribal cantons, villages, and city-states, such as Thessaly, Macedonia, and Epirus.[15] Some ethnē also maintained religious affiliations with outside polities through shared sanctuaries and cults. Such affiliations formed a distinct league of states. The most famous example is the Delphic Amphictyony that featured the Phocians so prominently from the late sixth century well into the third.[16] In sum, various state-forms combined in geographical ethnē to produce dynamic polities with their own peculiar features.[17]

Building on these corrective insights, beyond-the-polis scholarship has taken a renewed interest in the origins, development, and internal structure of fourth-century and Hellenistic federal states.[18] These studies have shown that long-standing religious practices and economic interactions dating back to the Archaic period and the fifth century shaped the political trajectories of later federal states. Put another way, Greek federal states were not strictly political phenomena. They encompassed and formalized a wide range of cultural, religious, and economic practices, and their success clearly stemmed from an earlier ethnos era.[19]

But this view suffers from one inherent weakness: it implies, if not states outright, that the formation of a formal federal state marked a key turning point in the sociopolitical development of ethnē and that without formal institutions, wide-scale collective action at the ethnos level would have been inconsistent and unreliable. For example, in Emily Mackil's view, "once the cooperation of multiple states had been achieved by the creation of a single federal state, its preservation and stability were largely determined by its institutions, for these provided the rules and structures according to which authority was distributed among the poleis and the koinon."[20] To date, no study has given serious consideration to ethnos-level statecraft that did not depend on formal institutions or the direction of a standing central government.

Furthermore, the military capabilities of ethnē during the fifth and fourth centuries have received almost no attention, and when they do, it is often in pursuit of different ends.[21] For example, boards of generals, the organization of armies, and military dedications have interested some beyond-the-polis scholars, but only insofar as they provide evidence of federal institutions, land divisions, or social networks within and across individual ethnē, primarily in Thessaly and Boeotia.[22]

Military historians have done little to correct this deficiency. The capabilities of upland ethnē are not featured in any part of Pritchett's five volumes on *The Greek State at War*, for example, to say nothing of the many handbooks and histories of ancient warfare.[23] This neglect is partly because the evidence for such capabilities is scant. Making matters worse, no ancient commentator ever associated developments in the military practices of ethnē with social and political change, as Aristotle did for the classical polis.[24] In addition, upland Greeks were mostly aloof from the major affairs of the rest of the Greek world. Although mercenaries from some upland ethnē took part in the so-called Persian, Peloponnesian, and Corinthian Wars, there was no state-level involvement to speak of.

As a result, ancient writers treated military encounters with upland ethnē as isolated, insignificant incidents, and modern historians of ancient Greek warfare have tended to follow suit. Such historians focus primarily on hoplite warfare and its relationship with the polis during the Archaic and classical periods. They then turn to the reforms of Philip II, the "rise of Macedon," and the nature of military change in the fourth century.[25] With that, the focus of military scholarship shifts from the practices of the polis realm directly to the Macedonians' innovative and brutally efficient methods of waging war. Left out of this narrative is the rest of the Greek world where these practices and methods did not prevail: the mountainous interior of the classical mainland.

Yet if the Greeks from upland ethnē used coins and official discourse to fashion themselves as part of a larger whole connected to a specific geographical space, it would follow that they also made some arrangements for protecting this whole. Jakob Larsen, a key figure in the study of Greek federal states, agreed with this view. He referred to these supposed arrangements as "concerted action on the conduct of war" (or some variation thereof), a capability that he thought must have been directed by a central power.[26] Otherwise, he did not elaborate, and subsequent scholarship has followed suit. As a result, three important questions remain open.

First, how did upland ethnē perceive external threats, and to what extent did they plan for defense? Second, how did these Greeks organize themselves for defense, and how do the defensive capabilities of upland ethnē compare across time and space during the classical period? Finally, how do these capabilities relate to the major insights and advances of beyond-the-polis scholarship?

By attending to these questions, this book will contribute to a more complete understanding of classical upland ethnē; in particular, their internal organization, collective capabilities, and relationship with the major centers of power during the classical period. As a series of defensive actions circa 490–370 shows, upland Greeks constituted well-organized polities that were thoroughly prepared to face the challenges of their respective geopolitical contexts, even without formal institutions or a central governing power.

The Defenses

On four occasions during the classical period, a large-scale army from the Greek lowlands invaded the realm of an upland ethnos; on each occasion, it was unsuccessful. The first is what I refer to as the Phocian Chalk Raid of the Thessalian camp circa 490; the second, the Aetolian Rout of the Athenians in 426; the third, the Defense of Acarnania in 389; and the fourth, the Defense of Arcadia in 370.[27] These military encounters share a number of important features. First, all four were documented by a contemporary writer who had access to eyewitness accounts and produced a narrative that is reconcilable to topography.[28] Additionally, the four encounters involve a coherent set of upland ethnē that defended themselves as a collective against aggressive and expansionary lowland polities.[29] Finally, the four defenses cover the chronological range of the classical period. As such, they are best understood in relation to each other.

Yet although the narratives of these military encounters document the collective capabilities of upland Greeks unlike any other ancient source, studying them faces a fundamental difficulty: Herodotus, Thucydides, and Xenophon were all outsiders of the ethnē whose activities they related. These writers also adhered to certain literary conventions, shaped their source material to convey a sense of accuracy, and may have even added details to their narratives for the sake of realism.[30] What we are left with in each case is a single, biased version of events reinforcing the writer's broader historiographical aims. Making matters worse, Herodotus, Thucydides, and Xenophon were also at pains to give the impression that encounters with upland Greeks unfolded exactly as written in their narratives. Furthermore, while these writers provide coherent narratives from the invaders' perspectives, at times they are imprecise, they overlook key features of individual engagements, and they assume and assert a great deal about defending ethnē.

But instead of abandoning these seemingly hopeless narratives, the analysis below uses them as a framework for telling an entirely different version of events. Individual chapters question what an ancient writer could have known, what he may have withheld from his narrative, and how he shaped his source material. Then, drawing on archaeological, topographical, and ethnographic research, they show what the narrative sources failed to appreciate about the defensive capabilities of upland Greeks. To understand the dynamics of these encounters, the analysis takes into account a variety of perspectives from invaders and defenders alike. At times, the analysis focuses on "the eye of command"; at others, on the grim view from below—but always in relation to the physical environment and the effects and limitations of ancient technology.[31]

This method traces its roots to the ancient face of battle—that is, to studies of morale and motivation, the use and effects of weapons, care of the wounded and dead, the physical circumstances of battle, and above all, the lived experiences of combatants.[32] Unlike past studies, however, this book treats the face of battle not as an end in itself, but as a foundation for inquiring into the social and political organization of the Phocians, Aetolians, Acarnanians, and Arcadians circa 490–362. Since effective wide-participation fighting presupposes good social and political organization, and effective wide-participation fighting is exactly what the subsequent chapters demonstrate, these encounters will reveal something even more significant about the social and political character of upland Greeks.

Key Terminology

Following the work of Richard White and James Scott, this book uses the terms "upland" and "lowland" as heuristics for assessing interregional interaction and conflict among disparate polities.[33] In contrast to the upland peoples of Scott's work, though, the upland ethnē of the classical Greek world did not constitute stateless societies. On the contrary, Phocis, Aetolia, Acarnania, and Arcadia circa 490–362 were combined political, cultural, and ethnic entities occupying a relatively distinct geographical space, much like modern nation-states. Yet scholars avoid referring to geographical ethnē as nations or nation-states, for good reason.

Unlike the city-state, the nation-state—with its centralized, bureaucratic structure—is generally regarded as a distinctively modern phenomenon.[34] Furthermore, with the possible exception of Athens, the evidence is simply insufficient for building a strong case for ancient nation-statehood in the classical Greek world, and nowhere more so than among upland ethnē.[35] Making matters even more complicated, a variety of political communities combined and overlapped in Phocis, Aetolia, Acarnania, and Arcadia during the time in question. Consequently, no single translation of ethnos can accurately describe these polities.[36] In light of this difficulty, and following the conventions of ancient Greek scholarship, I will retain the use of ethnos and ethnē throughout the book but detail in each case the political character of the ethnos under consideration.

By the existence of a formal, federal government, I mean the formation of officially federated states (koina), a phenomenon generally associated with the fourth century or later.[37] Unfortunately, the Greeks never developed consistent or precise terms for federal institutions or federal states. In the past, this terminological imprecision suggested to some that federal states did not exist in antiquity.[38] Subsequent scholarship has since softened this view but has yet to settle on a precise definition of an ancient Greek federal state (*koinon*).[39] The working definition for most is a formal union of self-governing states under the jurisdiction of a standing central power—that is, an elected council and representative assembly of citizens. In the case of Phocis circa 490, Aetolia circa 426, Acarnania circa 389, and Arcadia circa 370, the extent to which formal federal states existed is debatable. For this reason, I use the term "confederation" to distinguish between a formal federal state and a unified political entity that lacked a standing, stable central power.[40]

As for defensive strategy, I mean a standing ethnos-level plan that exploited known and developing advantages to repel potential invasions. Despite its roots in the Greek language, though, "strategy" is somewhat of an anachronistic term. In a modern context, strategy usually entails long-range planning and the development and allocation of a nation's resources to achieve major ends. This would be a nation's high or grand strategy.[41] Furthermore, as Colin Gray has argued, present-day strategies always form part of an even broader policy: "It is not possible to have a strategy without, ipso facto, having a policy end also."[42] As several studies have shown, ancient states clearly pursued strategic aims, and in some cases even grand-strategic ones, as in imperial Rome and fifth- and fourth-century Athens.[43] Unfortunately, if the Greeks of upland ethnē conducted this sort of thinking and planning, they left no direct evidence of it.

Nevertheless, this book argues that the defenses of circa 490, 426, 389, and 370 could not have been ad hoc, fortuitously successful responses to acute external threats. On the contrary, each encounter reveals an ethnos-wide capability of mobilizing and positioning personnel on short notice—often with the cooperation of civilian populations—and executing a sophisticated defensive action within the limits of their respective geographical realms. Put in Clausewitzian strategic terms, the Greeks of upland ethnē were adept at using battle to achieve a desired end—the annihilation or driving off of an aggressive, invading army.[44] The amount of foresight and coordination required to achieve this end makes "defensive strategy" the best term for understanding the collective capabilities of classical upland ethnē.

For far too long, these collective capabilities have been underappreciated both in modern scholarship and in ancient historical narratives. Herodotus, Thucydides, and Xenophon give only the slightest indication that lowlanders were aware of the dangers inherent in invading an upland *ethnos* or even understood the intricacy of the defenses they experienced. To date, modern scholarship has yet to find issue with their views, until now.

CHAPTER 1

The Phocian Chalk Raid
of the Thessalian Camp Circa 490

For most of the early Iron Age (ca. 1200–800), the Phocian ethnos comprised two distinct regions to the north and south of the Kephisos River. The northern region consisted of the Kephisos River Valley and eastern Phocis. The Phocians who lived in these areas were oriented more toward East Locris and Euboea and so resembled the Greeks of the central mainland in culture and politics. South of the Kephisos River was Mt. Parnassus and its coastal environs. The inhabitants of this southern region were involved less with the activities of the central mainland and more with the cultural and economic exchange of the Gulf of Corinth.[1]

Despite these differences, the Phocians of both regions shared a common ethnic identity that took shape between the Late Bronze Age and the eighth century.[2] Additionally, early in the eighth century, the Phocians established a network of sanctuaries that connected the northern and southern regions. This process intensified in the sixth century, mirroring developments in regional settlement patterns.[3] As the sixth century progressed, the Phocians overcame their geographical barriers and began building a common Phocian polity. Some have even argued that during the last quarter of the sixth century, the Phocians formed a *koinon* or federal state, most likely in response to the threat posed by neighboring Thessaly.[4] The supposed evidence for this koinon is twofold: the minting of coins bearing the ethnic *PHO-* or *PHOKI* [*KON*], and the building of what appears to be a common meeting house called the Phokikon.[5]

The problem, though, is that neither form of evidence fulfills the basic criteria for a federal state, namely, a formal union of self-governing states under the jurisdiction of a central power.[6] As several studies have shown, political communities minted coins for a variety of reasons in the Archaic and classical Greek world.[7] In this case, Williams has suggested that the Phocians minted coins primarily to celebrate their newly won independence from Thessaly.[8] Although the Phocian ethnos had become more unified by the end of the sixth century, coinage by itself does prove the existence of a formal council, assembly, and legal system with officials and a federal army requiring pay.

Furthermore, the exact location, date, and function of the original Phokikon are all contentious. Much of the debate surrounds the relationship between the later Phokikon that Pausanias described in the second century CE and the late Archaic or early classical building approximately one kilometer to the north.[9] The Phocians certainly could have established a common meeting hall around the turn of the fifth century, yet we have no clear evidence that this building housed a standing, federal government.

At the very least, though, standardized coinage and the building of the Phokikon provide good evidence for increased ethnos-wide unity during the late Archaic and early classical periods. By this time, the Phocians had indeed become an ethnically distinct political entity. If they had yet to establish formal federal institutions, they unquestionably had formed a loose confederation of independent poleis.[10] In the following, I will refer to the Phocians' confederacy simply as the Phocian ethnos and will focus on a major issue that all such polities had to deal with in the ancient world: defense.

Although nearly all Phocian defensive activity circa 525–475 was documented in later sources, Herodotus (8.27–28) preserves one significant exception: the defense of circa 490. According to his account, early in the fifth century the Thessalians and their allies invaded Phocis. In response, the Phocians withdrew to Mt. Parnassus, but the Thessalians did not relent. Effectively besieged, the Phocians waited until dark, covered their bodies and equipment with chalk, raided the Thessalian camp, and killed a large number of their adversaries.

This peculiar incident—the Phocian Chalk Raid of the Thessalian Camp—is the subject of the present chapter. It is the earliest joint action of the Phocian ethnos documented in a contemporary source, and as I will argue, the most illustrative example of the Phocians' collective capabilities during the late Archaic and early classical periods.

By focusing on the Chalk Raid, this chapter reconstructs a historiographically marginalized, violent encounter that involved some of the most unusual military tactics ever employed between Greeks. In all of Greek history, there is no other incident quite like the Chalk Raid; the encounter defies virtually every established convention of classical Greek warfare. Based on this recon-struction, the chapter argues that before the actual invasion of circa 490, the Phocians formulated an ethnos-level defensive strategy to guard against large-scale invasions and did so without the direction of a federal government.

Past Approaches and Sources

Studies of late Archaic and early classical Phocian history have yet to give the Chalk Raid serious consideration; the incident is even absent from some com-pendiums of ancient battles.[11] For the most part, scholarship from the Pho-cian perspective views the Chalk Raid primarily as an unplanned, almost miraculous triumph against all odds, as did the ancient writers who docu-mented the incident. For example, as Roderick Williams notes, "Herodotus (viii. 27) records that in the last campaign between [Phocis and Thessaly] . . . the Phokians were forced back into a narrow position on Mount Parnassos and were only saved by a trick devised by their seer Tellias."[12]

Part of the reason for this view could be that no extant writer considered the Chalk Raid particularly significant. In addition, as Pierre Ellinger has shown, the Chalk Raid became part of the Phocians' "national legend" (or "saga") that preserved and exploited memories of collective triumph in extreme situa-tions.[13] Subsequent generations of Phocians adapted these memories to fit their own historical circumstances to reinforce their ongoing project of self-fashioning. The Chalk Raid became part of this national legend, but the en-counter itself was not legendary.

We know this because the Phocians set aside a tenth of their profits from their victory over the Thessalians to fund "the large statues standing together around the tripod in front of the temple at Delphi and another set like these at Abae [in east Phocis]."[14] These same bronze statues of Herakles struggling with Apollo along with their accompanying inscription may have even been standing at Delphi in Pausanias's day, but it is difficult to say; the potentially extant fragments of the monument appear to date to the late fourth or early third century.[15] Be that as it may, Herodotus circa 450 could still speak of the statues at Delphi as a matter of fact, and a fifth-century author was quite un-likely to invent the existence of a highly conspicuous monument at a high-traffic, Panhellenic sanctuary. Furthermore, unlike the set at Abae, the Persians were unable to plunder those at Delphi during the invasion of 480, so Herodo-tus likely saw the monument for himself.[16]

Furthermore, the monument at Delphi suggests that the victory meant a great deal to late Archaic and early classical Phocians. Yet aside from investigating questions of later self-fashioning, past scholarship has virtually neglected the greater significance of the Chalk Raid. As a result, the defensive capabilities of the Phocians circa 490 remain unclear, and we are left with a series of questions about the character of the Phocian ethnos during the time in question.

First, since there is every indication that Thessalian aggression was a constant for the Phocians during the late Archaic and early classical periods, why do we see a seemingly ad hoc approach to defense if the Phocians had all of the resources needed for a more formidable system? Or did the Phocians have such resources?

Similarly, past treatments of the Chalk Raid portray the Thessalians as aggressive and well organized, and the Phocians as just the opposite. Will a careful analysis of the Phocians' success support such a view? For that matter, how and why were the Phocians successful in the face of the large-scale invasion circa 490? As a number of studies have shown, the Phocians' relationship to the land played a critical role in their collective development as an ethnos. Did the physical geography of the region shape their defensive methods? And why did an upland ethnos seemingly lack a light-infantry capability?

The analysis below seeks to answer these questions, but before doing so, we must consider the Chalk Raid's three narrative sources. The first is Herodotus, the sole contemporary source. Herodotus's sources of information and historical reliability remain controversial, especially regarding non-Greek affairs and events of the sixth century, yet his account of the Chalk Raid is less problematic.[17] First, unlike with many earlier events, Herodotus could have spoken with people who actually experienced the Chalk Raid, although if he did, these individuals were probably Phocian.[18] In addition, Herodotus gives little more than an outline of the encounter, and this outline is corroborated by the Phocians' dedication at Delphi.

More important, Herodotus has very little interest in the Chalk Raid per se. That is, from his perspective, the incident does not illustrate anything particularly profound about the Phocians, and Herodotus includes it in his writings only as an example of the hostilities between Thessalians and Phocians circa 480. According to Herodotus, those hostilities were the reason that the Phocians' sided with the Greeks during Xerxes' invasion: "The Phocians were the only Greeks in the central mainland that were not collaborating with the Persians, and as far as I can tell, this was only because they hated the Thessalians. In other words, had the Thessalians sided with the Greeks, I think the Phocians would have collaborated with the Persians."[19] In sum, Herodotus's bare-bones account of the Chalk Raid provides a reliable foundation on which to base further analysis.

The other two sources are much later and much less reliable. Pausanias and Polyaenus wrote approximately six centuries after the encounter took place.

Polyaenus documented the Chalk Raid as a "miscellaneous" stratagem, and he seems to have drawn primarily from Herodotus. The content of Polyaenus's account and Herodotus's narrative is the same, but as was his practice, Polyaenus reworked some of Herodotus's language to convey a sense of having done original research. Polyaenus also includes a few minor details that are absent from Herodotus's narrative, which may have been based on a separate source.[20]

In contrast, Pausanias's account is clearly based on a tradition that diverged from Herodotus. The structural features of the encounter are the same—the Thessalians invaded Phocis early in the fifth century, and in response, the Phocians pulled off their peculiar night attack—but the language of Pausanias's account differs both from Herodotus's and Polyaenus's in a number of key instances. Furthermore, Pausanias "is told" that the Chalk Raid occurred on the limits of Phocian territory, not on Mt. Parnassus as in Herodotus. Finally, in Pausanias's account, five hundred Phocians took part in the raid; the Phocians number six hundred in Herodotus's version.[21]

Like Herodotus, Pausanias provides only an outline of the Chalk Raid and attaches no broader significance to the incident. For Pausanias, the Chalk Raid is one of several collective achievements that the Phocians pulled off since their involvement in the Trojan War, and this is the only reason that he includes the Chalk Raid in his introductory sketch of Phocian history.

In light of these differences, the analysis below attempts to reconcile the Chalk Raid's three narrative sources while also evaluating how the physical geography and built environment of Phocis both limited and enabled the activities of Phocians and Thessalians alike. To achieve this end, the reconstruction integrates the insights of archaeological and topographical research into the analysis of the three narrative sources to cast new light on the Chalk Raid and its greater significance. With that, we turn to the encounter itself.

The Raid

"Only a few years before Xerxes' expedition." So begins Herodotus's account of the Phocian Chalk Raid of the Thessalian camp. Here, as elsewhere, Herodotus withholds the specifics, but based on this otherwise imprecise remark, we know that the incident occurred during the first or second decade of the fifth century.[22] Less clear, however, are the circumstances that led the Thessalians and their allies to attack the Phocians circa 490.[23]

"The Thessalians and their allies invaded with a full levy," says Herodotus, implying a large-scale invasion.[24] Yet no ancient writer documented the approximate size of the invading army, or even a motive for the Thessalians' aggression. It could be that the Thessalians were out to avenge a defeat suffered during the Phocian revolt circa 510, the incident that gave rise to the expression "Phocian Desperation."[25] Faced with a Thessalian invasion, the Phocians assembled all of their women and children and agreed that if the men lost the impending battle with the Thessalians, the rest would commit suicide by fire. Fortunately for the Phocians, the men won. But if this tale of desperation led to the invasion of circa 490, why did it take the Thessalians approximately two decades to respond? No later writer makes a connection between the two incidents, and Herodotus does not even mention the revolt.

For that matter, no ancient source explains why the Thessalians launched a large-scale invasion circa 490 when they could have harmed a number of Phocians north of the Kephisos River by raiding their settlements on horseback.[26] In fact, one such raid during the time in question led to a disaster for the Thessalians and may have even prompted the invasion circa 490. Near the town of Hyampolis, the Phocians had dug a large ditch, filled it with empty amphorae, and concealed the trap with loose dirt and natural vegetation to blend in with the surrounding surface. This stratagem devastated a sizeable contingent of Thessalian raiders who, unaware, rode their horses into the ditch, breaking the animals' legs.[27] The Thessalians, Herodotus says, were still smarting over this loss at the time of Xerxes' invasion.[28]

Unfortunately, the ancient sources disagree on the exact chronology of events. Pausanias says the Amphorae Trap caused the Thessalian invasion of circa 510, while Herodotus suggests that the Amphorae Trap took place only a few years before Xerxes' expedition. Yet neither writer makes a connection between the Amphorae Trap and the invasion of circa 490. In Pausanias's narrative, the Chalk Raid bears no discernable relationship with any other event in Phocian history. In Herodotus, the Amphorae Trap and Chalk Raid complement each other, but not because one led to the other; rather, the Chalk Raid explains how the Phocians once devastated the Thessalians' infantry, and the Amphora Trap explains how they harmed the Thessalians' cavalry.[29] Furthermore, neither writer questions why the Thessalians and their allies invaded "Parnassus" if the Thessalians sought to repay the Hyampolitans who inhabited the eastern lowlands of Phocis on the other side of the Kephisos River (map 2). We will return to this.

The large-scale invasion and subsequent Chalk Raid circa 490 stand alone as comprising one of the more violent encounters between Thessalians and Phocians during the late sixth and early fifth centuries, but there likely was much more to the story.[30] After all, the Thessalians circa 490 seemed less concerned with seizing or destroying Phocian territory and more intent on cap-

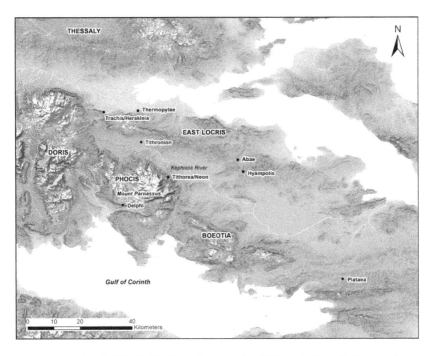

MAP 2. The Phocian Chalk Raid of the Thessalian Camp (ca. 490). Created by D. Matthew Buell.

turing or killing actual Phocians. For now, the Thessalians' primary motive must remain speculative.

Less speculative is the route taken by the invading army. For over a decade, archaeologists of the Phokis-Doris Expedition investigated routes of communication between the northern and southern Greek mainland. They concluded that the modern-day Dhema Gap, or "the Pass through Trachis" as it was known in antiquity, was the most likely route taken by the invaders into Phocian territory.[31] The Dhema Gap provided the northern access point to what the Phokis-Doris Expedition deemed the Great Isthmus Corridor Route. The Isthmus Corridor offered the most traversable route into central Greece from the north for a major cavalry force—presumed from the Thessalians' involvement in the incident—or an army with an extensive baggage train. In fact, the settlement of Trachis may have been where the allies of the Thessalians assembled.

Pausanias suggests as much when he notes that the Chalk Raid took place "when the armies were encamped across from each other near the pass into Phocis."[32] Presumably, he means the main pass into the upper Kephisos Valley, as opposed to the passes in the east that led primarily into the central mainland beyond Phocian territory. Kleonai, for instance, was the site of another entrance into Phocis north of the Kephisos River. This was where the revolting Phocians defeated the Thessalians circa 510. However, most Phocian territory during the time in question was south of the river. The Thessalians and their allies could have invaded from the east, but they would have then had to march back toward the northern Kephisos Valley, since Tithronion was the only suitable crossing site connected to the Parnassus region.[33]

Among the Thessalians' allies, the Euboeans, Dorians, Opuntian (or East) Locrians, and even Boeotians could have contributed individual contingents.[34] The latter three shared borders with the Phocians, as did the Thessalians to a lesser extent. For the invaders, then, there would have been no hiding the invasion, unless the Phocians were somehow oblivious to the activities of their aggressive neighbors.

Yet no ancient narrative mentions any subdivisions of the Phocian ethnos. We hear only of "the Phocians," and this may have been all that an inquiring outsider could have learned during the fifth century.[35] "The Phocians" does not necessarily mean that the entire Phocian ethnos gathered in defense, but it does suggest that the Thessalians were targeting more than just a few Phocian poleis. If so, the Phocians needed to coordinate their efforts across the entire ethnos if they hoped to repel the Thessalian-led invasion. Even with some advance notice, the Phocians still had to act on relatively short notice, especially those in the upper Kephisos River Valley closest to Trachis. Phocian poleis in that region were too small to offer any significant resistance on their own—hence the proliferation of defensible mountain refuges within close proximity to these settlements.[36]

One such refuge could have been the site of the Chalk Raid. Herodotus says the Phocians "were forced into a narrow space on Parnassus," and Polyaenus corroborates Herodotus's account by noting that the Phocians were "shut in by the Thessalians on Parnassus."[37] Both suggest that the Phocians were besieged in some sense.[38] Herodotus also reports that during the Thessalian-led Persian invasion of Phocis in 480, a number of Phocians climbed Parnassus to an isolated peak known as Tithorea, a haven suitable for a large number of people.[39]

If the Thessalians and their allies followed the same route into Phocis as the Persians, as the Phokis-Doris Expedition suggests, Tithorea would have been the most accessible and accommodating mountain sanctuary for the Phocians who lived north of the Kephisos River and for those who inhabited the northern foothills of Parnassus.[40] No other site could have supported and protected such a large number of Phocians.

But what of Pausanias's claim that the incident took place "near the pass into Phocis"? It is difficult to reconcile this remark with Herodotus's version.

The simple solution in instances of disagreement between a fifth-century account and one written approximately six centuries after the fact would be to rely on the testimony of a writer who could have spoken with the individuals involved in the incident. That is reasonable enough, but Pausanias's version is suspect for different reasons.

First, consider how flattering Pausanias's account of the Chalk Raid is from the Phocian perspective. Instead of whole populations of Phocians abandoning their settlements, a Phocian army assembles and then repels the invading force at the very entrance into the region: no violation of Phocian territory, no hasty retreat to the mountains. This sounds too much like a competing version of the incident that the later Phocians adapted to their own national legend.[41] But there is a more practical problem with Pausanias's account: the source of the Phocians' chalk.

I will discuss the particulars of the raid in a moment, but we must first consider where hundreds of Phocians could have found enough chalk to cover their bodies and equipment. If the Phocians were on Parnassus, as Herodotus claims, then the answer is simple: anywhere. The mountain itself is made of gray to gray-white compact limestone that was quarried extensively in antiquity. Importantly, the limestone from Parnassus is rich in white calcite, meaning that every outcropping of limestone offered a potential source of chalk for the Phocians; the sedimentary rock can be pulverized relatively easily and mixed with water to form a white to light-gray adhesive paste.[42] Of course, there could have been limestone exposed in "the pass into Phocis," assuming this is the Dhema Gap, but "near the pass" in Phocian territory, there is nothing to compare with the massive outcroppings characteristic of Parnassus.[43] It is "on Parnassus," then, that we locate the Chalk Raid.[44]

Again, in light of the Phocians' response to the Persian invasion in 480, the only place to look is the mountain refuge of Tithorea just above the town of Neon.[45] The deep ravine of the Kachales River and a sheer rock face protected Tithorea in every direction except toward the west, the direction from which the Thessalians and their allies would have invaded Parnassus.[46] Just as the ancient narratives suggest, with the Thessalians and their allies occupying the town of Neon only a short distance below, the Phocians were indeed "cooped up" and "shut in" on Parnassus with seemingly little hope of escape.

But why would the Phocians put themselves in such a situation? One explanation is that they assumed the Thessalians and their allies were only out to plunder and destroy Phocian settlements, as the Persians would do only a few years later.[47] The Phocians may have expected the invaders to continue toward the east and south once they had devastated Neon. And maybe that was the Thessalians' plan until they noticed that they had cornered a large number of Phocians. Then again, the Thessalians may have finally had the real object of their invasion in reach: "to spare no men of fighting age and sell the women and children as slaves."[48] That is, they intentionally drove the Phocians into a tight spot.

But there is another possibility. What no ancient narrative mentions is that the confined space around Tithorea neutralized the aggressors' numerical advantage and, significantly, prevented the Thessalians from employing their cavalry against the defenders. In this light, it is more likely that the Phocians deliberately abandoned their settlements. If pressed to fight at Tithorea, they could do so on a relatively level playing field, so to speak, and even with a few key advantages.

From an outsider's perspective, the Phocians appeared to be in a desperate situation once again. According to Herodotus, a foreign seer, Tellias of Elis, solved the Phocians' problem: "He had 600 of the best Phocians chalk their bodies and equipment and set them upon the Thessalians at night, ordering them to kill whomever they saw who was not whitened."[49] As elsewhere in Herodotus's work, the literary *topos* of the seer should give pause.[50] Perhaps a foreign seer actually contrived the stratagem. Perhaps we should consider other factors.

Above all, night activity of this nature was not unprecedented in Phocian history, even during the time in question, but the evidence comes only from Pausanias. During the Phocian revolt, three hundred Phocians under the command of a certain Gelon allegedly went at night to gather intelligence on an invading Thessalian army but were caught and annihilated by a number of Thessalian cavalrymen.[51] This encounter occurred at Kleonai, an ideal arena for cavalry, much unlike Parnassus. Incidentally, no ancient account of the Phocian Chalk Raid mentions Thessalian cavalry, and as noted above, Herodotus emphasizes instead that on this occasion the Phocians routed the Thessalians' army.[52]

In addition, as one commentator has observed, the incident does have a "faintly ritual or magical quality" to it: the Titans also plastered their faces before destroying Dionysus, and as Plutarch observes, early comic performers lacking masks instead chalked (or "plastered") their faces.[53] That a seer allegedly prescribed the chalking of the Phocians' bodies and equipment would seem to support a quasi-religious interpretation of the nighttime raid. We could even consider a mythical interpretation. The opportunistic incursion of Odysseus and Diomedes into the Trojan camp comes to mind, although the Phocian Chalk Raid was far less furtive and on a much larger scale.[54]

In comparison, a series of more mundane considerations offers an entirely different perspective. As Thucydides observed, in nighttime conditions, even with decent moonlight, combatants at best could only distinguish the outline of figures. But crucially, they still could not be sure if these figures belonged to their own side. The hesitancy and confusion inherent to this situation contributed to the Athenian disaster at Epipolae in 413, "where there were great numbers of hoplites on both sides moving around in a small area."[55] The only way the Athenians could recognize each other was by asking for a watchword; this was no easy task, since their opponents, the Syracusans, were communicating via loud shouts.

At Tithorea, not only did chalking solve the problem of identification for the Phocians, but it also eliminated the need to communicate verbally. For this to work, each Phocian had to chalk not only his skin and weapons but other equipment that was less susceptible to perspiration. According to Herodotus, this is exactly what the Phocians did. Properly whitened, the Phocians could distinguish their enemies from every direction and angle—behind and front, left and right, whether looking up or down.[56] No chalk, no questions asked. Yet chalking inevitably worked both ways, and the whitened Phocians undoubtedly made themselves clearer targets.[57] So why risk a chalk raid? Because surprise greatly enhanced the tactical advantages that Tithorea offered the defenders. A conventional engagement during the day was a possibility, but it would have been far riskier, especially as the Phocians were likely outnumbered.

According to Herodotus, the Thessalians and their allies invaded "with a full levy." Herodotus may have meant a full levy of Thessalians combined with a full levy of allies, that is, the largest force possible. Then again, "a full levy" may have consisted of a contingent of Thessalians combined with various contingents of allies. "Full," in this sense, would convey that all of the Thessalians' allies participated. In a less technical sense, "a full levy" may have meant "a really large force," larger than preceding ones. The Phocians ended up killing about 4,000 of the invaders, so assuming that this number represents approximately 25 to 50 percent of the invading army—a generous estimate from the Phocian perspective—it is possible that approximately 8,000 to 16,000 of the Thessalians and their allies invaded Phocis circa 490.[58] On Tithorea, only a portion of this force would have been able to face the Phocians at any given time, but with such a substantial reserve of combatants, the invaders could eventually wear down the smaller defending force.

As for the Phocians, Herodotus and Pausanias disagree about the number involved in the incident. Herodotus says six hundred of the "best" Phocians executed the Chalk Raid, while Pausanias says it was five hundred "picked men."[59] The figure of 1,000 Phocian hoplites appears elsewhere in Herodotus's history, so Pausanias's five hundred would represent half of the usual number, assuming the "best" were armed as hoplites.[60]

Even more important, a selection of five hundred to six hundred raiders means that an even greater number of Phocians participated indirectly in the Chalk Raid—anywhere from 1,000 to 2,000 total, including nonhoplites. Since no single Phocian community could have organized a raid force in such numbers, the Phocians must have coordinated their defensive efforts as an ethnos against the invading army.[61]

In addition to the combatants at Tithorea, there likely was a sizeable civilian population present. It made no sense for Phocian civilians to remain in the settlements through which the Thessalians and their allies were about to march on their way up Parnassus. It is even possible that the Phocians moved their women and children to the mountain haven, went to meet the Thessalians at the pass into Phocis, but then retreated to Tithorea when they saw the size of the invading army. Interestingly, the 1,000 Phocian hoplites at Thermopylae who volunteered to protect the Anopaia Path did just that: surprised by the Persians and assailed by arrows, they fled to the peak of a nearby mountain and made preparations for battle there.[62]

A more likely possibility, though, is that the Phocians collectively moved to Tithorea as they did during the Persian invasion, preferably to wait out the storm but ready to defend themselves if necessary. In this case, once the Phocians realized that they were under siege, they prepared to fight. There was no shortage of resources at Tithorea. The Phocians had a considerable fighting force at their disposal, and the massive amount of exposed limestone from the rock faces protecting the refuge provided an ideal source of chalk.

The five hundred to six hundred raiders with their arms and equipment represented the most able-bodied of the Phocian hoplites; they provided the bodily strength and equipment required for the task at hand. Nonraiders and noncombatants also could have helped by pulverizing limestone and applying the chalky paste to the skin, garments, weapons, and equipment of the raiders. In addition to a spear and short sword, the Phocians would have carried their shields, breastplates (whether of metal, leather, or linen), and some form of headgear, although not necessarily a full-faced metal helmet.[63] Any more equipment would have hindered their speed and mobility.

According to both Pausanias and Polyaenus, the Phocians waited until they had a full moon to attack.[64] Some moonlight would have been necessary to reflect off of the chalk and provide enough of a contrast for the raiders to see, but not necessarily the light of a full moon. Although absent from Herodotus's account, this detail regarding moonlight suggests a sense of timing on the part of the Phocians that was necessary for a successful raid. That is, in addition to a competent raid force, the Phocians needed the right conditions for their attack to work; in particular, a relatively clear sky with sufficient moonlight.

We must also assume some degree of organization within the raid force, at least in pairs, given the number of individuals involved.[65] The success of the raid depended fundamentally on surprise and speed, and this is part of the reason that the Phocians limited the number of raiders. Their goal, it seems, was to kill as many Thessalians as possible and as quickly as possible. The raid also needed to be decisive. If unsuccessful, the attack surely would have prompted an assault of Tithorea, and the remaining Phocians would have been without their best fighters.

All of this suggests that what the Phocians executed on Parnassus circa 490 was far from some harassing, "ritual" raid. It was equally unlikely that some hastily chalked up, unorganized mob of hoplites charged downhill at night into the Thessalian camp. Fighting for their survival, the Phocians were far more deliberate and cunning than that.

Once again, chalking eliminated the need for the raiders to communicate verbally; this is especially important, since all accounts agree with Herodotus that as the Phocians descended upon their invaders, "the Thessalian sentries who saw them first were terrified and thought something supernatural was happening."[66] The sight of the whitened warriors certainly would have appeared strange on the mythologically charged peaks of Parnassus, even if the Phocians were not gleaming from head to toe as Pausanias suggests. But the appearance of the Phocians would have been positively unnerving if combined with a silent advance, that is, with little indication that the whitened figures were mortal beings.

Yet the natural rattling of Phocians' arms and armor still would have been audible. This only would have added to the sentries' confusion. In fact, according to Polyaenus, a few of the Thessalians supposed that they were being attacked not by phantom soldiers but by Phocian reinforcements.[67] Then again, there is a hint of revisionism in this qualification, almost as if Polyaenus (or his source) wanted to emphasize that not all of the Thessalian sentries fell apart so easily at the sight of the attacking Phocians.[68] Startled and confused, the sentries still needed to alert the rest of the camp, and here the fortunes of the Phocians' were about to turn.

"After the sentries [were spooked], so was the invading army itself," writes Herodotus.[69] The stationing of sentries indicates that the Thessalians were on guard against the Phocians and at least felt the need to monitor their nighttime activities, possibly recalling the Phocians' nighttime activities from previous encounters. The Thessalians and their allies should not have been surprised if the sentries raised an alarm according to procedure. But that was not what happened.

The chalked Phocians terrified the sentries, who then stirred up the rest of the army with what must have been a disturbing report. The sentries' flight into the camp only would have led to further confusion as the Phocians descended upon the camp. And so what started as a raid became a rout, and a vicious one at that.

The Phocians may have caught and killed some of the sentries; we have no idea of the number of sentries posted around Tithorea, or of how they were armed, but enough of them escaped the Phocians' initial advance to "inform" the rest of the army. Within the confines of the camp, that is, in and around Neon, the Phocians would have encountered a mass of alarmed and confused individuals who, partially armed, were likely disorganized, scrambling, and still trying to make sense of the situation. In fact, "battle" or even "rout" may be too euphemistic for what ensued. According to Herodotus, the Thessalians and their allies "were defeated by the Phocians and treated savagely," or in Pausanias's words, the Phocians slaughtered the Thessalians, implying that the Phocians killed armed and unarmed alike.[70]

Well protected, working in teams, easily distinguished from their enemies, the chalked Phocians capitalized on their now enhanced advantage of surprise. The Phocians may have supposed that the chalking would terrify the invaders, but they could not have depended on this effect for the success of the raid.[71] Chalking was in fact a practical solution to a pressing issue: the raid was a matter of survival for the Phocians, at least in the short term. But if some sort of collective survival instinct accounts for the viciousness of the Phocians' treatment of the Thessalians, it does so only in part.

We need to consider an additional factor: the Chalk Raid could have been the Phocians' only opportunity to kill such a large number of their menacing neighbors without any legal, political, or religious scruples. This may have weighed on the minds of Phocian leaders and heightened the Phocians' sense of urgency as they pressed their attack. Given the equipment at hand, the slaughter would have consisted of the Phocians thrusting their leaf-shaped spear blades into the chest cavities, necks, and faces of the invaders, hacking the limbs of the wounded and unarmed with swords, and dropping spear butts onto the heads of those lying on the ground.[72]

"In the end the Phocians took possession of about 4,000 bodies and shields," says Herodotus.[73] If this number is reasonably accurate, the ratio of Thessalian causalities to Phocian raiders was seven to one. This means that the raid and ensuing slaughter may have taken approximately an hour or two and most likely was confined to hours of darkness. It is unlikely that the Phocians pursued the fleeing invaders down mountain paths at night; instead, it seems that they concentrated their efforts on the camp itself to eliminate those unfortunate enough not to have escaped. In this way, the Phocians took possession of the Thessalian dead not because they refused to honor a universal Hellenic convention, but because all of the survivors had fled Parnassus. Indeed, for the Thessalians, the encounter could have been nothing short of a "trauma."[74]

But why does Herodotus (or his source) specify that the Phocians seized both the corpses and the shields? Is it to emphasize that the Phocians actually killed 4,000 invaders and did not merely collect 4,000 discarded shields, or to imply that the Phocians fought honorably, at least to a certain extent—that is, that they did not slaughter half-asleep and half-armed or unarmed men struggling to disentangle themselves from each other and their equipment and bedding? Both are possibilities.

Herodotus also states that the Phocians immediately dedicated 2,000 of the shields at Abae, the Phocian sanctuary close to Hyampolis, and the rest at Delphi.[75] The dedication at Delphi speaks to a growing national identity among Phocians, and the one at Abae far from the site of the incident reinforces further the view that the successful defense circa 490 required coordination and cooperation across the Phocian ethnos.

Then again, the Delphians may have refused all 4,000 shields, and the sanctuary at Abae may have had limited space. True, the Phocians had every reason to advertise their victory to the rest of the Greek world, but in more practical terms, they may also have needed to spread their load of gore-spattered memorials across the region, as no single sanctuary could accommodate such a mass of equipment. At any rate, the 2,000 shields at Abae—and presumably the other spoils taken from the Thessalians and their allies—certainly would have furnished the Phocians with a substantial reserve of equipment for any future emergencies.[76]

Aftermath

In 480, approximately five to ten years after the Chalk Raid, 1,000 Phocian hoplites joined the Greeks defending Thermopylae. Shortly thereafter the Thessalians led the Persians through Phocis, pillaging and destroying settlements and sanctuaries. Then in 479 another Phocian contingent of 1,000 hoplites led by Harmocydes had to fight beside the Thessalians for Mardonius at Plataea. Allegedly, the Phocians had to do so "under compulsion and against their will."[77]

Herodotus, or his source for this incident, is quick to add that not all of the Phocians were collaborating with the Persians in 479. Some had taken refuge on Parnassus and were using the mountain as a base from which to raid and harass Mardonius's army in Boeotia.[78] By Pausanias's day, the Phocians had actually deserted Mardonius and fought with the Greeks allied against the

Persians—yet another example of a competing, national version of Phocian history preserved in later sources.[79]

Despite these disagreements, Herodotus and later writers agree that the Chalk Raid circa 490 effectively ended Thessalian aggression against the Phocians for the rest of the fifth century. After Xerxes' invasion, the next serious threat to the Phocian ethnos would materialize in the middle of the fourth century in the form of the Third Sacred War.[80] Yet if the success of the Phocians during the early decades of the fifth century is clear enough, less so is the exact nature of their defensive capabilities and its greater significance.

Analysis

At first glance, the Chalk Raid appears to permit a range of interpretations. According to the conventional view of the incident, one could attribute the Phocians' success primarily to a foreign seer. By this view, the Phocians lacked a coherent defensive capability, aside from flocking to the mountains and hoping for the best.

But there are a few problems with this interpretation, starting with the size of the Phocian raid force. The Phocians selected five hundred to six hundred of their best fighters to raid the Thessalian camp, so we can assume that even more hoplites were ready at Tithorea, perhaps 1,000 or more. A thousand Phocian hoplites appear elsewhere in Herodotus's history as the rough total of what individual Phocian poleis could contribute for a joint action. Since this fighting force represented a number of Phocian communities, the same mechanism that brought together 1,000 hoplites circa 480–479 must also have been in effect circa 490. Interestingly, this same mechanism may have survived into the fourth century. In reference to events circa 371, Xenophon referred to it as the Phocians' ability to bring together fighting forces "from all quarters."[81]

Mobilizing such a force circa 490 would have required a high level of organization and communication across the Phocian ethnos, and as the Chalk Raid shows, this was fully within the Phocians' capabilities. The Chalk Raid also reveals that the Phocians had formulated a defensive strategy to guard against potential invasions. This strategy ran along the following lines. First, the Phocians of the Kephisos River Valley and eastern Phocis were to abandon their settlements, move inland, and notify the Phocians of Parnassus and its environs. Collectively, the Phocians would then converge at Tithorea—a centrally located, naturally defensible site—and prepare to fight. This was the same strategy that the Phocians enacted in response to the Persian invasion of 480, but on that occasion there was no fighting on Parnassus. Additionally, Herodotus mentions that some Phocians moved to nearby Amphissa in West Locris since Tithorea could not accommodate the entire ethnos; the Phocians may have done the same in response to the invasion circa 490.[82] From an outsider's perspective, enacting this strategy may not have appeared particularly impressive, but as the Thessalians learned, the Phocians' defensive capabilities were far from ineffective.

In fact, if the Phocians had not developed such a defensive strategy and instead were only fortuitously successful against the Thessalians and their allies, we are faced with a curious series of coincidences. First, faced with a large-scale invasion threatening their very existence, all of the Phocians who inhabited the more vulnerable settlements north of the Kephisos River managed to flee inland in advance of the invading army. The escapees then ended up at the most defensible site on Parnassus where other Phocians joined them before the invading force arrived at Neon. Furthermore, by chance, at least 1,000 fully equipped hoplites were included in this group. The cliffs surrounding Tithorea also happened to provide an ideal source of calcite-rich limestone that the Phocians could use for a nighttime raid. There were also competent enough individuals at hand to organize and execute such a raid—whether a foreign adviser, Harmocydes, or some other anonymous Phocians—and all of this happened to come together in extremis.

A far more likely interpretation is that by circa 490 the Phocians had fully appreciated the threats that surrounded them in the central mainland and had taken steps to defend themselves should the need ever arise. Recall that in Herodotus's account, the Chalk Raid was only the latest of a series of "woundings" that the Thessalians had suffered at the hands of the Phocians, implying that a number of limited-scale incidents starting circa 510 culminated in the invasion circa 490. Although the details of this protracted conflict are hazy, the Phocians of the late Archaic and early classical period unquestionably lived with the threat of invasion. If their powerful and aggressive neighbors to the north ever wanted to escalate the conflict, as they likely would, the Phocians needed to be prepared. The Phocians, in short, had every reason to develop a defensive strategy during the late sixth and early fifth centuries, and as the reconstruction of the Chalk Raid shows, they did so to great effect.

It is even possible that the Phocians fostered the appearance of vulnerability on Parnassus to lure the Thessalians to Tithorea. Tithorea neutralized every advantage that the Thessalians and their allies could bring to bear—namely, the possibility of tactical maneuvering, the employment of cavalry, and the invaders' numerical advantage. Additionally, a nighttime raid—far from being an act of desperation—actually offered the Phocians the greatest chance of success. And while it may be somewhat of a speculative point, perhaps the Phocians attributed their success to the impromptu solution of a foreign seer in order to conceal the full extent of their shrewd defensive methods.

But why did the Phocians seemingly lack a light-armed capability during the late Archaic and early classical period when small-scale pastoral conflict with the West Locrians was a relative constant for the inhabitants of Parnassus?[83] This seeming deficiency could be merely a function of the sources. That is, the Phocians actually had such capabilities, but since they were involved very little in the broader affairs of the fifth-century Greek world, we hear nothing of light-armed Phocians.

This is a possibility, yet the Chalk Raid clearly shows that the Phocian ethnos did not depend on light-armed fighters for matters of defense circa 490. On the contrary, the Phocians had adapted the technology and tactics of the polis-centric Greek world to their upland environment in the central mainland. The Phocians' defensive strategy, then, reflects a sound understanding of the potential threats that surrounded their ethnos.

And so to return to the issue raised at the outset, does the Phocians' success mean we are dealing with a federal state? That is, did a standing central power mobilize an army of various Phocian contingents that were led by elected generals? Not necessarily. The best evidence of federal organization along these lines during the late Archaic and early classical periods comes from much later sources and, crucially, from events documented only by Pausanias and Plutarch. Admittedly, Pausanias and Plutarch could have had access to local sources that were unavailable to Herodotus, but if they did, these sources are no longer extant. For that matter, they may not have even existed in Herodotus's day.[84] Furthermore, the Phocians of the late classical and Hellenistic periods attached a great deal of importance to the achievements of the fifth-century ethnos. Thus, it is likely that they related these achievements in terms familiar to the formal league structure of their era—hence the development of a national legend.

Nevertheless, the Chalk Raid certainly attests to the workings of a protofederal state or confederation during the time in question. Phocian poleis were fully capable of concerted action for matters of defense, even those that concerned the entire ethnos. At the very least, the defense of circa 490 shows that individual poleis had articulated a commitment to defend each other; interestingly, this commitment corresponded to the common identity articulated by the Phocians' coinage circa 510–478.

But an argument for the existence of a particular political entity—in this case, a federal state or *koinon*—requires particular evidence. Ideally, this evidence should originate from the political entity itself in the form of epigraphic records of administrative appointments, alliances, grants of citizenship, or judiciary proceedings. Such evidence is relatively abundant for the Phocian koinon of the mid-fourth to the early third century; it simply does not exist for the Phocian ethnos circa 510–480.[85]

Yet why does it matter if there was a formal koinon in Phocis during the time in question, and what is at stake with the existence of an early Phocian federal state? The answer, it seems, is that an early Phocian koinon, a complex "and imaginative response to the changing circumstances of the Archaic period," as Jeremy McInerney describes it, would effectively invalidate the Thucydidean view of upland ethnē as backward, at least for the case of Phocis.[86] Invalidating this view is an important correction for understanding the development of the Phocian ethnos in the late Archaic and classical periods, but it does not require the existence of a koinon to be valid.

The defense of circa 490 illustrates that even without a formal federal structure, the Phocians still constituted a well-organized and effective political entity. Since an ethnic affiliation, common coinage, and a common meeting place distinguished later koina, the possibility remains that a federal state existed in Phocis during the time in question.[87] But the point is that there did not need to be a formal federal state in Phocis for an effective defense, and this collective capability also invalidates the notion that the Phocians were somehow playing catch-up with the rest of the Greek world.

Perhaps a better indication of the existence of a federal state is the Phocians' territorial aggression circa 458–57. In 458, the Phocians attacked the Dorian towns of Boion, Erineon, and Kytineon, captured one of them, but then withdrew when the Spartans came to the Dorians' aid.[88] Around the same time, the Phocians also attacked and seized the sanctuary of Delphi, were involved in hostilities against the Thessalians, and may have formed an alliance with the Athenians.[89] These incidents suggest that a more coherent central power was acting on the perceived interests of the Phocian ethnos and that these interests now included more than defense and survival. At the time of the Chalk Raid, the Phocians were indeed on this trajectory, but their political institutions were still a work in progress.

By way of conclusion, it is worth considering why we never hear of chalking again in ancient Greek history, especially since the tactic was so successful on Parnassus circa 490. There is no shortage of historical comparanda for the use of paste or body paint in war, whether for protection, camouflage, or some ritual purpose. The Celts are perhaps the most well-known example from antiquity.[90] But chalking was not a standard practice for the Phocians. If it had been, the Chalk Raid could be interpreted along these quasi-ritual lines.

One explanation for the uniqueness of chalking, then, is that such a tactic could have worked only under very specific conditions and that these circumstances were never met elsewhere in the Greek world. But if so, what about the rest of Phocian history? Why is there only one chalk raid if there were subsequent invasions of Phocis?

Recall that when the Persians invaded Phocis in 480 they did not attempt to dislodge the Phocians, who were once again "shut in" at Tithorea. Crucially, the Thessalians were the ones guiding the invasion. Whatever the aims of the Persians, the Thessalians could have persuaded their foreign allies to help them exact revenge for the slaughter of circa 490. But was it worth the risk?

Tithorea neutralized virtually every advantage that an invading army could bring to Phocis, and the prospects of defending against another nighttime raid would have been uncertain at best. Perhaps this is why we never hear of another chalk raid: the Chalk Raid circa 490 worked so well that no enemy of the Phocians ever dared to press the issue.

Yet without Herodotus's account and the dedications at Delphi, the Chalk Raid could easily have become part of the somewhat fanciful embellishments of later accounts, and we would still be in the dark regarding the Phocians' defensive capabilities. As it stands, though, the Chalk Raid provides the sole contemporary glimpse into the Phocians' defensive actions during the time in question and reveals a defensive strategy that the Thessalians clearly failed to appreciate.

And so maybe it is only fitting that the Phocians' defense was based on the peaks of Parnassus. The imposing geographical barrier that had earlier divided the Phocians had now become the source of their collective survival.

CHAPTER 2

The Aetolian Rout of the Athenians in 426

The ancient literary tradition produced a wide range of characterizations for the Aetolians. They were "steadfast in battle" and "great-hearted" in Homer; in Pindar, they were strict overseers of competition at Olympia.[1] Outsiders considered their land isolated and nearly impenetrable.[2] Herodotus, for instance, relates how a certain Titormus, the "strongest man in Greece," went to live on the limits of Aetolian territory solely to avoid other people.[3] According to Thucydides, the Aetolians were apolitical, plundering pastoralists—relics of a past age still scattered across mountain villages.[4] In the eyes of some Greeks, the Aetolians were also "semi-barbarous," assuming Euripides' description of the mythical Tydeus represented Athenian attitudes toward actual Aetolians.[5] A couple of centuries later, Polybius characterized the Aetolians as violent, cruel, impious, haughty, inhuman, revolutionary, greedy, and even cowardly (among other things).[6] Ultimately, by Livy's day, the Aetolians had become full-fledged barbarians, at least from the perspective of elite Romans.[7]

In response, a great deal of scholarship has attempted to discredit or at least qualify these ancient stereotypes. For example, the practice of raiding was relatively constant in Aetolian history, but it was not a way of life for all Aetolians, and the Aetolians never constituted a pirate state.[8] As for pastoralism, given the limited amount of arable land in the region, we should expect that the ancient Aetolians relied more on animal husbandry for sustenance.[9] Additionally, although archaeological research in Aetolia is still developing, there is no evidence of urbanism in the region until the late fourth and early third centuries.[10] As several scholars have argued, however, the lack of poleis and monumental architecture during the fifth and fourth centuries did not result from a cultural failure on the part of the Aetolians. On the contrary, the Aetolians were adapting to the demands of their mountainous environment and geopolitical context, and these demands did not call for cities, fortifications, or grandiose temples.[11]

Besides qualifying ancient stereotypes, another branch of Aetolian studies has focused on a more local issue, namely, the relationship between the Hellenistic Aetolian League (koinon) and the fifth-century Aetolian ethnos. As one leading researcher put it, "History presents an enigmatic problem in the rise to dominance of the ancient Aetolians. How could these backward mountaineers, living in their poor, harsh and hardly penetrable territory, develop into a successful cohesive political formation, which was to be one of the most prominent Hellenistic powers opposing the Macedonians and the Romans?"[12] Solving this "enigmatic problem" has proven to be difficult.

The Aetolian League of the Hellenistic period is relatively well documented and has been studied in depth, but the earliest indication of a formal koinon in Aetolia is an Athenian decree dated to 367/366 that protested the treatment of Athenian emissaries.[13] Before this decree, scattered references in ancient historical writings suggest that the fifth-century Aetolian ethnos amounted to a loose confederation.[14] Consequently, most scholars agree that the Aetolian koinon circa 367 emerged from a gradual ethnos-wide shift toward greater legal and political cooperation under the direction of a central governing council.[15]

Yet the gradual development of the fourth-century Aetolian koinon raises a series of fundamental questions. If the Aetolians constituted a relatively coherent "people" or "nation" during the fifth century, what capabilities did they have as a collective, and what might these capabilities reveal about the structure and organization of the Aetolian ethnos? Past scholarship would answer that the fifth-century Aetolians were capable of rudimentary concerted action. That is, they sent representative embassies abroad and concluded alliances (there is one instance of this on record), they fought to retain and then regain the coastal settlement of Naupactus, they participated in at least one limited-scale conflict outside of the territorial limits of Aetolia, and they also made some allowance for "national" defense.[16] These actions suggest that something more than an ethnic group existed in Aetolia during the fifth century—something like a confederation.

But what has yet to be given serious consideration is the nature and broader significance of these actions vis-à-vis our understanding of the fifth-century

Aetolian state. Part of the reason for this neglect could be that the Aetolians were mostly aloof from the major affairs of the rest of the Greek world during the time in question. The status of the evidence has also discouraged the investigation of this topic: what little evidence there is before the middle of the fourth century all originates from non-Aetolian sources.

Nevertheless, an underappreciated defensive action against the Athenians and their allies in 426 stands to change the prevailing notions of the Aetolians' fifth-century collective capabilities.[17] This action, the Aetolian Rout of the Athenians, reveals a high level of coordination and strategic planning within the Aetolian ethnos during the time in question, despite the absence of a central directing power.

Past Approaches and Sources

The Aetolian Rout of the Athenians has surfaced in a variety of debates, beyond focused investigations of ancient Aetolia. Historiographical analyses, for instance, have shown that the incident illustrates important aspects of Thucydides' overarching methodology.[18] A branch of this approach, the study of individuals in Thucydides, has placed special emphasis on the Aetolian experiences of the general Demosthenes, a key figure in later Athenian successes and failures.[19] The development of Aigition, the location of the Rout itself, has raised questions of urbanization and the nature of polis formation during the fifth and fourth centuries.[20] And for some, the incident speaks to ancient attitudes regarding political and cultural differences within the ancient Greek world, especially toward the Aetolians.[21]

Historians of ancient Greek warfare have discussed the Aetolian Rout of the Athenians mostly to refine or illustrate a particular view of things. For example, it is a "classic demonstration of the folly of taking hoplites into terrain that suited light troops," in Lazenby's view.[22] According to van Wees, Thucydides' narrative of the Rout is allegedly "the most remarkable failure to acknowledge the presence of light-armed rowers" fighting on land in any classical source, and by another view, the incident is one of the earliest indications of developing trends in Greek warfare that would prevail in the fourth century.[23] Finally, in Hanson's interpretation, the incident illustrates the classical hoplite disdain for those who fight from afar, that is, not face-to-face.[24]

Although not flawed per se, these approaches have obscured the illustrative significance of the Rout, in part by focusing on particular aspects of Thucydides' narrative, but more significantly by neglecting the Aetolians' perspective. As a result, in the eyes of modern researchers, the incident has become an Athenian mishap—the culmination of a series of errors and misjudgments. Very little consideration has been given to the Aetolian perspective of the encounter.

The difficulty with studying this perspective, though, is that Thucydides is the one source for the Aetolian Rout of the Athenians. No other ancient source has survived for comparison.[25] Additionally, as is well known, Thucydides' historical enterprise was thoroughly enmeshed in his philosophical and literary one. That is, he selected and shaped historical material to cast individuals and events in a certain light, often to establish and reinforce his general, predictable patterns of human behavior.[26] For the year 426/425, for instance, Thucydides only related the deeds of the Athenians and their allies and those who fought against them—in other words, only the ones he deemed worthy of his history.[27] Thucydides also could have distorted or added details to fit his own broader narratives, and his account of the Athenians' experience in Aetolia is no exception.

As usual, Thucydides does not specify his sources for the Aetolian Rout of the Athenians, and there are no indications that he took part in the expedition under Demosthenes and Procles.[28] Thucydides would have learned of the incident from Athenian survivors, and as a number of scholars have argued, Demosthenes likely was his principal source.[29] Nevertheless, we can assume that the Athenians attempted to cast their actions in as favorable a light as possible, and in light of the pathos that Thucydides exhibits at the end of his Aetolian narrative, they appear to have had a sympathetic listener.

All of these considerations call for a measured perspective. With this in mind, the reconstruction below considers various interpretations of Thucydides' language. To mitigate the single-source problem, the analysis also draws on the published results of archaeological, ethnographic, and topographical research in the region of ancient Aetolia.[30] At times this research enhances aspects of Thucydides' narrative. At others, it calls into question the assertions that Thucydides and his sources made regarding the Aetolians' activities. Overall, these different forms of evidence provide an opportunity to reconstruct the dynamics of the incident in great detail.

But before turning to the Aetolian Rout of the Athenians, some context is helpful: The sixth year of the war between the Spartans, Athenians, and their respective allies (426/425) began with a flurry of activity. A series of earthquakes turned back a Spartan invasion of Attica, and the Athenians in Sicily resumed their operations from the previous winter, defeating the Mylaeans and forcing the surrender of nearby Messania. Meanwhile, a sizable detachment of ships under Nicias left the Piraeus to subdue the Melians, and another under Demosthenes and Procles departed to sail around the Peloponnese.[31]

At the same time, the Spartans were establishing and fortifying their colony of Heraclea in Trachis, a cause of strategic concern for the Athenians and a source of irritation and eventual conflict for the Thessalians and Euboeans.[32] In the western mainland, no comparable activity preceded the arrival of the Athenians. The Athenians had been active in the region a few years before, and around the same time, there is some evidence of conflict between the Ambracians and Amphilocian Argives involving neighboring non-Greeks.[33] Although no single polity was attempting to control the entire region, the western Greeks were far from being at ease with each other.[34] Whether they realized it or not, the Athenians under Demosthenes and Procles were about to involve themselves in a complex of regional affairs.

The Rout

The Athenians had no reason to be in Aetolia during the early summer of 426.[35] Their allies might have, but the Athenians did not.

Earlier in the year, a force of thirty Athenian ships under the command of Demosthenes and Procles had sailed around the Peloponnese into the Ionian Sea. The Athenians first ambushed some guards at Ellomenos and then, with the help of the Acarnanians, Zacynthians, Cephallenians, and fifteen Corcyraean ships, attacked the island of Leucas. In response, the Leucadians withdrew into the polis of Leucas on the northern end of the island.

According to Thucydides, the Acarnanians urged the Athenians to besiege the Leucadians and rid the region of what they perceived to be a perennial nuisance.[36] The Athenians, however, had no desire to conduct a siege, but they did remain near Leucas. While they were there, a contingent of Messenians from Naupactus arrived and suggested that Demosthenes consider an invasion of Aetolia. Demosthenes likely took great interest in this proposal. For one, the Aetolians were the enemies of Naupactus, a coastal polity where the Athenians had helped settle a number of rebel helots approximately thirty years prior. The settling of the helots—and the existence of Naupactus itself—still grieved the Spartans, as Demosthenes would have known.[37] In addition, with the Aetolians subdued, the Athenians could potentially take control of the entire western mainland and use the region for their own expansionary purposes. All of these prospects appealed to Demosthenes for a variety of reasons.

First, from a practical perspective, the land force at his disposal was immense. Anything was possible, or so it seemed. Demosthenes also had every reason to grant the Messenians' request. The Messenians were key allies in the escalating conflict between the Athenians and Spartans, and it was in the Athenians' interest to remain in good standing with a population of Greeks dedicated to the defeat of their adversaries. Furthermore, with the Aetolians out of the way, or even as allies, Demosthenes could lead a land force against the Boeotians from the west without further aid from Athens. The accolades that would follow such an achievement surely excited the young Athenian general.[38] Finally, Demosthenes lacked experience in this part of the Greek world and so was a poor judge of advice. In this case, the Messenians gave him these assurances: "Although the Aetolians were a large and warlike *ethnos*, they lived in villages without walls that were dispersed at great length. Also, as they fought with a light armament, they could easily be subdued before uniting in defense."[39]

From an outsider's perspective, the Aetolians constituted an *ethnos*—a people or nation. Thucydides typically reserves this term for large populations of non-Greeks and Greeks of the mountainous and remote northern mainland.[40] There were some built settlements in Aetolia, and a very important one as we will see, but Aetolian poleis were scarce during the time in question and located south of the Daphnos River.[41] As for political organization, the Aetolian ethnos consisted of three tribal groups: The Apodotians occupied most of southern Aetolia and shared borders with the Ozolian or Western Locrians. The Ophionians—subdivided into the Bomiensians and Kalliensians— inhabited the rest of southern Aetolia and the area north and east of the Apodotians. The Eurytanians lived north of the Daphnos River in the southern Pindus region, the most mountainous and geographically expansive part of Aetolia (map 3).[42]

In Thucydides' view, the Aetolians were relics of a past age: they dwelt in unfortified settlements, carried weapons at all times, and relied on brigandage for subsistence. This way of life suggested that the Aetolians had only limited communication between settlements—hence the Messenians' advice. Also, as the Messenians seem to have known, the Aetolians fought without heavy equipment, since the rugged terrain of the region favored a lighter fighting load.[43] The Messenians considered this an advantage for the Athenians. Additionally, the Messenians claimed that the Aetolians "speak a most unintelligible dialect, and are said to eat their meat raw."[44] Were it not for the fact that the Aetolians spoke Greek and could claim a share of the Homeric tradition, one could consider them full-fledged barbarians.[45] But the Aetolians were Greeks, no question about it—only in the eyes of the Messenians the Aetolians' backward way of life was somewhat of a weakness, and certainly exploitable.[46]

Demosthenes was convinced: "With the rest of the land force— Cephallenians, Messenians, Zacynthians, and three hundred marines from

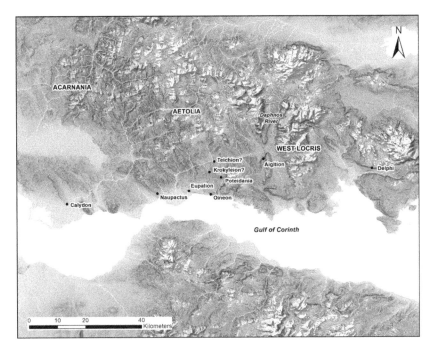

MAP 3. The Aetolian Rout of the Athenians (426). Created by D. Matthew Buell.

the Athenian fleet (the fifteen Corcyraean ships had departed)—he initiated the attack against the Aetolians, setting up base at Oineon in Locris."[47]

The Cephallenians and Zacynthians were islanders. What they brought on the expedition in terms of armament and equipment is unknown. Also unknown is how they organized themselves in defense, although they likely relied on the protection of city walls when faced with an external threat, as did the Leucadians. This, however, was an aggressive incursion, and Thucydides, if he knew at all, regarded whatever they added to Demosthenes' land force as unremarkable. The Messenians, we learn later, at least provided a guide in the region, but the manner in which they fought, if they fought at all, is unknown.

What we do know is that the Athenians contributed three hundred of their own *epibatai*, conventionally referred to as marines. Each Athenian vessel carried ten of these sea hoplites. Their duties ranged from boarding and capturing enemy ships to security and internal administration when not underway.[48] These ancient marines could have organized themselves in ranks by vessel once on land—a phalanx thirty across and ten deep would have been a considerable force—or they could have fought in a less rigid formation. As the incident unfolds, the latter seems to be the case.

The Corcyraeans did not take part. Presumably they left with about one hundred and fifty of their own marines, or at least with some contingent of light-armed troops or archers that performed similar duties. The Acarnanians refused to join the expedition, upset by Demosthenes' refusal to besiege Leucas. But luckily for Demosthenes, the Athenians had other resources in the region: "The Ozolian Locrians were allies of the Athenians, and they were to meet the Athenians with their whole force in the heart of the country."[49] Ozolian (or Western) Locris, in a literal and figurative sense, provided a bridge to Aetolia. The Ozolian Locrians occupied approximately thirty kilometers of coast on the northern Gulf of Corinth, and their settlement at Oineon offered the only harbor in the region that could accommodate the Athenians and their allies. Conveniently, the northern and western limits of Ozolian Locris bordered southern and eastern Aetolia. This meant that the Athenians and their allies did not have to fight their way into Aetolian territory.[50] Instead, they could acclimate to the climate and terrain, prepare their equipment, and ready themselves in case the Aetolians decided to resist. Furthermore, writes Thucydides, "as [the Locrians] shared borders with the Aetolians, were armed in a similar fashion, and knew the Aetolians' way of fighting and their territory, they seemed likely to be of great value as allies on the expedition."[51]

Put another way, the Locrians had an essential ingredient to success in this part of the Greek world, one that Demosthenes lacked: experience. Whether from plundering activities, pastoral conflict, or other less violent forms of interaction, the Locrians were well acquainted with the land of Aetolia and the practices of its inhabitants, and they agreed to meet the Athenians further inland as reinforcements.[52] Their support in all likelihood was a key aspect of the invasion. Like the Aetolians, the Locrians also lived in a mountainous environment, so their take on the situation may have gone something like this: "Demosthenes, you really shouldn't do anything without us. The Aetolians are not to be trifled with, especially in their own territory, and you don't have the sort of light-armed troops that can match the Aetolians' abilities on foot." If the Locrians actually imparted their intimate knowledge of the region and its people to Demosthenes, there are no indications that he took their cautions to heart.

The Athenians and their allies were content to follow the council of their Messenian advisers. At dawn, they launched their invasion of Aetolia: "On the first day they took Poteidania, on the second Krokylion, and on the third Teichion. Demosthenes stopped there and sent the booty to Eupalion in Locris."[53] The Athenians and their allies covered approximately fifteen kilometers of Apodotian territory over the course of three days, seized three village settlements, yet faced no resistance.[54] This was almost too easy, and whatever the intentions of the Ophionions to the north, Demosthenes now had a toehold in Aetolia and some options for future operations[55]—or so it seemed. The Apodotians may have conceded their settlements to the invading force, but they had not capitulated, nor had they been caught unaware. On the contrary, writes Thucydides, the Athenians' "preparations did not escape the Aetolians' notice, even in the initial stages of planning, and once the army invaded their territory, the Aetolians gathered in great force for defense."[56]

This part of Thucydides' narrative raises a series of important questions. How could the Aetolians have known Demosthenes' plans from the very start, and how did they assemble themselves so quickly and in such great numbers? For that matter, how did Thucydides know that the Aetolians knew, given that his sources were decidedly Athenian? One possibility is that Thucydides did not know but that he (or his source) supplied this detail to account for the prompt response of the Aetolians and to lessen the embarrassment of the Athenians. Put another way, if the Aetolians had gained knowledge of Demosthenes' plans, the Athenian defeat would have been more excusable. They could argue that for no fault of their own they had been victims of treachery.

Yet it is quite unlikely that someone close to Demosthenes successfully deserted the Athenians at Oineon, and it is just as unlikely that the Aetolians somehow infiltrated the Athenian camp. There is also no record of Demosthenes or any other Athenian laying a charge against the Locrians for treachery. In fact, Athenian-Locrian relations remained strong even after what happened in Aetolia. But an even bigger issue with Thucydides' narrative is that we have no indications that Demosthenes ever had a clear plan for conducting the actual invasion, aside from advancing northward into Aetolia and moving from settlement to settlement. So what exactly could the Aetolians have known from the start?

It could be that knowing from "the initial stages of planning" helped Thucydides make sense of the incident (or apologize for the Athenians), but this does not explain the speed, scale, and effectiveness of the Aetolians' response, which clearly surprised the invading army. Since the explanation that the Aetolians gained access to Demosthenes' plans is untenable, we have to consider another possibility—namely, that the Aetolians deduced the Athenians' intentions for themselves.

Consider the geopolitical situation of the fifth-century Aetolians: they were surrounded by Athenian allies. To the west were the Acarnanians, to the south and southeast the Naupactians and Ozolian Locrians, and to the east the Dorians and Phocians. A force of Athenians gathering in the region would have suggested only one thing to the Aetolians—a potential invasion. But to have recognized such a threat, the Aetolians needed to be watching the Athenians and their allies from the moment they landed in the region, or shortly thereafter. Was this possible?

Here the work of archaeologists comes to the forefront, in particular the Aetolian Studies Project and its investigation of the intervisibility of sites in southern Aetolia.[57] This intervisibility study revealed that the Aetolians of Kallieis, who comprised a smaller Ophionian community bordering on Ozolian Locris, were fully capable of clandestinely observing activity in and around Oineon from the heights surrounding the harbor. The Kallieansians could have then informed the neighboring Aetolians in Apodotia. The Apodotians who lived closest to the Corinthian Gulf also could have observed the activities at Oineon and then notified their fellow Aetolians to the north and east of the impending invasion.

In addition to the threat of invasion, the Aetolians also needed to be on guard against neighboring populations who "were armed in a similar fashion" and familiar with the Aetolians' way of fighting. At stake were the resources and the safety of their fellow Aetolians. To borrow from a different tradition: "When someone asked why Sparta lacked fortification walls, [Agesilaus] pointed to the citizens bearing arms and said, 'These are the Spartans' walls.'"[58] The Aetolians, in short, had every reason to maintain an active watch on their territory, which they apparently did.

In the year 280, for instance, Aetolian shepherds observed a hostile Spartan army from the surrounding hills of the coastal lowlands and summoned a force of about five hundred Aetolians to attack the would-be invaders.[59] Also, in 208, Aetolians "in the field" were the first to observe the landing of Philip V on the Ozolian Locrian coast. The Macedonians managed to seize some sheep and goats, but the Aetolians escaped into the forests and mountains.[60] Additionally, Aetolian beekeepers could have initially spotted the arrival of the Athenians since, for good reason, bees were usually kept at a distance from settlements.[61] Although Thucydides makes no mention of sheep, goats, or bees in his narrative, the Apodotians from Poteidania, Krokylion, and Teichion clearly were not surprised. Instead, they withdrew inland, seemingly forewarned, to make preparations of their own, and "even the most distant of the Ophionians, the Bomieansians, and Kallieansians who reach to the Malian Gulf, came to help."[62] A distance of approximately fifty kilometers over mountainous terrain separated these more distant Aetolians from the Apodotians to the south, so how did the Aetolians assemble so quickly?

One possibility put forth by the same intervisibility study is optical relay signaling. Where line-of-sight communication was restricted, runners could quickly have filled in the gaps. To that end, the transhumance routes and paths of exchange that cut across ancient and modern Aetolia would have provided ease of movement from region to region. The distances were such that over the course of three days the Bomieansians, Kallieansians, and the rest of the Ophionions could easily have made their way to the heart of Apodotian territory.[63] Interestingly, Thucydides does not mention the Eurytanians. These northern Aetolians may have been too distant to help, or they could have been defending Aetolian territory north of the Daphnos River and so indirectly taking part in the defense.

In the Athenian camp at Teichion, Demosthenes faced somewhat of a dilemma. Things were going well, but he had yet to encounter his Locrian reinforcements, and as Thucydides makes clear, the Athenian expeditionary force was most deficient in light-armed troops.[64] That the Aetolians fought as javelineers was no secret, and Demosthenes would have known that his heavily armed hoplites were more vulnerable in mountainous terrain. The Athenians needed their own light-armed contingent, but the Locrians were nowhere to be found.

The Messenians advised Demosthenes to continue the invasion regardless and capture as many villages as possible. They emphasized once again that it would be an easy victory for the Athenians and their allies provided they advance before the entire Aetolian ethnos united in defense.[65] Demosthenes made his decision: "He advanced against Aigition, stormed the place, and took it by force."[66]

The Athenians and their allies traversed approximately fourteen kilometers of mountainous terrain to reach Aigition from Teichion. This was roughly the combined distance they had covered since setting off from Oineon.[67] Thucydides refers to Aigition as a polis, or urban center, and recent studies of settlement patterns in the region have corroborated his account.[68] Built on high ground, centrally located, highly visible, and connected with a network of paths that ran throughout the region, Aigition was a hub of communication and movement for the Aetolians. The site would have been an ideal mobilization point for the entire ethnos.

In fact, the centrality of Aigition helps to explain why the Messenians guided the Athenians and their allies there after Teichion. From the Messenians' perspective, controlling Aigition was essential to limiting the Aetolians' collective abilities. This would also explain why the Athenians stormed the place: they were expecting resistance. It must have puzzled the Messenians and Demosthenes when they found Aigition deserted. Thucydides describes the setting: "The men, women, and children had withdrawn and were encamped on the heights above the town," joined in all likelihood by the residents of Poteidania, Krokylion, Teichion, other Apodotians, and the rest of the Aetolians, "who by now had come to the rescue at Aigition."[69]

At this time, from the perspective of the invaders, the Locrians would have been particularly helpful, because once the invading force entered Aigition, the Aetolians "attacked the Athenians and their allies, some running down from one hill, some from another, all hurling javelins."[70] The Aetolians had concealed themselves on the surrounding heights well enough to time their ambush as they saw fit.[71] The unexpected attack and barrage of javelins would have startled the Athenians and their allies, but it does not seem to have resulted in many casualties, nor in a significant advantage for the Aetolians.

"When the army of the Athenians advanced the Aetolians withdrew, and when the Athenians retreated, they attacked,"[72] writes Thucydides. The Aetolians kept themselves out of range. They had no choice. They still kept the pressure on the invaders, baiting them forward, and then attacking as they withdrew, but they were not inflicting much damage. Apparently, the shields and armor of approximately three hundred hoplites provided sufficient protection.

For some reason, the allies temporarily drop out of the narrative here. Thucydides, it seems, would have his readers believe that the Athenian marines were the ones doing the advancing and withdrawing, while the allies contributed little to the effort. Another possibility is that Thucydides slanted his account to favor those closest to his own sociopolitical status. There is no way to tell. Yet in the absence of further evidence, the possibility remains that the allies were in fact worthless at Aigition. Either way, allies or Athenians, no one was accomplishing much in Aetolia.

"Such was the battle for a long time, pursuits and tactical withdrawals, and in both the Athenians were the weaker party," according to Thucydides.[73] Which is to say, the Athenians were growing tired, mentally and physically. The Aetolians, "fit for battle," were not. Following Krentz's recent reconstruction, each marine could have been carrying as little as twenty-five pounds of equipment and so would have had plenty of mobility.[74] Furthermore, most of them would have been fit for battle, at least in some contexts, but the suitability of their conditioning in Aetolia was a different matter.

The Athenians and their allies would already have expended a significant amount of energy covering the distance between Teichion and Aigition, and this could not have been lost on the Aetolians who were waiting silently on the surrounding heights. It should come as no surprise that Thucydides' language of pursuits and tactical withdrawals brings to mind the practice of hunting, an activity presumably familiar to most Aetolians.[75]

Thucydides tells us that "as long as the archers had arrows and were able to use them, the Athenians held out—the light-armed Aetolians, assailed by arrows, were held in check."[76] Thucydides does not say whether those archers were Athenians assigned to individual vessels or an allied contingent. If the former, there would have been approximately 120. The Athenians had employed their own archers before, famously at the Battle of Plataea.[77] At Aigition they may have been involved in the fighting from the very start. But even if they were not involved, this raises an important question: Had the Athenians and their allies by this time consolidated under the protection of the archers, or were the archers covering the Athenian advances and withdrawals described above?

The language of holding out suggests that the Athenians and their allies had in fact consolidated, just as the Spartans did when pressed at Sphacteria the following year.[78] Recall, though, that the Athenians and their allies had stormed Aigition. Since archers were not the individuals of choice to spearhead an assault, at some point after the initial attack, the archers must have taken up positions close to the front where they could target the Aetolians. To their credit, the Athenians did this with enough skill and coordination to check the Aetolians' initial assault. The Athenian marines were protected in part by their own equipment, but the archers diminished the effectiveness of the javelins by keeping the Aetolians at a distance of at least sixty meters.[79]

Aside from his marines, who evidently were not up to the task, Demosthenes still lacked a contingent of troops capable of dislodging the Aetolians from their positions on the heights. The light-armed Locrians never made it to Aigition. From the Aetolians' perspective, then, it was only a matter of time before the invaders ran out of arrows or broke from exhaustion. From the Athenians' perspective, what was to happen now?

"When the leader of the archers was killed, the rest scattered," Thucydides writes.[80] The Athenians now had an even bigger problem. Yet how random was the killing of the *toxarchos*? Since the other archers came undone when their leader was killed, the toxarchos clearly was playing a key role in controlling and directing the efforts of the archers. The Aetolians may have picked up on this. The toxarchos could have been dressed differently, he certainly would have been issuing verbal commands that the Aetolians could have heard and understood, and he likely was not stationary during the actual fighting. The archers were quite effective, and the Aetolians needed to do something about them. Eliminating the toxarchos would have been an ideal place to start.

Furthermore, continues Thucydides, "the Athenians themselves were exhausted, and to a great extent, were collapsing from the repetitious exertion."[81] Now without the protection of the archers, they had to work that much harder to defend themselves. We do not know if heat played a role in the Athenians' exhaustion, although the Athenians' previous exertions and the Aetolians' tenacity over the course of what was presumably an hour or more certainly did.

Interestingly, the language of "collapsing from the repetitious exertion" also allows for an actual contraction of individuals into a mass.

"The Aetolians continued to attack and hurl javelins," reports Thucydides.[82] Hard-pressed and now within range of their assailants, the Athenians and their allies broke and fled. "Some fell into gullies that they could not climb out of while others lost their way."[83] A number of small ravines surrounded Aigition— the polis, after all, was built on high ground—and their steep banks, combined with the brush that grows in them during the summertime, would have been difficult for the Athenians to escape. More significantly, the gullies would have been one of the few avenues of escape available to the Athenians, but "their guide, Chromon the Messenian, had been killed."[84]

This short notice should give pause. What Thucydides is about to relate regarding the actions of the Athenians is by no means flattering. But if the Athenians lost their guide, again, through no fault of their own, they at least had some sort of excuse for their disordered retreat. Does this mean that Thucydides invented the death of Chromon? Probably not. But details like this suggest that there was more to Thucydides' narrative than factual reporting.

As before, we must consider the randomness of a leader's death. Did Chromon stand out among the Athenians and their allies, or had he drawn attention to himself as someone with authority? Did some Aetolians know who he was? In light of the toxarchos' fate, the killing of Chromon suggests a pattern. What comes to mind is the connection that Keegan made with warfare and the tactics of flock management. In Keegan's view, those who practiced a predominantly pastoralist way of life "knew how to break a flock up into manageable sections, how to cut off a line of retreat by circling to a flank, how to compress scattered beasts into a compact mass, how to isolate flock-leaders, how to dominate superior numbers by threat and menace, how to kill the chosen few while leaving the mass inert and subject to control."[85] The Aetolians relied heavily (though not entirely) on animal husbandry for many of their everyday needs as well as for surplus production; Aetolia simply could not support extensive agricultural practices.[86] To a certain extent, the Aetolians may have adapted the tactics of animal husbandry to their own way of war.

Thucydides continues: "The Aetolians, swift-footed and light-armed, were hurling javelins, and they caught and killed many [of the invaders] in the rout itself."[87] "Swift-footed" is one of Homer's epithets for Achilles.[88] In the context of Thucydides' narrative, the word implies that the Aetolians were naturally fast, and more significantly in this context, faster than the Athenians and their allies. By this time, the Aetolians could have been recycling javelins as they pursued their invaders. Thucydides once again employs the language of hunting—a graphic metaphor for sure, but the Aetolians were running down the invaders, knocking them over, and then presumably hacking or clubbing them to death.[89]

Such a grim fate awaited only those who fled. Those who stood their ground likely were killed first. Yet for most of the Athenians and their allies, the experience surely would have been terrifying: "Even more strayed from the paths and rushed into a forest from which there were no ways out. The Aetolians torched them."[90] Why would the Athenians rush into the woods? At first glance, this seems to have been a bad move, but the speedy and light-armed Aetolians could have run down the invaders with relative ease on the paths. The forest was the invaders' only other option. And while having "no ways out" likely was an exaggeration, the point is that the Athenians were chased into such thick brush that they could no longer evade their assailants.

The Aetolians were determined to rid their territory of the Athenians and those who had accompanied them, and perhaps even send a message to the neighboring communities who facilitated or contributed to the invasion. There would be no prisoners, and there would have been no survivors if the Aetolians had had their way. Ruthless and determined, the Aetolians torched not just the forest itself, but the actual individuals who stumbled into the woods.

Past commentators have shied away from the full import of Thucydides' language here, yet this is the most likely sense of the Athenians suffering "every form of flight and death imaginable," beyond mere hyperbole.[91] That is, in addition to the deaths brought about by conventional military implements in the rout itself, the trapped Athenians and their allies died from asphyxiation or burning to death, not to mention whatever grim fate awaited any potential escapees who fell into the hands of the Aetolians.

The successful escapees, without a guide, somehow made their way back to Oineon, possibly harassed or threatened the entire way.[92] "Many of the allies fell, and of the Athenian hoplites, about a hundred and twenty [died] . . . in the flower of youth." According to Thucydides, they were "the best men of the Athenian polis that died during this war."[93]

An unspecified number of allies perished in the rout, but Thucydides' narrative is too vague to venture an estimate. Demosthenes either dismissed the rest of the allies, or the survivors returned home on their own accord. From this point on, they are absent from the narrative. The most telling measure of the scale of the Athenians' defeat, according to Thucydides, was that nearly half of the original three hundred marines lost their lives in the encounter. One hundred twenty dead marines represented a 40 percent casualty rate among the Athenian hoplites at Aigition, assuming all three hundred took part in the invasion. If some of the marines stayed at Oineon to guard the Athenians' ships, an even higher percentage could have perished in Aetolia.[94] Along with the 120 marines, "Procles, one of the two generals, was also killed."[95] It was relatively common for a Greek general to die in battle, but this reinforces the pattern identified above regarding the Aetolians' way of war.[96]

Thucydides concludes: "After they had received the bodies of the dead under a truce from the Aetolians, the Athenians went back to Naupactus, and returned in their ships to Athens."[97] The Athenians acknowledged their defeat by asking to recover their dead. The Aetolians, adhering to what was virtually a universal Hellenic custom, granted their request.[98]

Although we are spared the details, the nature of this task had to have been nothing short of gruesome. The Athenians would have been dealing with an extensive scatter of stripped, bludgeoned, transfixed corpses, and possibly even a concentration of charred remains still smoldering in the woodlands near Aigition.

Aftermath

At some point before the Athenian invasion of 426, the Aetolians had sent an embassy to the Spartans and Corinthians to request assistance in regaining Naupactus. Toward the end of the summer, after the Athenian invasion, Sparta finally granted the Aetolians' request. The Spartans assembled a sizable contingent of 5,000 hoplites, five hundred of whom originated from Heraclea in Trachis, and set off from Delphi to be reinforced by the Aetolians near the border of Aetolia and West Locris.

Fearing the consequences of defeat in Aetolia, Demosthenes had chosen to stay in the western mainland and maintain a low profile. Once he learned of the Aetolians' and Spartans' intentions, he persuaded the Acarnanians to commit 1,000 hoplites of their own to defend Naupactus. The presence of these armed defenders at Naupactus was enough to dissuade the Aetolians and Spartans from attempting an assault, and this minor victory for Demosthenes marked the beginning of a new trend in his career.[99] With a string of successes in the west, he was soon to redeem himself in the eyes of his fellow Athenians.

Nevertheless, Demosthenes unquestionably failed in Aetolia, and the reasons for his failure remain unclear. Did he fall prey to bad advice and rush into Aetolia unprepared, or did the Athenians, reasonably well informed and well prepared, encounter too formidable of an opponent?

Analysis

Demosthenes clearly put a great deal of thought into launching the invasion, and he entered Aetolia with a purpose. After subduing the Aetolians, he planned to invade Boeotia. He also made arrangements for the West Locrians to supplement the allied contingents and Athenian archers, and he methodically advanced from settlement to settlement after setting off from Oineon. Furthermore, the Athenians stormed Aigition prepared to face some form of resistance. Finally, even without the Locrians, the Athenians and their allies successfully checked the Aetolian attack, at least initially.

In sum, Demosthenes and the rest of the Athenians did not stumble clumsily into the mountains of Aetolia. They intentionally launched an aggressive invasion with a well-coordinated force of archers and marines ready to fight. Had Demosthenes or Procles organized a hoplite assault of the heights surrounding Aigition, the Athenians could have had even more success against the light-armed Aetolians. If anything, then, the Aetolian rout of the Athenians demonstrates not the folly of leading "heavy" infantry into mountainous terrain, but the versatility of hoplites.[100]

According to the Messenians, what mattered most in Aetolia was not heavy or light equipment or certain battle formations, but speed and aggression. As the incident unfolded, the Messenians' advice to advance before the Aetolians could assemble turned out to be perfectly sound. But beating the Aetolians in Aetolia was no easy task. Xenophon, for instance, observed that without the Aetolians' consent in 389, a Spartan army would never have been able to march through Aetolia, regardless of the army's size.[101] Unfortunately, we cannot verify Xenophon's claim. No large-scale army ever invaded Aetolia with success—perhaps not a minor point.

As for bad advice, it is difficult to find fault with the Naupactian Messenians. They at least knew that the Aetolians could assemble in large numbers, and they reminded Demosthenes that the Aetolians fought without heavy equipment. In these two respects, the cautions they conveyed to Demosthenes were accurate to the best of their knowledge. At the time, a large-scale invasion of Aetolia was unprecedented, so no one, not even the Messenians, knew the full extent of the Aetolians' defensive capabilities. Even Thucydides, the former Athenian general ever concerned with the intelligent conduct of war, found no fault with Demosthenes for following the Messenians' advice. Like most of the Greek world, the Athenians were in the dark regarding the structure, organization, and capabilities of the fifth-century Aetolian ethnos, but the Aetolian Rout of the Athenians sheds new light on the subject.

We learn that the Aetolian response to the invasion of 426 represented only two-thirds of what the Aetolians could have accomplished as an ethnos. Thucydides makes no mention of the Eurytanians in his account of the fighting, but earlier in the year the Aetolians sent an embassy to Sparta and Corinth consisting of one representative from each of the three tribes of Aetolia. The Ophionions sent Tolophus, the Apodotians Tisander, and the Eurytanians Boriades. If there had been some sort of falling out between these groups in the interim, the Messenians were unaware of it, since they included the Eurytanians in their sketch of the Aetolian ethnos. So if there had been no falling out, and if the Eurytanians did not take part in the Rout, where were they?

There are two possibilities. First, the Eurytanians could have remained north of the Daphnos River in case the invading army chose to advance in that direction. The other possibility is that some Eurytanians actually were involved in the defensive effort, but not at Aigition. Instead, they were preventing the Locrians from entering Aetolia from the east. In both cases, while the Ophionians and Apodotians faced the threat from the south and west, the Eurytanians dealt with any threats from the north and east—the Aetolians' version of defense in depth. Incidentally, the absence of the Eurytanians means that the Athenians and their allies were spared from contending with the mighty, "raw-meat eating" Aetolians of the north. In other words, as horrific as it was to fight the Ophionians and Apodotians, the Athenians' experience actually could have been worse.

Whether the Eurytanians were at Aigition or not, the Aetolian Rout of the Athenians reveals that the Aetolian ethnos circa 426 could organize and execute a sophisticated and ruthless defense on short notice. This defense relied on the cooperation of Aetolian civilians to alert the rest of the ethnos of an invasion, abandon the vulnerable settlements of southern Aetolia, and assemble at Aigition. Aigition was centrally located, and the high ground and steep terrain in its vicinity offered the Aetolians a number of advantages against potential invading armies. If the Aetolians had to fight in Aetolia, they needed a site that played to their collective strengths; a loss within their home territory was too costly. With such high stakes, the Aetolians chose to concede the villages of southern Aetolia, but with strategic intent: they were in fact luring the Athenians and their allies to Aigition.

As we saw, the only harbor in the region that could have accommodated the Athenians and their allies was Oineon, but a quick glance at a map shows that an imposing mountain separates Oineon from Aigition. This means that a large-scale, conventional army had only one reasonable option for advancing north through southern Aetolia: a circuitous route in a clockwise direction following the foothills of the mountain. Along this route such an invading army would have encountered three Aetolian villages: Poteidania, Krokyleion, and Teichion.

In other words, the invading army's route from Oineon to Aigition was far from arbitrary: the invaders were following a major line of communication in southern Aetolia. This route began in the vicinity of Poteidania, continued on to other smaller settlements, and ultimately led to Aigition. Had such a route not existed through southern Aetolia, it would have been extremely difficult, if not impossible, for the Athenians and their allies to have made the fourteen-kilometer movement from Teichion to Aigition in such a short amount of time.

From the Aetolians' perspective, a large-scale invasion from the coast was going to follow a predictable route. Furthermore, this route was going to be relatively slow for the invading army, and without resistance, it would naturally end at Aigition. If the Aetolians who lived closest to the coast spotted a large number of warships at Oineon, they could alert the rest of the ethnos through visual signals and runners. The Ophionians and Apodotians could then abandon their unfortified and more vulnerable villages and make their way to Aigition and prepare an attack. And should the invaders choose to bypass Aigition and cross the Daphnos for some reason, the Eurytanians would have been there to greet them. In a way, then, the Aetolians did know Demosthenes' intentions from the start: they knew better than the Athenians and their allies.

The Aetolians did more than just capitalize on a series of blunders in response to the invasion of 426. They were not fortuitously successful against the Athenians and their allies, and they certainly did not defend themselves on a whim. On the contrary, the fifth-century Aetolians, as an ethnos, had developed a defensive strategy that they enacted shortly after the Athenians and their allies arrived at Oineon.

No other explanation accounts for the Aetolians' speed and sophistication in response to the invasion of 426. The only alternative is that Thucydides somehow made the Aetolians appear informed to soften the embarrassment of the Athenians. But the reconstruction of the Aetolian Rout of the Athenians shows that the Aetolians did not need such information to execute a successful defense.

Yet we must ask, what motive did the Aetolians have to develop such a defense strategy? What was the large-scale threat? At first glance, there would seem to be no clear answer. There were no aggressive or expansionary polities in the western mainland during the time in question, and limited-scale raiding and skirmishing with neighboring communities, though dangerous and potentially costly, did not threaten the existence of the Aetolian ethnos as a political entity.

We must remember, though, that late fifth-century Aetolia was an insulated, inland version of the Aetolia from previous generations, due primarily to the loss of Naupactus late in the sixth century or earlier in the fifth.[102] Furthermore, it was no secret that the Messenian Naupactians had wide-reaching connections, and in particular with the Athenians and their various allies. On their own, the Messenians of Naupactus were incapable of invading Aetolia, but they could bring a sizable group of allies to the region.

The threat of such an invasion may have been more immediate to the Ophionians and Apodotians, but the Eurytanians had every reason to assist in maintaining the integrity of their ethnos. At some point around the turn of the fifth century, then, the three Aetolian tribes needed to address the possibility of invasion.

The solution was an ethnos-wide system of defense that involved observing, evading, and then surprising potential invaders by exploiting geographical advantages—the mountains and woodlands—while relying on the cooperation and participation of a mobile civilian population.[103] It was a capability along these lines that the Messenians aimed to overwhelm with the help of the Athenians and their allies, not some feeble scatter of unfortified villages. Yet even then, the Messenians clearly underestimated the full extent of the Aetolians' collective capabilities.

In stark contrast to the prevailing practices of their day, the Aetolians developed a sophisticated way of war that complemented, and was not determined by, the advantages of their physical environment.[104] Collectively, the Aetolians recognized potential large-scale threats and made arrangements to protect themselves, and they did this not as a formal koinon, or federal state, but as an ethnos.

Larsen supposed that the Aetolians' defensive action in 426 required the existence of an "efficient central government," but what he meant by "government" is ambiguous.[105] He was not suggesting that the federal state recognizable in later periods also existed in the fifth century, but based strictly on the Aetolian Rout of the Athenians, he concluded that the fifth-century Aetolian ethnos must have constituted some sort of political entity. Larsen called this entity a "tribal state," and subsequent treatments of the fifth-century ethnos and the emergent Aetolian koinon have found no reason to disagree with his conclusion.[106] The earliest evidence of a formal council, assembly, and a possible system of magistrates in Aetolia dates to 367, although even then the source is non-Aetolian. As for Aetolian coinage and Aetolian epigraphic evidence of the workings of a federal state, both were third-century phenomena.[107]

But if there is no debate to speak of regarding the existence of a fifth-century koinon in Aetolia, there is also no denying that the Ophionians, Apodotians, and Eurytanians made a commitment to defend each other and formulated a plan as to how they would do so. These three groups even sent representative embassies abroad, suggesting that the Aetolian ethnos also had something along the lines of a foreign policy. From this it would follow, as Larsen suggested, that the fifth-century Aetolians had developed some form of government for deciding on issues that impinged on the entire ethnos.

Evidently, though, this loose confederation did not require a formal constitution or even standing institutions or offices to function. Without formal political structures, the Aetolians may have appeared backward to the polis-centric Greek world, but that mattered very little to the Aetolians. The Aetolians in fact constituted a coherent political entity thoroughly adapted to the demands of their geopolitical environment. The intricacies of this system may never be known, but the reconstruction of the Aetolian Rout of the Athenians shows that it was far from ineffective, "primitive," or out of touch with the dynamics of the rest of the Greek world.

By way of conclusion, it may be worth comparing the success of the fifth-century Aetolians with that of Aetolians from the late fourth century and then the third. Although aggressive and expansionary, Aetolians from later generations never spread themselves too thin. That is, the Aetolian League remained firmly rooted in the same mountainous environment as the fifth-century ethnos. Ironically, the way of war that the fifth-century Aetolians developed turned out to be better suited to the shifting demands of the fourth and third centuries, and aspects of it are recognizable in later generations.[108]

Perhaps this was no coincidence. The Aetolian League had every reason to retain the geographical advantages that the Aetolians from earlier generations exploited to such great effect. Furthermore, if the Aetolians of the late fourth century and the Hellenistic period did in fact build on the foundations of the fifth-century ethnos, their rise to power during this time should be less enigmatic. After all, they would have been building on what was already a relatively cohesive political formation, one with proven success in achieving desired ends in war.

CHAPTER 3

The Defense of Acarnania in 389

During the sixth and early fifth centuries, Acarnania consisted of three geographically and politically diverse regions: a large plain around the Acheloos River, a rugged mountainous region further inland, and a stretch of coastland extending from the Gulf of Corinth into the Ionian Sea.[1] Before the classical period, this coastal region and its adjacent islands hosted a series of Corinthian colonies. The colonists, however, interacted minimally with the inland inhabitants of Acarnania, of whom we know very little before the fifth century.[2]

By the middle of the fifth century, some of these regional divisions had dissolved. In terms of politics, most of the coastal colonies on the mainland were oriented toward the Acarnanians of the interior. But the islanders of Leucas, Kephallania, Ithaca, Zacythus, and Corcyra chose to remain independent. On some occasions, their independence led to conflict with the Corinthians and the Athenians, who viewed the Ionian Sea as a gateway to the Italian peninsula, Sicily, and the western Mediterranean.[3] As a result, the Athenians went to great pains to establish and maintain influence in the region. Eventually, their interests in the Ionian Sea came to involve the Acarnanians of the mainland.

These mainlanders constituted an ethnos of Acarnanians—that is, a people recognizable to outsiders—but the internal structure of their polity by the middle of the fifth century remains unclear.[4] There were a number of Acarnanian poleis both in the coastal region and further inland, and various populations lacking urban centers inhabited the region's mountainous interior.[5] Nevertheless, questions remain about the extent of political integration in Acarnania, and in particular whether a koinon, or federal state, existed at this time.

Proponents of a fifth-century koinon point to Stratos—a centrally located, inland polis—as clear evidence of a federal state.[6] That the fifth-century Acarnanians developed an impressive urban center can only suggest that they were fashioning a federal capital for themselves, or so the argument goes. In addition, Thucydides mentions the existence of a common court that existed at Olpae on the northern limits of Acarnanian territory circa 426. Some have taken this court as evidence of a federal judiciary.[7] Furthermore, Xenophon says that in 389, Agesilaus sent an embassy to *to koinon* of the Acarnanians at Stratos.[8] To some, *to koinon* must mean the Acarnanian federal government.

But there are a few problems with these views. First, although Stratos occupied an unambiguously central location and was unusually developed among Acarnanian settlements during the time in question, Stratian coinage circa 450–400 gives no indication of the existence of a federal state, let alone a shared Acarnanian identity. In fact, Acarnanian coinage in general does not exhibit a common ethnic inscription until circa 350–330.[9] As for epigraphic evidence of federal activities from Stratos, or from any other place in Acarnania, there is none.

Furthermore, as proponents of an early koinon reluctantly admit, the court at Olpae may not have been the location of a federal judiciary at all, but a site where the Acarnanians settled disputes with their Amphilocian neighbors to the north.[10] The language of Thucydides' narrative is too ambiguous to say with certainty.[11] As for Xenophon's notice of an Acarnanian koinon, it is clear that Agesilaus's embassy addressed a diplomatic congress of Acarnanians, but there are no indications that this congress formed part of a standing government with jurisdiction over the entire region. Since Xenophon may have had only a rudimentary understanding of the Acarnanians, his brief notice by itself cannot be taken as definitive evidence of a formal federal structure.

More important, we have no internal evidence from Acarnania that indicates the existence of a federal state during the fifth and early fourth centuries—nothing, that is, comparable to the inscriptions from the second half of the fourth century and the Hellenistic period.[12] Based on events documented by outsiders, a loose confederation of Acarnanian political communities clearly existed as early as the second half of the fifth century.[13] At the very least, by the first quarter of the fourth century, the Acarnanians were well on their way to establishing the federal state recognizable in the Hellenistic period.

Otherwise, the Acarnanians constitute yet another case of a somewhat aloof upland ethnos on the classical Greek mainland. They rarely took part in major Greek affairs during the fifth and fourth centuries until circa 375, and only when Athens, Corinth, or Sparta took interest in their region, which was not often. In fact, as a collective, the Acarnanians had to deal with external aggression on only two occasions. The first was Phormio's brief incursion into the Acarnanian interior in the winter of 429 when, for some reason, Thucydides was more interested in detailing the course of the Acheloos River than the activities of the Athenians and Acarnanians.[14] The other was the Spartan-led invasion of 389 documented by Xenophon. Xenophon, unlike Thucydides, took great interest in the actions of the invaders and defenders alike. His narrative is the most extensive account of the Acarnanians' collective activities for the entire classical period, and the analysis in this chapter seeks to answer a series of questions relating to it.

First, given that the Acarnanians constituted some sort of political entity during the time in question, what does the Defense of 389 reveal about their internal organization and collective capabilities during the early fourth century? Building on this, can we identify continuities between the defensive activities documented by Xenophon and those from earlier periods? Furthermore, if the distinction between the Acarnanian ethnos and koinon is unclear, are there any indications that the Defense of 389 was a federal defense? Ultimately, the chapter will show that not only had the Acarnanians developed a sophisticated defensive strategy that predated the invasion of 389, but their collective capabilities were rooted in the pre-koinon era of their history.

Past Approaches and Sources

Despite a relatively shallow depth of analysis, no study of the fifth- and fourth-century Acarnanians has ever overlooked the Defense of Acarnania in 389. But beyond referencing the Defense as the earliest mention of an Acarnanian koinon, no scholarly approach has investigated what the incident itself might reveal about the collective capabilities of the Acarnanians during the early fourth century. Why? Because Xenophon's usage of *to koinon* says very little about the internal structure and organization of the Acarnanian polity, and if that structure and organization is the main point of interest, the incident has little else to offer.

In topographical studies, the Defense of Acarnania has been the focal point of a centuries-long debate regarding the location of the violent encounter between Acarnanians and Spartans in 389. This debate will be important for our understanding of the incident and so is discussed in depth below. At present, suffice it to say that as illuminating as these studies have been, not a single one has ever considered whether the Acarnanians engineered the site of their encounter with the Spartans.

Studies of the so-called Corinthian War of 395–387 have treated the Spartan-led invasion of Acarnania in 389 as a sideshow to more important developments in the northern Peloponnese.[15] In some ways, this is a legitimate perspective. After all, the ramifications of the Defense vis-à-vis broader affairs within the Greek world appear to have been slight.

But what is troubling about this perspective is that it views the outcome of the Defense as a Spartan success, and in particular a success of Agesilaus.[16] Since Xenophon provides the only narrative account of the encounter, this interpretation still prevails. Plutarch, Pausanias, and Polyaenus summarily treat the Defense, but they are in full agreement with Xenophon and make no additions to his account in the *Hellenica*.[17] In fact, the language and structure of each of these later narratives are so similar to that of Xenophon's that all three were likely derivatives thereof. To complicate matters even further, no other contemporary source exists for comparison with Xenophon.

This source situation raises a series of concerns. The first has to do with Xenophon's methodology. As is well known, Xenophon based his historical writings almost entirely on memory. Furthermore, there are few indications that he conducted his own investigation of events in which he did not participate or that did not involve his close associates. As a result, Xenophon tended to remain silent on matters for which he had no information.

Given the basis of his historical method, the material Xenophon did relate was subject to the vagaries of memory and the various interests and agendas of his sources.[18] Most important, Xenophon was an open admirer of the Spartans. He could be critical of particular actions, but in general he was sympathetic toward the Spartans' cause and wrote about them favorably. Furthermore, Xenophon positively adored Agesilaus and cast the actions of the Spartan king in as positive a light as possible. His account of what Agesilaus allegedly accomplished in Acarnania in 389 is no exception. In addition, and not surprisingly, Xenophon is effectively silent on the organization and leadership of the Acarnanian defense. Consequently, he offers only a one-sided perspective of the encounter slanted entirely in favor of the invading army.

Despite these concerns, Christopher Tuplin has demonstrated that there are rarely grounds to doubt Xenophon's accuracy in relating the dynamics of actual military engagements, especially in the *Hellenica*.[19] In this case, Xenophon's narrative of the Defense of Acarnania is internally coherent, contains descriptions of terrain that are reconcilable to the topography of the region, and is based on eyewitness accounts.[20] If Xenophon did not take part in the Spartan-led invasion of Acarnania in 389 (and it is possible that he did), he certainly had direct access to Agesilaus, the commander of the invading army.[21] In short, no aspect of the narrative appears to have been the work of Xenophon's imagination. To reconstruct the dynamics of the Defense and evaluate its greater significance, the analysis below uses archaeological and topographical studies to read Xenophon's narrative against the grain.

Before turning to this narrative, some context is necessary: Toward the end of the first decade of the fourth century, the fifth year of the Corinthian War, the Spartans found themselves pitted against the recently formed quadruple alliance of Athens, Boeotia, Argos, and Corinth.[22] By 390, most of the fighting centered on the northern Peloponnese, where the Spartans were experiencing a mix of minor successes around Corinth. They also suffered a few setbacks, first in Arcadia and then a disaster near Lechaeum engineered by Iphicrates and his peltasts.[23]

In contrast, the Acarnanians were mostly aloof from the conflict. They were allied with the Athenians and Boeotians as early as 394, when they sent a contingent of light-armed fighters to support the Corinthians at Nemea.[24] Short of that, they kept to their own affairs, although not peacefully. Making good use of their alliance, the Acarnanians were pursuing their own territorial interests in the western mainland, namely, the settlement of Calydon. Eventually, their aggression prompted a response from the coalition opposing the Athenians and Boeotians and brought the fighting of the Corinthian War to the Acarnanians' own borders.

The Defense

In the late summer of 389, an embassy of Achaeans gained an audience in Sparta and asked for help. The Acarnanians were attacking Calydon, had compelled the Achaeans to maintain a garrison there, and now, with assistance from the Athenians and Boeotians, were threatening to seize the Achaeans' sole "overseas" possession.[25] The Achaeans did not merely request aid from their Spartan allies. They threatened to send the majority of their military resources across the Gulf of Corinth should the Spartans refuse. In other words, the Achaeans were going to abandon the Spartans' war in the Peloponnese. And if the Achaeans still could not protect the Calydonians, they had plans to make peace with the Acarnanians and their allies.[26]

According to Xenophon, "The ephors and the assembly decided that they had to launch an expedition with the Achaeans against the Acarnanians, so they sent Agesilaus with two *morai* and a contingent of allies."[27] This was no token gesture on the part of the ephors. At this time, the entire Lacedaemonian army consisted of only six *morai*, conventionally referred to as regiments. Each *mora* consisted of anywhere between 600 and 1,100 hoplites.[28] The Spartans sent at least one-third of their standing army under the charge of their most competent commander. The threat worked.

Accompanying the two *morai* would have been approximately 120 to 300 Lacedaemonian horsemen (*hippeis*), meaning that the Spartan force totaled about 1,400 to 2,500 individuals.[29] The rest of the allies are unnamed in Xenophon's narrative, but whoever they were, there is no indication that they contributed much to the effort.[30] In comparison, "the Achaeans joined the expedition in full force."[31]

The capabilities of the Achaean ethnos at this time are somewhat vague. The twelve "divisions" of Herodotus's day provided a means of summoning and organizing resources on a large scale, but estimating even an approximate size of the Achaean contingent is speculative.[32] Assuming the Achaeans at full force numbered at least five hundred, the entire expeditionary force would have ranged between 2,000 and 4,000 individuals. At its lowest estimate, the army about to cross the Gulf of Corinth was menacing, and it certainly made an impression on the Acarnanians who observed its arrival.

Xenophon reports, "After Agesilaus crossed, all of the Acarnanians from the country districts fled into the towns [*astē*], and they withdrew their livestock inland to prevent their animals from being captured."[33] The Acarnanians took two precautionary measures in response to the pending invasion. They headed toward their fortified and more defensible settlements, and they sent their valuable livestock to the mountainous interior of Acarnania, well outside of the invading army's reach. Xenophon does not specify the actual landing site, but given the Acarnanians' response, there are only two possibilities. The first is somewhere along the Calydonian coast, or more likely, somewhere in the Paracheloitis region, a spacious and fertile plain near the mouth of the Acheloos River (map 4).[34]

But Xenophon's description of the Acarnanians' response should give pause. A powerful army arrives, and the natives head for the hills; this sounds very much like a literary trope. Given the circumstances, though, such a response on the part of the Acarnanians actually made the most sense. First, the Acarnanians simply could not have been oblivious to maritime activity along their coastal borders, especially the Acarnanians at Oiniadai.[35] Additionally, if the Acarnanians were preparing another attack on Calydon, there already would have been an increased Acarnanian presence near the coast. In each case, a large number of non-Athenian vessels transporting personnel, horses, and military equipment meant trouble.

For the Acarnanians, abandoning the countryside in favor of fortified inland settlements likely was a standard response, as it was during the fifth

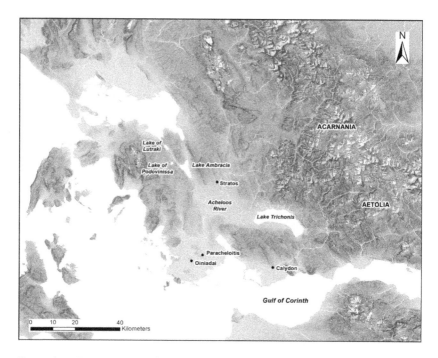

MAP 4. The Defense of Acarnania (389). Created by D. Matthew Buell.

century. For instance, when the Spartans under Eurylochus made their way through Acarnanian territory in the winter of 426, they found the land empty of its inhabitants: the Acarnanians who had not gone to the aid of Amphilocian Argos were garrisoned at Stratos.[36]

To return to Xenophon's narrative of the invasion of 389: "When Agesilaus arrived at the border of enemy territory, he sent an embassy to the congress [*koinon*] of the Acarnanians at Stratos."[37] Stratos was a large, inland polis, approximately fifty kilometers from the coast, well developed during the classical period, and evidently, also the location of the Acarnanians' decision-making assembly. Importantly, the geographical distance from the coast and the time it would have taken to gather the Acarnanian assembly gave the Acarnanians more time to prepare their defense, even if the embassy went on horseback. Once both parties were assembled at Stratos, Xenophon writes that Agesilaus's embassy "announced that if the Acarnanians did not renounce their alliance with the Boeotians and Athenians and become allies of the Spartans and Achaeans he would ravage their entire country—one portion after another—and would spare nothing."[38] Before responding to the Spartans' ultimatum, the Acarnanians had to take into account a variety of factors—above all was their long-standing affiliation with the Athenians and enmity with the Achaeans.

Would there be serious repercussions if the Acarnanians broke their alliance with the Athenians? For that matter, with a force of Spartans and their allies poised to devastate the Acarnanians' agricultural resources, would the Athenians offer assistance? If not, could the Acarnanians sustain the consequences of the imminent invasion? That is, how confident were the Acarnanians in their own defensive capabilities?

The extent to which the congress of Acarnanians weighed these contingencies is unclear, but the embassy clearly failed to make a persuasive case: "Since the Acarnanians refused, Agesilaus did as he said he would: he advanced no more than ten or twelve stadia per day, devastating the land methodically."[39] The invaders covered approximately two kilometers per day, destroying whatever agricultural resources they encountered, such as grains, fruit trees (including olive trees), and vines.[40] Systematically destroying these resources in the fertile Paracheloitis region would have been an intensive and time-consuming task, especially east of the Acheloos where the invasion most likely began[41]—hence the slow advance.

"Because of the army's slowness, the Acarnanians thought it was safe to drive their livestock down from the mountains and to go on cultivating the greater part of the countryside."[42] Xenophon's description seems like a natural enough response. After all, most Acarnanian territory was west of the Acheloos River, well out of the invading army's reach, and the Acarnanians could withdraw their livestock again if necessary. Notice, though, what the Acarnanians did not do, namely, marshal support from their Athenian and Boeotian allies. Why? Is this merely a function of Xenophon's limited knowledge? Perhaps, but as the defense of Acarnania unfolds, the Acarnanians' allies are nowhere to be found, at least not in Acarnania.[43]

It could be that the invading army prevented the Acarnanians from reaching their allies; this is unlikely, however, because it required only a single messenger to summon aid. Perhaps the Acarnanians underestimated the intentions of the invading army. In fact, maybe they were overconfident, as Agesilaus thought.

Xenophon continues: "On the fifteenth or sixteenth day after the start of the invasion, when it seemed to Agesilaus that the Acarnanians were now overly confident, he made a sacrifice early in the day and marched the army 160 stadia before evening to the lake around which nearly all of the Acarnanians' livestock was located."[44] If the invaders maintained their two-kilometer-per-day pace, at this point they would have advanced approximately thirty to thirty-two kilometers. If they advanced north in a relatively straight line, as opposed to a more realistic meandering route, they would have been approaching the southern limits of the Stratike region—that is, the district surrounding the polis of Stratos.[45]

This means that the 160-stadia march matched the distance that the army had covered in two and a half weeks. Without question, a certain amount of scouting enabled Agesilaus to learn of the location of the Acarnanians' livestock, and the individuals who gathered this information likely were the same ones who led the army to the lake.[46]

Yet the lake itself is unnamed. Its identification has generated some controversy, but its location is actually less important for understanding what unfolded in Acarnania in 389.[47] At present, it is important to note that the Acarnanians only seemed overly confident to Agesilaus. This is a crucial distinction. In the past, scholars have all too easily ascribed a complacent state of mind to the Acarnanians, based solely on Xenophon's account.[48]

When Agesilaus reached the Acarnanians' herds, Xenophon writes, "he seized great numbers of cattle and horses, all sorts of livestock, and many slaves."[49] Why do we hear only of slaves? What happened to the rest of the Acarnanians? Did a hostile army numbering in the thousands march through the heart of Acarnanian territory over the course of an entire day and go unnoticed? Why were the Acarnanians so careless as to leave their valuable herds and slaves unguarded?

In the context of Agesilaus's invasion, the animals and slaves were indeed booty, "taken by the spear," but there is no indication that the invaders faced any resistance in seizing the Acarnanians' resources.[50] On the contrary, Xenophon continues, "after the seizure, [Agesilaus] remained there for the next day, and sold the booty."[51] The individuals to whom Agesilaus sold the booty remain a puzzle. The most reasonable explanation is that merchants accompanied the invading army.[52] If so, where did they go after they bought the livestock and slaves? Did they stay with the army and witness the Spartan commander's own case of overconfidence?

"While Agesilaus was camped on the mountain slopes," writes Xenophon, "many Acarnanian peltasts arrived."[53] Consider what this development presumes. Within twenty-four hours of Agesilaus's arrival at the lake and the seizure and sale of the livestock and slaves, a specialized contingent of Acarnanians, undetected, had assembled and approached the army's camp.[54] By this time, the Acarnanians had had almost three weeks to observe the size, activities, and disposition of the invading army, a task ideally suited to the light-armed peltasts native to the region. The 160-stadia cross-country march simply could not have gone unnoticed and in fact may have been unopposed for a very good reason.[55]

From the invaders' perspective, the arrival of the peltasts was the first hostile act encountered since landing in Acarnania, but it was not the Acarnanians' first defensive activity. On the contrary, after Agesilaus crossed the Gulf of

Corinth, what seemed to Xenophon (or his source) as essentially a fear response on the part of the Acarnanians was just the opposite. Rather than "fleeing" to the safety of their fortified settlements, the Acarnanians were rushing to mobilization points to prepare their defense.[56] That Agesilaus met with no resistance when capturing the livestock and slaves only reinforces this view—the Acarnanians responsible for defending their ethnos were attending to just that. Now it was time to attack.

"Hurling and slinging projectiles from the ridge of the mountain, they remained unharmed and forced the army down onto the level ground, even though the invaders were already preparing their evening meal."[57] Xenophon goes on to use five separate verbs for discharging missiles. The first two here indicate that the Acarnanians' initial volleys consisted of javelins, light spears, and clay, stone, or lead bullets fired from slings.[58]

The Acarnanians attacked when the invaders were preparing a meal, which suggests a sense of timing based on direct observation of the invading army. Agesilaus's army seems to have responded effectively, at least to a certain extent, since it took the Acarnanians some time to force the invaders off the mountain slope.

From the invaders' perspective, the attack may have seemed like mere harassment. The Acarnanians disturbed their meal, forced them to change the location of their camp after they had settled in for the evening, and perhaps even wounded a few individuals, but they did not follow up on their success. They did just the opposite: "At night the Acarnanians went away."[59]

The Acarnanians did not trouble the invaders after nightfall. Instead, they kept quiet, remained out of site, and evidently, refrained from making fires. Such is the import of "went away," but the Acarnanians had not gone anywhere. In fact, forcing the invading army down into the level ground was the first openly hostile act in a sophisticated, well-coordinated attack.

"The soldiers posted sentries and slept."[60] With this remark, Xenophon suggests that Agesilaus, contrary to the Spartans' customary practice, had not posted sentries on the mountain slope. Perhaps he was relying on the security of the terrain before the Acarnanians' arrival.[61] This seeming complacency may be an indication that the accumulated exhaustion of the two-and-a-half-week invasion, the devastation of the Acarnanian countryside, and the thirty-kilometer march cross country was taking its toll on the Spartans and their allies. If so, this could not have been lost on the Acarnanians and may have indicated to them that it was time to attack. But with sentries now posted, the invaders passed the night uneventfully.

"The next day Agesilaus started to lead the army away. But the route out of the meadow and plain around the lake was narrow because of the encircling mountains."[62] Xenophon's description of the terrain is quite clear: the army camped in a relatively flat, grassy area next to a lake, surrounded by mountains, and from the invaders' perspective, this basin had only one narrow exit. Given this description and the approximate distance that the invading army had covered since its arrival in Acarnania, nineteenth-century topographers identified three likely candidates for the lake of Xenophon's narrative, all within three to five kilometers of each other: Lake Ambracia, the Lake of Lutraki, and the Lake of Podovinissa.[63] Pritchett conducted his own survey of the region and backed the identification of the Lake of Lutraki, but most recently, Landgraf and Schmidt have argued for the southern tip of Lake Ambracia.[64]

This debate is highly significant not because researchers have been unable to identify with certainty the site of the violent encounter in 389; rather, because there are at least three lakes that are reconcilable to Xenophon's narrative. In other words, the Acarnanians could have executed their attack in any number of places within their territory. It was no coincidence that the Acarnanians sent their livestock to the site described by Xenophon. Evidently, Agesilaus took the Acarnanian bait.

The Acarnanian peltasts had ensured that the invading army moved away from the encircling heights and down into the bottom of this natural basin. Even more Acarnanians had escaped Agesilaus's notice in occupying these heights, because as the invading army attempted to advance out of the natural basin, Xenophon explains, "the Acarnanians, in control [of the high ground], were launching projectiles and hurling javelins from the heights above the right of the army."[65]

Xenophon gives no indication that the Acarnanians surprised the army to great effect, but if they did, the invading force weathered the attack. It appears that the assailants kept themselves at a distance just as they had done the previous day, but instead of merely harassing the invaders, "the Acarnanians gradually descended to the lowest slopes, pressed their attack, and made things so difficult that the army was no longer able to advance."[66] The invaders could no longer rely on their individual shields to deflect sling stones and javelins from their right flank as they moved toward the exit of the basin. They had to turn and respond to the attack. At first glance, this may have seemed like a simple task from the invaders' perspective, since the Acarnanian slingers were likely the ones spearheading the assault.

The closer the Acarnanian slingers could get to the army, the higher the impact velocity of their sling stones would be, and the slingers needed to be within at least 100 to 150 meters of their targets to inflict significant damage.[67] Furthermore, because of the high velocity and consequent flat trajectory of the sling-fired projectiles, the slingers also needed to remain above the peltasts and javelineers on the slope, or at least rush in front of them to fire at the army. On relatively level ground, the javelineers could lob their projectiles over the heads of the slingers, but the reverse was not the case.

The gradual descent that Xenophon mentions would have made room for more Acarnanians to join the fight, although the Acarnanians would not have wanted to flood the slope with slingers and javelineers in case they needed to retreat. In response, the invaders formed a phalanx, and some actively countered the Acarnanian attack, but "the hoplites and *hippeis* who broke out of the phalanx in pursuit of their attackers were doing no damage since the Acarnanians were always quick to fall back to strong-points."[68]

There are no indications that the hoplites and hippeis attempted a coordinated assault. If they did, it did not matter, since the Acarnanians quickly withdrew to what would have been unassailable positions and presumably continued to shoot at those who had rushed out of the phalanx.[69]

Given Xenophon's silence on the matter, one has to wonder about the fate of these bold attackers. Outside of the phalanx, they would have been easy targets for the slingers and javelineers who were not currently being chased up the slope. Perhaps the Acarnanians were aware of this. By approaching the army now consolidated in defense, they may have been attempting to draw individuals out from the protection of the phalanx just as Iphicrates' peltasts did against the Spartans at Lechaeum the previous year.[70] In the wake of Lechaeum, Agesilaus's apparent lack of light-armed troops is curious. The explanation of silence on Xenophon's part will not suffice: Xenophon knew and appreciated the value of peltasts like no other contemporary source, and he mentioned their contributions throughout his writings.[71] Without peltasts or other light-armed troops, the Spartans were at a major disadvantage.

"Realizing that it would be difficult to exit the narrow pass under these conditions, Agesilaus decided to go after the large number of attackers pressing hard from the left."[72] Here we learn from Xenophon that Agesilaus was dealing not only with the Acarnanian slingers and javelineers to the army's right, but an even larger-scale attack from the other side of the basin. Using the terrain to their advantage and remaining undetected, the Acarnanians had surrounded and attacked a sizable invading army led by one of the most seasoned commanders in the Greek world at the time.[73] Although that is remarkable in itself, we have yet to see the full extent of the Acarnanians' defensive capabilities.

First, though, a few observations on the current situation: The exact nature of the Acarnanian attack from the army's left is unclear. The hoplites and horsemen who were rushing out of the phalanx were targeting only the slingers and javelineers on their right. Perhaps, then, the Acarnanians attacking from the other side of the basin were keeping their distance, although still "pressing hard" with sustained volleys of sling stones and javelins.[74]

By this time, Agesilaus would have realized that he needed to move the army out of the basin as soon as possible. The pass appeared to be unguarded— although the Acarnanians may have had a surprise waiting for anyone who attempted to exit it—but as we saw, the army could no longer advance in that direction. In the opposite direction was the lake, and the army as a whole could not traverse the steep and well-guarded terrain to the right. The only remaining option was the other side of the basin, since, as Xenophon explains, "the mountain in this direction was more traversable for both hoplites and horses."[75]

Agesilaus made a plan to break out of the basin, circulated it to the rest of the Spartans and their allies, and prepared a sacrifice. The Acarnanians could have observed this activity, and they may have responded in some way.[76] On this point, Xenophon mentions that "while Agesilaus was making the sacrifice, the Acarnanians continued to launch projectiles and hurl javelins, and coming in close, they were wounding many."[77] The Acarnanians in both directions were still attacking. The Acarnanians on the more traversable slope were now closing with Agesilaus's army and firing sling stones and javelins from a closer distance—again, as close as 100 to 150 meters. The notice that the Acarnanians were wounding many is the first of only two indications in Xenophon's entire narrative that some of the invaders actually bled in Acarnania. Despite Xenophon's potential understatement, it does seem that the invading army was holding up well. Nevertheless, the Acarnanians were wearing down the army that they had trapped in the basin and by all accounts were steadily subduing the invaders.

"But when Agesilaus gave the command, the fifteen-year class rushed out from the hoplites, the *hippeis* charged, and Agesilaus himself followed with the others."[78] By "gave the command," Xenophon likely meant that Agesilaus ordered a *salpinx* call. The cries of the wounded and the shouting of those still fighting combined with the impacts and reverberations of Acarnanian projectiles on shields and armor would have made a verbal signal inaudible, especially one intended for a large portion of the army.[79]

The fifteen-year class—those aged twenty to thirty-five—would have been the most physically competent of the Spartan hoplites, and this time, the hippeis advanced on their horses. Xenophon cannot resist adding that Agesilaus also advanced, but with the unnamed "others" behind the leading wave. Given the nature of the Acarnanians' weapons, the hoplites would have needed to retain their shields and helmets for the assault. In addition, the Spartans' lightweight pilos helmets would have been no burden, and importantly, they offered additional protection.[80]

"The Acarnanians who had advanced down the mountain and were throw-ing missiles turned around quickly but were killed to a man as they fled."[81] Agesilaus's tactical acumen here is remarkable. He waited for the Acarnanians to approach and signaled the assault while the Acarnanians were launching— or more likely, preparing to launch—another volley of javelins.[82] In the pro-cess of firing, the Acarnanians would have been least prepared to run back up the mountain. As the uncoordinated and ineffective Spartan rushes from earlier in the encounter revealed, the invaders needed every possible advantage against their speedy assailants.

The annihilation of the slingers and javelineers was the invaders' first suc-cess, but not the end of their difficulties: "On the summit, Acarnanian hop-lites were drawn up for battle as was the majority of the peltasts, and they stood firm."[83] The intricacy of the Acarnanian attack is now on full display: the Acarnanians had prepared a phalanx of their own, supported presumably by the same peltasts who had initiated the Acarnanians' attack so effectively the previous day. But this development also raises a number of questions.

First, was it the Acarnanians' intention to lure the invading army up the slope so the Acarnanian hoplites could attack with the aid of the peltasts and an extraordinary terrain advantage?[84] If so, this would explain why the Acar-nanians initially kept their distance on this side of the basin and pressed the attack from the other. Then again, were the slingers and javelineers meant to soften up the army so these hoplites and peltasts could attack at the most op-portune time? For that matter, were Acarnanian hoplites drawn up for battle all around the basin or just on this side?

Either way, it bears emphasizing that the Acarnanians had not only as-sembled and deployed this coordinated force in a relatively short amount of time—roughly from the time the Acarnanian peltasts located the invading army camped on the mountain slope—but also executed their sophisticated attack undetected. As Xenophon writes, "They launched various projectiles and threw their spears, wounding the cavalrymen and killing some horses."[85] To the credit of the Spartan fifteen-year class and hippeis, they continued the assault up the slope, and by doing so, prevented a rout. Had they hesitated, and if the Acarnanian hoplites and peltasts then advanced, a fight on the slope would have ensued.

Notice that the Acarnanian—quite unusually—threw their spears. Xeno-phon may have included this detail to convey a sense of desperation, that is, the undeterred Spartan assault rattled the Acarnanian phalanx. Yet it is entirely possible that each Acarnanian hoplite carried two spears, threw one, and con-tinued to stand firm with the other. (Xenophon does not say who did the actual throwing.)[86] The Acarnanians would have known that they were up against a contingent of Spartan cavalry, so it is possible that the peltasts brought heavier spears for this very reason.

"But when they were almost within reach of the Lacedaemonian hoplites, they retreated."[87] Note the slight discrepancy in Xenophon's narrative. Earlier he claimed that the fifteen-year class was to lead the assault up the slope, but it is clear that the horsemen were the first to engage with the Acarnanian hoplite and peltast contingents. Despite Xenophon's best efforts to downplay the Acarnanians' actions—they wounded the cavalrymen (all of them?) and killed "some" horses—the hoplites and peltasts in fact stopped the cavalry charge and were still standing firm.

But in the end, the Acarnanians wheeled around and retreated.[88] The persistent assault of the Spartan fifteen-year class with the rest of the Lacedaemonian and Achaean hoplites in tow was too much.[89] The Acarnanian hoplites may have been outnumbered, or perhaps the unnamed Acarnanian generals were smart enough to avoid fighting the Lacedaemonian army on equal footing.

To answer some of the questions raised above, it does not appear that Acarnanian hoplites stood ready out of sight on the other side of the basin. If they were, one has to wonder why they did not attack when they saw the invading army launch its assault. Instead, it seems that the Acarnanian slingers and javelineers on the steeper slope withdrew when they saw that the invaders were making their way out of the basin. Since these particular Acarnanians were also preventing the army from moving toward the narrow exit, it is most likely that they were attempting to compel (or lure) the invading army up the slope for a decisive engagement. In other words, the Acarnanians left Agesilaus only one option.

"On that day, about 300 of them died."[90] The significance of this number is difficult to gauge. For one, although Xenophon has hinted at the high casualty rate sustained by Agesilaus's army, he does not relate the number of invaders slain or the status of the wounded for comparison. It would be helpful to know, for instance, how many of Agesilaus's wounded were still able to fight and how many could no longer contribute to the invasion. Xenophon also does not specify the various contingents to which the three hundred Acarnanians who died in the encounter belonged. Modern scholarship has yet to treat this as a problem. But the rest of Xenophon's narrative provides enough information to discern who these Acarnanians were, and this sheds light on a significant aspect of the Acarnanian defense.

First, as there is no indication of a rout and pursuit of the Acarnanian hoplites in Xenophon's narrative—on the contrary, Xenophon clearly states that they withdrew before coming within reach of the Lacedaemonians—very few Acarnanian hoplites would have been included in the three hundred. In addition, the Acarnanian peltasts who were drawn up for battle out of sight could have easily outrun the Lacedaemonian hoplites just as the Acarnanian slingers and javelineers on the army's right had evaded the hoplites and hippeis who broke out of the phalanx.

This means that the wave of slingers and javelineers "great in number," caught and killed to a man in the army's charge out of the basin, constituted the most significant portion of the three hundred Acarnanian dead.[91] These individuals were some of the youngest, poorest, and least specialized members of the Acarnanians' defensive repertoire, and from a commander's perspective, the easiest to replace.[92]

Furthermore, to judge from Xenophon's account, the Acarnanians did not even admit defeat by requesting to recover their dead, a detail that Xenophon tended to include in his narratives of military encounters.[93] Nevertheless, "after that, Agesilaus set up a trophy, and going around from there, cut down and scorched the countryside."[94] Destruction by fire was absent from the army's earlier devastation activities. Perhaps Xenophon meant to convey a sense of heightened aggression on the part of the invaders in response to the disaster that they had nearly suffered. Or maybe Agesilaus ordered the scorching to elicit a response from the Acarnanians, that is, to fight in the open. If the latter, he was unsuccessful.

"Compelled by the Achaeans, he even attacked some of the *poleis*, but he did not take a single one."[95] The distinction, if any, that Xenophon made between the Acarnanian *poleis* here and the *astē* from earlier in his narrative is unclear, as is the nature of these attacks and the Acarnanians' defensive methods.[96] Given the logistical constraints of the invasion and the time that had already passed, the burning and "besieging" portion of the invasion could have lasted only two to four weeks.[97] The Acarnanians refused to fight Agesilaus on his terms, and Agesilaus avoided fighting the Acarnanians on theirs.

Logistics aside, Agesilaus did not want to stay in Acarnania once the colder seasons started to approach. Heavy rainfalls would have restricted his army's mobility, leaving the invaders vulnerable to yet another Acarnanian attack.[98] And so "when autumn was coming on, he left the country."[99]

Aftermath

The Achaeans were less than pleased with the outcome of the invasion. They had asked Agesilaus to stay in the country long enough to prevent the Acarnanians from sowing their fields, but he refused, claiming that the more the Acarnanians sowed their fields, the more willingly they would come to terms with the Spartans and their allies the following year. Unimpressed, and citing Agesilaus's inability to gain control of a single Acarnanian polis, the Achaeans concluded that the expedition had accomplished nothing. (Xenophon kept his own view of the matter to himself.)[100] Was there anything to the Achaeans' claim?

Analysis

Part of the Achaeans' grievance with Agesilaus was that not only had he failed to win over a single Acarnanian polis by force, but that he was unable to do so through diplomacy. Agesilaus left the region without the Acarnanians having agreed to anything—no truce with the Achaeans, no alliance with the Spartans, not even a pledge to cease from attacking the Calydonians.

Beyond the Achaeans' grievances, there are some additional factors to explore. First, did the invasion bring about economic ruin for the Acarnanians? Without question, the crop destruction and disruption of the harvest in 389 would have been significant, but the Acarnanians should have been prepared for at least one bad year. Preventing the Acarnanians from sowing their fields would have been far more devastating. In fact, with their harvest partially destroyed and the invading army blocking them from sowing their fields, the Acarnanians might have been willing to consider an offer from Agesilaus. Given the Acarnanians' initial response to the Spartan embassy at Stratos, though, Agesilaus probably figured that they would refuse any terms and instead prepare another attack. If so, the Spartans needed to be cautious; they had barely escaped their first engagement with the Acarnanians.

The fate of the Acarnanians' livestock and slaves raises additional questions. As with the disruption of the harvest, the loss of these possessions would have been significant, but did the Acarnanians actually lose them? It is difficult to say. The first and last that we hear of the livestock and slaves is the brief notice in Xenophon's narrative. In addition, not only is the identity of the supposed merchants unknown, but Xenophon gives no indication as to where they went after buying the livestock and slaves. (To be fair, he may not have known.)

Nevertheless, whoever the merchants were, they could not have gone far in the span of a day or two, and wherever they went, they still would have been near the heart of Acarnanian territory. Burdened with Acarnanian livestock and slaves, these merchants would have been easy targets as soon as they left the protection of the invading army. Xenophon and his sources had no way of knowing what happened to the livestock and slaves after Agesilaus sold them near the lake. But the Acarnanians were already in the vicinity of whichever direction the merchants actually went. We know this because the Acarnanians attacked the Spartans and their allies the following evening.

It is possible that some merchants remained with Agesilaus and then followed the invading army out of Acarnania. Some of the merchants could have even been Calydonians. Again, though, the army's protection would have lasted only until the Spartans left the region. And once the invading army left, the Acarnanians easily could have regained their livestock and slaves. As events leading up to the invasion of 389 showed, the Acarnanians were fully capable of attacking coastal settlements beyond their own borders. Consequently, it is difficult to sustain the notion that the invasion brought about agricultural or economic ruin for the Acarnanians.

That said, the Acarnanians did send an embassy to Sparta the following spring to make peace with the Achaeans and become allies of the Spartans. According to Xenophon, they did so because Agesilaus was making preparations for another invasion, and the potential ramifications of further crop destruction worried the Acarnanians.[101] But this is Xenophon talking. In his view, the Acarnanians must have feared another invasion. Why else would they have capitulated?

There are a few reasons. First, very little was at stake for the Acarnanians by making peace with the Achaeans and becoming allies of the Spartans. They had to stop attacking Calydon, at least temporarily—that was about it. In addition, the Athenians and Boeotians had shown little concern for what was happening in Acarnania; evidently, they were dealing with more pressing issues. If coming to terms with the Achaeans and Spartans was going to prevent further destruction and keep the Spartans from meddling in Acarnania, the Acarnanians had no reason to sustain another invasion.

Furthermore, there are few indications that the Acarnanians' newly pledged loyalty to the Spartans was anything more than a calculated move. Never once does Xenophon mention that the Acarnanians took part in subsequent engagements during the Corinthian War—that is, they offered no support to the Spartan cause. And the next record of Acarnanian involvement in Greek affairs is in 375 when the Acarnanians joined the Second Athenian League allied against Sparta, and then in 370 when they joined the Theban invasion of Sparta.[102] So much for Acarnanian loyalty.

But to return to the encounter of 389, in what way could the incident be understood as a Spartan victory? What exactly had the Spartans accomplished? They had secured no terms of peace with the Acarnanians, and perhaps even more importantly, they had not even quieted the Achaeans. Was it a military victory? Again, it is difficult to say. Xenophon is curiously silent on the number of Spartan and Achaean dead and wounded. This silence suggests that Xenophon downplayed Spartan and Achaean casualties to give the impression that only the Acarnanians suffered losses in the encounter. Xenophon notes that Agesilaus set up a trophy after the attack at the basin and did not seek a truce to recover his dead. Agesilaus claimed victory, and the Acarnanians made no response, so perhaps it was a Spartan victory.

In a technical sense, Agesilaus was right. But the Spartans did not need a truce to recover their dead and set up a trophy because all of the Spartan and Achaean dead were confined to the limits of the basin. Since there was no truce or exchange of dead, Xenophon and his sources could afford to omit the extent of the Spartans' and Achaeans' losses. The encounter may have been a victory in the eyes of Agesilaus and Xenophon, but the real achievement of the Spartans and their allies was that they managed to survive the Acarnanian attack.

From the Acarnanians' perspective, the Defense of 389 could have been nothing short of a success. They had sustained the trauma of a large-scale, destructive invasion while almost annihilating the invading army. Then, drawing on the advantages of the region's physical environment and aided by their own network of fortified settlements, the Acarnanians drove off the Spartans and Achaeans in time to sow their fields. Furthermore, they did all of this without granting the invaders a single concession, at least not until shrewdly "capitulating" the following spring. The Defense of Acarnania also reveals that the Acarnanians circa 389 could organize and execute a wide-scale, intricate defense on short notice under conditions of uncertainty.

The attack at the lake was a coordinated effort of Acarnanian peltasts, hoplites, and an array of slingers and other javelineers—in all, a considerable force displaying great tactical sophistication. Additionally, since most of the peltasts and at least some of the slingers and javelineers would have originated from the mountainous interior of Acarnania, while the hoplites presumably represented the poleis of the plain and coast, we can conclude that the Acarnanian defensive force spanned the entire region. Not only had the Acarnanians assembled this force in response to the Spartan embassy at Stratos, but they kept it out of sight as the invaders made their way through Acarnanian territory. Crucially, the Acarnanians initiated their attack only after securing every geographical and tactical advantage against Agesilaus and his army.

That the Acarnanians managed to coordinate this attack without fully knowing the intentions of the invading army is remarkable. True, Agesilaus had announced that he would ravage the countryside should the Acarnanians refuse his offer, but the Acarnanians had no way of knowing the exact course that the invaders would take or how fast they would be moving through the coastal region and plain. The Acarnanians, in short, needed to be prepared for anything, and they were. But the analysis here suggests that the location of the attack was no coincidence, and specifically, that the Acarnanians used their livestock and slaves to bait Agesilaus to the site of the attack. This calls for elaboration.

First, Xenophon (or his source) could not have known exactly where the Acarnanians removed their livestock when the invading army arrived in the region. As a result, the notices in Xenophon's narrative of the Acarnanians "withdrawing the livestock inland" and then "driving the livestock down from the mountains" should be understood not as matters of fact but as deductions. According to Xenophon, since the livestock initially disappeared from the invaders' sight but then reappeared by the lake, it "must have been the case" that the Acarnanians drove their livestock to the interior and then brought the animals back to the plain because they felt safe.

That is reasonable enough, but this deduction prompts a question: Why would the Acarnanians return their livestock from the mountains, even if they felt safe? The invasion took place in the late summer, and there would have been no shortage of water and pasture for the animals in the Acarnanian interior. Put another way, nothing was stopping the Acarnanians from keeping their livestock well out of the invaders' reach. That they left their animals under the care of slaves in an area fully visible and accessible to the invading army can only suggest that they wanted the Spartans to notice them. Consider the location and timing of the Acarnanians' highly coordinated attack: it occurred directly after the invaders seized the livestock and slaves at a site that gave every advantage to the Acarnanian defensive force. This sophistication reveals that the Defense of Acarnania was in fact a strategic response to the Spartan-led invasion.

Yet the invading army had been in Acarnania for a little over two weeks by the time of the attack; that should have been enough time for the Acarnanians to organize a response. If the Defense was more than a series of reactive measures strung together on an ad hoc basis, are there clear indications of high-level planning on the part of the Acarnanians?

There are. The first is the response of the Acarnanian congress at Stratos to Agesilaus's unmistakable ultimatum. Even though the Spartans and their allies were already in the region and poised for an invasion, the Acarnanians rejected the embassy's terms of peace. It is unlikely that the Acarnanians would have done so without some form of defensive plan. Given the sophistication and aggressive nature of the Acarnanians' subsequent activities, the Acarnanians clearly were undaunted by the prospects of a large-scale invasion and had full confidence in their defensive capabilities.

Perhaps a better indication of the existence of a defensive strategy in Acarnania is the course of the defense itself, which reveals a multiscalar contingency plan. This plan ran along the following lines: First, in response to the invading army's arrival, the occupants of the coast and plain were to abandon their settlements, withdraw inland, send their movable goods to a remote location, and then notify the rest of the Acarnanians, just as they had done in 426. This set the defense in motion.

From there, the Acarnanians were to remain within their fortified inland settlements, most of which were also protected to the east and north by the region's mountainous interior. An open engagement with a large-scale army like that of the Spartans and their allies simply was not an option. Instead, the Acarnanians would concede their fields, monitor the invading army's activities, and wait for the invaders to depart after they destroyed whatever agricultural resources were within their reach. As the Acarnanians would have known, it was not a given that the invaders would depart, and in 389, the Spartans and their allies decided to stay.

The next step, then, entailed luring the invading army to one of the various locations that favored the Acarnanians. In this case, the Spartans took the bait, and the Acarnanians attacked. This was the third step. If the attack was unsuccessful, the Acarnanians were to return to their fortified settlements, where the cycle could begin again. In this way, although the attack at the lake was not wholly successful, the Defense of 389 was.

The next question is what motive the Acarnanians had to develop such a high-level plan. In this case, the answer is relatively clear. The Acarnanians had taken great interest in gaining control of Calydon, and it was no secret that the Spartans were allied with the Aetolians and Achaeans. In short, the potential consequences of attacking the Calydonians were clear to the Acarnanians.

Furthermore, the Spartans had ventured into Acarnania in recent decades. The possibility remained that they would return, and in any case the Athenians were unreliable allies and had even launched their own invasion in the past to interfere with Acarnanian internal affairs. When it came to defense, the Acarnanians could count only on themselves, and they would have realized this by the second quarter of the fifth century at the latest. In response, they developed a defensive strategy to protect their ethnos from external aggression.

By way of conclusion, we must consider whether a federal government or the Acarnanian "people" coordinated the Defense of 389. Although the full extent of political organization in Acarnania during the time in question cannot be known in detail, the reconstruction in this chapter has revealed a high level of coordination among Acarnanians writ large. Such organization would support the view that the Acarnanians had formed a federal state by 389. Furthermore, the solidarity that the Acarnanians exhibited after the attack suggests that the bonds connecting the loose confederation of the fifth century had indeed become tighter by the first quarter of the fourth century.

It is also clear that the sophistication and solidarity of the Acarnanians was unexpected, at least from an outsider's perspective. The Spartans and Achaeans knew that an Acarnanian decision-making assembly was located at Stratos, but this could have been all that they knew about the Acarnanians. In any case, Agesilaus clearly underestimated the solidarity of the Acarnanians, which suggests that he was unaware of the full extent of their collective capabilities. Overall, Xenophon's narrative is ambiguous, and we have no other evidence to confirm that the Acarnanians had formed a federal state by the time of the invasion. As a result, the possibility that a koinon did not exist during the time in question must remain on the table.

But why does it matter if a federal state existed in Acarnania circa 450–389? As in the case of the Phocians circa 525–475, an early koinon would fly in the face of the Thucydidean view of upland ethnē. This correction would be particularly important in the case of the Acarnanians, since Thucydides named them in his assessment of the western mainland. The forming of an early koinon in Acarnania would show that the Acarnanians were not centuries behind the polis-centric Greek world in the realm of political development.

Yet here we arrive at the greater significance of the Defense of Acarnania. Even if Xenophon's use of *to koinon* referred to an actual federal government—a real possibility—the Acarnanians' successful defense of 389 was possible without the structure of a formal federal state and the direction of a central power.

The Defense of 389 certainly required leadership, and notwithstanding Xenophon's silence on the matter, there is no question that Acarnanian generals were directing the individual contingents of slingers, javelineers, peltasts, and hoplites that attacked the Spartans and their allies. In fact, Thucydides mentions such generals as early as 425.[103] These individuals must have been leading figures within individual Acarnanian communities, and they may have constituted the Acarnanian congress at Stratos. Yet we have no grounds to conclude that they were also federal magistrates constituting or supervised by a standing, central government.

Even if a koinon did not exist in Acarnania at the time of the Spartan-led invasion, the Defense of 389 still negates the Thucydidean view of upland ethnē for the case of Acarnania. By the first quarter of the fourth century, the ethnos of the Acarnanians constituted a well-connected, well-organized, and efficient political entity that was thoroughly adapted to the broader geopolitical context of the Greek mainland. The polis-centric Greek world of the late fifth and early fourth centuries may have been ignorant of the collective capabilities of this political entity, but as the Spartans and their allies learned in 389, the reverse certainly was not the case.

CHAPTER 4

The Defense of Arcadia in 370

At the dawn of the Archaic age, Arcadians had already laid claim to the landlocked, mountainous interior of the central Peloponnese.[1] Then as now, mountains reaching as high as 2,300 meters gave shape to a number of expansive upland plains. The largest of these was the so-called central Arcadian plain. It was here that the region's largest city-states, Mantineia and Tegea, came to power during the classical period.

Before the classical period, "Arcadia" was nothing more than a shorthand expression for "land inhabited by Arcadians."[2] There was some regional cooperation in the religious sphere as evidenced by a network of Archaic sanctuaries, but whatever political significance these sanctuaries may have had, if any, has left no traces.[3] By the late sixth and early fifth centuries, a more coherent regional identity began to take shape. Herodotus, for example, spoke of an ethnos of Arcadians—that is, a "people" composed of various city-states and tribal communities.[4] Additionally, around the same time, outsiders had come to recognize Arcadians as ideal mercenaries.[5] And later in the fifth century, the Arcadians attempted to politicize their shared identity by circulating coinage throughout the region that bore a common ethnic inscription.[6] But small-scale conflicts with Argives, Spartans, and Eleans led most Arcadians to identify first with their local communities and only secondarily with "Arcadia." The Arcadians may have formed an ethnos-wide symmachy against

Sparta during the fifth century, but that is the only evidence of sustained political cooperation on a regional scale.[7]

All of that changed in the fourth century. During the summer of 370, the Arcadians formed a formal koinon known to us as the Arcadian League.[8] According to Xenophon and Diodorus, the primary elements of the league were a council and assembly of 10,000 voting citizens. Collectively, the council and assembly could pass resolutions binding on all constituent polities, whether poleis, smaller towns, or tribal communities.[9]

In addition to the notices in Xenophon and Diodorus, we have an Arcadian inscription found at Tegea that attests to the existence and political structure of the koinon by 369.[10] This epigraphic evidence means that the Arcadians constitute the first unambiguous case of a federal state among the upland ethnē considered in this book. Also, unlike the Phocians circa 490, the Aetolians in 426, and the Acarnanians in 389, the Arcadians provide the only example of intra-ethnos conflict. In fact, internal dissent would play an important role in the development and eventual demise of the Arcadian koinon circa 370–362.

Before that, at the very interface of the transition from ethnos to koinon, the Arcadians had to face a Spartan-led invasion that threatened the existence of their nascent league. The Arcadians' response to this invasion—the Defense of Arcadia—was the first collective action of the Arcadian League documented in a contemporary source. But past scholarship has virtually ignored the dynamics and greater significance of this encounter, leaving a series of questions open for investigation.

First, to what extent were the collective capabilities of the Arcadians in 370 related to those of pre-league Arcadians? During the fifth and early fourth centuries, for instance, Mantineia and Tegea had been allied off and on with the Spartans, yet both played a key role in the Defense of 370. Was it the case, then, that the founding of a formal league finally enabled widespread collective action in Arcadia?

Similarly, was the organized force of Arcadians opposing the Spartan invasion of 370 a federal army? The Arcadians did eventually form a standing army in the 360s, but it is unclear whether this force existed at the founding of the koinon. Were pre-league Arcadians also capable of mobilizing, organizing, and positioning personnel as an ethnos? If so, to what extent did the Arcadian "federal" army exist before 370, and what might this tell us about the relationship between the Arcadian koinon and the ethnos that preceded it?

This chapter seeks to answer these questions by reconstructing the intricacies of the Arcadians' defense primarily from the defenders' perspective. Such an approach reveals that the Arcadians enacted a sophisticated defensive strategy that existed before the invasion of 370. This strategy made use of the basic infrastructure of the region, exploited a number of geographical and tactical advantages, and relied on the cooperation of civilian populations to observe, control, menace, attack, and ultimately drive off the invading army.

Past Approaches and Sources

To date, modern scholarship has mentioned the Defense of Arcadia only in passing; the incident has yet to be given serious consideration.[11] This neglect stems from a series of factors: there are no major discrepancies between sources to debate, no topographical puzzles to solve, and no indications that the encounter between Arcadians and Spartans in 370 had major repercussions vis-à-vis the rest of the Greek world. In addition, the Defense took place between the Battle of Leuctra in 371 and the Invasion of Laconia in 370.[12] In a way, the Defense of Arcadia remains in the shadows of these two monumental events.

Yet when scholars do discuss the Defense, they usually treat the encounter as a nonevent: the Spartans invaded Arcadia, the Arcadians refused to fight, the Spartans went home. Modern scholarship claims that the Arcadians did not fight because they were scared of the Spartans. But this is the same explanation given by Xenophon and Diodorus, the encounter's two narrative sources. Since these narratives are central to the study of the Defense, they call for some discussion.

Xenophon provides the main source for the Defense of Arcadia, and the same considerations discussed in chapter 3 are still in effect. Once again, Xenophon's extensive and detailed narrative is internally coherent, it contains descriptions of terrain that are reconcilable to the topography of the region, and it is based on eyewitness accounts. Furthermore, although Xenophon offers an outsider's perspective of the Defense, he would have known comparatively more about the Arcadians than he knew about some of the Spartans' other adversaries. After all, Xenophon dealt with Arcadians extensively during his mercenary exploits in Anatolia, and he lived for a number of years in Elis close to the central Peloponnese.[13]

As before, Xenophon's narrative focuses primarily on the decisions and actions of Agesilaus.[14] And even more so than in other incidents, Xenophon goes to great lengths to show that Agesilaus and the Spartans maintained the initiative against their adversaries. As a result, it is clear that he has omitted, obscured, and downplayed a number of significant features pertaining to the Arcadians.

But these biases can be overcome. Recent archaeological, topographical, and ethnographic research casts in a different light most of what Xenophon related about the Arcadians' defense. By reevaluating his account from the perspective of this research, Xenophon's one-sided narrative becomes an illustrative source for understanding the collective capabilities of the Arcadians circa 370.

The other source for the Defense of Arcadia is far less illustrative. Not only was Diodorus writing approximately three hundred years after the fact, but he was also epitomizing material from Ephorus's fourth-century universal history. To make matters worse, the pertinent material drawn from Ephorus's history appears to have been based on secondhand sources at best.[15] Consequently, Diodorus relates several details about the Arcadians that are clearly anachronistic, and his summary account diverges from Xenophon's narrative in a few instances.

As for context, the Defense of Arcadia took place a little less than two decades after the King's Peace of 387. The King's Peace ended the Corinthian War and guaranteed political autonomy for participating Greeks, but it also allowed the Spartans to administrate the terms of the decree.[16] Not surprisingly, under the guise of enforcing the Peace, the Spartans continued to attack their political enemies. The Thebans were of particular concern for the Spartans, and hostilities between the two powers were both frequent and violent.

This conflict culminated in 371 with the Thebans' decisive victory over the Spartans at Leuctra.[17] Leuctra effectively ended Spartan hegemony on the Greek mainland and established the Thebans as the leading power of the Greek world. By the summer of 370, though, the full impact of the Theban victory had yet to reach the rest of the Greeks. Amid this uncertainty, a few polities took steps to secure their place in a changing world, in particular the Arcadians. Their response to the events of 371 soon made the central Peloponnese a hub of further conflict.

The Defense

At some point during the summer of 370, in an unspecified location, an assembly of Arcadians created a formal federation of towns and cities that encompassed most of the geographical realm of Arcadia. A few Arcadian poleis refused to join the league, opting instead to remain loyal to their foreign allies and independent within the central Peloponnese. Tegea was one of these poleis, at least at the start.[18]

Stassipus, a leading Tegean politician with a sizable following, had persuaded the Tegean assembly to maintain the status quo in external matters, that is, to remain allies of Sparta. But his opponents in Tegea took to arms, overthrew the council's decision, summoned aid from Mantineia, and ended up killing Stassipus and a large number of his followers.[19]

After this particularly violent bout of political upheaval, the polis of Tegea became part of the Arcadian League, and, according to Xenophon, "about 800 of the Tegeans loyal to Stassipus fled to Sparta."[20] This number may have represented approximately a third of Tegea's total population of male citizens at this time.[21] Those who remained still made a significant addition to the nascent Arcadian League, and the city-state's territory of about 385 square kilometers in southern Arcadia would have been welcome also.[22]

For the Tegeans who were forcibly exiled, Sparta was the only refuge within reason that they could have sought. They quickly gathered an audience in Sparta and detailed their injustice. In response, writes Xenophon, "the Lacedaemonians decided that in accordance with their oaths they had to provide assistance on behalf of the dead and exiled of the Tegeans, so they organized an expedition against the Mantineians on the grounds that they had violated their oaths by attacking the Tegeans."[23] The oaths mentioned may have been the terms of peace sworn by a number of Greek polities after the Spartans' defeat at Leuctra.[24] The cities that took part in this agreement—including, evidently, Tegea and Mantineia—were entitled to protection from the others.

Yet the relationship between the Mantineians and Spartans was deteriorating, and in recent decades the Mantineians had resisted Spartan domination in the Peloponnese, usually with a violent and unsuccessful end for the Mantineians.[25] Earlier in the year 370, for instance, the Mantineians had once again reasserted their independence from Sparta, this time by rebuilding the fortifications that the Spartans had once demolished. The fortifications made the Spartans uneasy, but they could do nothing about it.[26] Now that the Mantineians had aided the Tegeans in killing and exiling those loyal to Stassipus, the Spartans had a legitimate pretext to attack.

According to Xenophon, "The ephors ordered a levy and the voting citizens placed Agesilaus in command."[27] Agesilaus was the natural choice for this expedition: he was a seasoned (though aging) commander, he was familiar with the land of Arcadia, and he had personal ties with some Mantineians.[28] It is worth noting that the Spartans singled out the Mantineians for retaliation. Perhaps they thought that they could invade Arcadia without dealing with the rest of the Tegeans, or the rest of the Arcadians. But were the Spartans in any position to be campaigning in Arcadia one year after Leuctra?

It is difficult to say. We learn later that the invasion occurred in early to midwinter (roughly December or January), well after the traditional campaigning season had ended for the Greeks. At least one scholar has pointed to the timing of the invasion as an indication of how desperate the Spartans had become to maintain their influence in the Peloponnese.[29] It would seem, then, that the Spartans felt pressured to respond to the threats developing in Arcadia, whatever the costs.[30] Additionally, as arrogant as Spartan decision makers traditionally were, they must have known that the winter of 370 was a poor time for risking the lives of their remaining citizens, especially against a large number of Arcadians with a long-standing reputation as fierce soldiers.[31] If anything, the unconventional timing of the campaign suggests that not only were the Spartans desperate to maintain their influence in the region, but also that they were somewhat ignorant or dismissive of the Arcadians' collective capabilities. Depleted of manpower, the Spartans still figured that they could invade Arcadia with relative impunity.

Then again, perhaps they were attempting to catch the Mantineians and the rest of the Arcadians off guard with the timing of their invasion. If so, they failed. As Agesilaus was organizing his army, Xenophon writes that "most of the Arcadians were assembling at Asea."[32]Asea was a large settlement in southern Arcadia with a fortified acropolis and a population of approximately 2,000 to 3,000 during the first half of the fourth century (map 5).[33] Upwards of a third of this population may have been scattered across the polis's sixty square kilometers of mountainous high country, which included the Asea Valley itself.[34]

Furthermore, the polis of Asea was unusual in that it had an extensive network of paths, roads, and mountain passes that connected the valley to the rest of Arcadia.[35] Since Arcadians from across the central Peloponnese could reach Asea rather quickly, the polis was an ideal point of assembly for an army numbering in the thousands, especially one about to face an invasion from the south.

To judge from Xenophon's narrative, the Arcadians assembled in response to the levy in Sparta—that is, they were not permanently mobilized at Asea.[36] How Xenophon (or his source) knew this is unclear, but he could have deduced where the Arcadians initially assembled after the fact. Later, he also would have realized that not all of the Arcadians had gathered at Asea before the Spartan invasion. On the contrary, "the Mantineians remained in place to keep a watch on the Orchomenians who had refused to join the *koinon* of the Arcadians out of enmity with Mantineia and who had received into their city the mercenary force assembled at Corinth that was led by Polytropus."[37] From the Arcadians' perspective, the Orchomenians were threatening the political integrity of the rest of the nascent league by remaining independent. By accommodating a considerable mercenary force led by a Spartan commander, they were also threatening the physical security of the league's constituent polities.[38]

The Mantineians—themselves yet another powerful Arcadian polis—were approximately fifteen kilometers south of Orchomenos and fully capable of defending at least part of the northern limits of the league's territory until assistance could arrive.[39] But by this time, the Arcadians would have realized

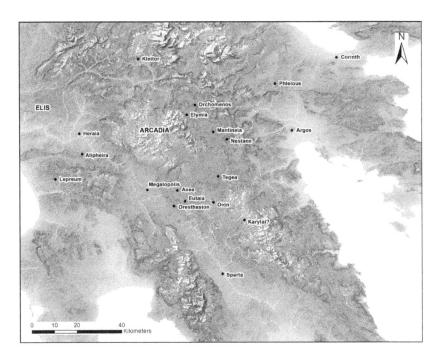

MAP 5. The Defense of Arcadia (370). Created by D. Matthew Buell.

that they were facing an invasion from two fronts: to the south was the Spartan army under Agesilaus, to the north the Orchomenian and mercenary one.

According to Xenophon, "The Heraians and the Lepreans also campaigned with the Lacedaemonians against the Mantineians."[40] The Lepreans originated from Tryphylia, the coastal region in the western Peloponnese between Elis and Messenia; the Heraians were Arcadians dwelling on the Alpheios River on the western edge of Arcadian territory during the time in question.[41] Both had long-standing ties with the Spartans. What the Lepreans and Heraians added to Agesilaus's army is unknown, and Xenophon does not mention them again during his account of the invasion.

"As soon as the crossing sacrifices turned out favorably for him, Agesilaus advanced into Arcadia," reports Xenophon.[42] Based on Agesilaus's first stop in Arcadia and the subsequent route of his campaign, his most likely point of entry into Arcadia was through Oresthasion on the northwest edge of Laconian territory.[43] There was also a narrow pass at Oion in Sciritis that led directly to Tegea; the Spartans would have faced no opposition there.[44] That Agesilaus avoided Oion suggests that he was attempting to surprise the Arcadians. Then again, the Tegeans who had remained in Arcadia were now hostile to the Spartans, so perhaps Agesilaus simply wanted to bypass them on his way north. Xenophon continues: "He seized the neighboring town of Eutaia and there discovered that the old men, women, and children were still living in their homes."[45] Agesilaus entered Eutaia prepared for a fight. He expected the Arcadians to oppose his entrance into their territory but instead found an entire civilian population going about its everyday business.

Eutaia itself seems to have been more of a dependent town of the tribal Mainalians than an independent polis, so its inhabitants would have posed no threat to the invading army, as Agesilaus likely knew.[46] He could subdue the Eutaians, gain a foothold in Arcadia, and proceed from there—only there was no one to subdue: "the men of fighting age had departed to join the assembling Arcadians [*to Arkadikon*]."[47]

Presumably Agesilaus learned this information from the Eutaians. This remark also suggests that the Eutaians withheld precise information from Agesilaus pertaining to the Arcadians' collective capabilities. Agesilaus's dealings with the Eutaians may have gone something like this: Where are the men? They left. Where to? To the Arkadikon. Where's that? Could be anywhere by now. How big is the Arkadikon? Depends. And so on.

Lending further support to this interpretation of the Eutaians as passively uncooperative is this: a large group of Arcadians was assembling at Asea only five kilometers to the northwest of Eutaia across an open mountain valley, and there are absolutely no indications that Agesilaus was aware of it. "Nevertheless he did not harm the city; rather, he allowed them to go on living there and his men paid for whatever they needed. Agesilaus also found and returned whatever was taken when his army initially assaulted the city."[48] Xenophon rarely misses an opportunity to praise Agesilaus, as he does here, yet in the process he also confirms that the Spartans attacked Eutaia expecting a fight. Xenophon also reinforces the interpretation of the Eutaians as uncooperative by insisting that Agesilaus did no injustice to the Eutaians, even though they did nothing to assist him.

Xenophon continues: "He passed the time waiting for Polytropus's mercenaries by having the city wall repaired where it was needed."[49] Repairing the wall served a number of functions for Agesilaus: it gave his otherwise idle and potentially fidgety army something to do, it strengthened his toehold in Arcadia, and given Agesilaus's treatment of the Eutaian civilians, it laid the groundwork for a potential ally.[50] Xenophon's narrative suggests that the Spartans remained in Eutaia for at least a few days, if not a few weeks.

But this wall building raises an important question: Why was Agesilaus waiting for Polytropus in the southernmost region of Arcadia if the Spartan mercenary commander was already at Orchomenos and the alleged aim of the invasion was to punish the Mantineians? Why not move to Polytropus? While Agesilaus weighed these options, "the Mantineians attacked the Orchomenians."[51]

Even without direct observation of the Spartans at Eutaia, the Arcadians at Asea would have realized that the Spartans were now delayed in the south, and they could have relayed this information to the Mantineians via runners. The mountainous subregion of western Arcadia with its various routes of communication allowed the Arcadians to communicate easily with each other. To judge from the speed with which the Arcadians mobilized prior to the invasion, this system worked quite well.[52]

In addition, without precise knowledge of the invaders' intentions, the Arcadians had to assume that the Orchomenians and Polytropus were planning to attack from the north in conjunction with an attack from the south. And so, from the Arcadians' perspective, the time to act was now, while the invaders from the south were camped at Eutaia rebuilding a wall. "But their attack on the wall [of Orchomenos] was unsuccessful, and some of them died."[53] Xenophon does very little to illuminate the nature of this attack, but his narrative contains a few important details: First, the mention of a wall suggests that the Mantineians attacked the urban center, or *asty*, of Orchomenos. The *asty* was situated on the top and southern slope of the modern-day Kalpaki Hill at an elevation of approximately 929 meters.[54] The hill divides and overlooks the northern and southern subplains of Orchomenian territory and so would have been an ideal location for a fortified defensive position.[55] It was here that the Mantineians found the Orchomenians and Polytropus's peltasts.

But what did the Mantineians do? Try to scale the wall? They certainly were not settling in for siege, and according to Xenophon, only a few of them died in the encounter, so the attack could not have been too involved. The bulk of the Mantineians would have been hoplites, perhaps upwards of 1,000, but they gave up the attack without accomplishing anything[56]—or so it seemed.

"When the Mantineians withdrew to Elymia, the Orchomenian hoplites were no longer following them, but Polytropus' mercenaries were still in hot pursuit."[57] Elymia was a small town built against the mountainous Arcadian interior, only about five kilometers away across the southern Orchomenian subplain near the limits of Orchomenian and Mantineian territory.[58] The route back to Mantineia was still open, and the Mantineians seem to have withdrawn together without any apparent confusion. This orderly retreat suggests that the Mantineians planned to withdraw toward Elymia after the attack.[59] In light of this, it is interesting to note that the Orchomenian hoplites did not pursue the Mantineians to a great extent. Perhaps they suspected something.

In contrast, Polytropus and his peltasts pressed the attack as if to follow up on a seeming victory. "The Mantineians, realizing that many of them would be cut down by javelins if they failed to drive off the mercenaries, turned and closed with their attackers."[60] So far, Xenophon's narrative of the incident has given the following impression: the Mantineians, seemingly on their own accord, launched a half-hearted and probably disorganized attack on a rival of the Arcadian League, were completely unsuccessful, retreated before suffering any major losses, and then, pursued by a mass of aggressive hoplite-killing mercenaries led by a Spartan general, at the very last moment, with no other option, turned to make a desperate stand. What Xenophon left out of his narrative is that the Mantineians were led by the thoroughly competent and exceptionally shrewd Lycomedes, the architect of the Arcadian League, who, it would follow, was now responsible for maintaining the watch on Orchomenos.[61]

The Orchomenians and Polytropus's mercenary force had occupied a virtually unassailable position, and from Lycomedes' perspective—and that of the Arcadians in general—were poised to invade Arcadia from the north. The Mantineians' aim all along, then, may have been to wait for an opportune time to draw the Orchomenians and Polytropus's peltasts out from behind the walls to a place where the Mantineians could fight under more favorable conditions. What better way to prompt a chase than feigning incompetence and a lack of resolve, especially when the other half of the invading force was busy building a wall in Eutaia?

"Polytropus died fighting at Elymia. The others who fled would have died to a man had not the Phliasian cavalry arrived and ridden round the Mantineians' rear forcing them to give up the pursuit."[62] Again, Xenophon's narrative provides very little detail regarding the nature of the fighting, but it is clear that Polytropus failed to keep a safe distance between his peltasts and the Arcadians. They were so close, in fact, that when the Mantineians turned and closed with their attackers, the peltasts' javelins were useless against the Mantineians' armor, shields, and spears.[63] In this way an actual rout ensued.

The Mantineians' success required skillful coordination and an expert sense of timing, and this suggests that the entire action against Orchomenos was intentional from the start. But it would not have been the first time in ancient Greek history that a hoplite army's feigned retreat surprised a mass of overly confident pursuers to great effect, as a Spartan commander such as Polytropus ought to have known.[64] As for the Phliasians, by riding in between the Mantineians and Elymia they managed to redirect the efforts of the Mantineians and thereby gave the routed peltasts a chance to run.[65] Incidentally, the arrival of the Phliasian cavalry confirmed the Arcadians' suspicions that they were facing an invasion from the north in conjunction with one from the south.

"After accomplishing these things, the Mantineians went home."[66] Xenophon mentions no exchange of dead, no trophy, no offer of a truce.[67] What the Mantineians had just accomplished bears emphasis: they killed a Spartan general, decimated his mercenary force that had been poised to invade Arcadia, and returned to their original defensive position virtually unscathed. This was no minor victory for the Arcadians, but they had not entirely eliminated the threat from the north, and Agesilaus was still in the south. "After Agesilaus heard of this he figured that the mercenaries from Orchomenos would not be joining him, and so he advanced."[68]

Apparently, Agesilaus wanted to move through Arcadia with more peltasts, or perhaps Polytropus was to supply him with a light-armed contingent that he otherwise lacked. That Agesilaus "heard" of what happened suggests that he had some sort of communication with his allies to the north, unless he simply advanced after waiting longer than he figured was necessary.[69]

"On the first day they spent the evening in the territory of Tegea," Xenophon writes.[70] The territory of Tegea covered approximately 385 square kilometers to include the southern portion of the central Arcadian plain and its surrounding mountains. This means that the army would have advanced approximately ten kilometers to the northeast of Eutaia over fairly mountainous terrain to reach the western limits of the Tegean countryside. Since the Tegeans were now part of the Arcadian League, Agesilaus likely did not advance too far from the security of the mountains before setting up camp. After all, the Tegeans could have had potentially immense resources at their disposal.[71]

Xenophon continues: "The next day they passed into the territory of Mantineia and set up camp at the foot of the mountains west of the city of Mantineia."[72] Agesilaus skirted the Maenalian Mountains, which formed the western limit of the central Arcadian plain. He would have covered a distance of approximately twenty kilometers if he had set up camp due west of Mantineia. As with Tegea, the territory associated with Mantineia was rather large. Since it occupied most of the northern half of the central Arcadian plain, the invading army may have advanced as little as fifteen kilometers, still a good distance from the region's urban center.[73] In fact, this seems to have been the case, because according to Xenophon, "there they ravaged the land and plundered the farms."[74]

The invading army destroyed or carried off the Mantineians' resources seemingly without fear of being attacked, which suggests that the Lacedaemonians were closer to the southern limits of the vast Mantineian countryside. But one day's worth of destruction during the wintertime could not have done too much damage given the size of the Mantineians' territory.[75] At any rate, they did not trigger a response from the Mantineians. The abandonment of the farms indicates that the Mantineians had left well in advance of the army's arrival. For that matter, the Lacedaemonians had yet to encounter any Arcadians since they left Eutaia, but this was about to change.

"During the night the Arcadians assembled at Asea moved to Tegea," writes Xenophon.[76] Tegea was more than capable of supporting an army of Arcadians numbering around 5,000.[77] Preparing this force for a nighttime movement across twelve to fifteen kilometers of mountainous terrain required time. In light of this, it would follow that the Arcadians at Asea did in fact have the Spartans at Eutaia under some form of observation—even if direct observation was impossible—and were simply waiting for them to make a move. But a large, conventional army like Agesilaus's only had one place to go in Arcadia: the central plain. The Arcadians did not need to lure the Spartans into the plain. If the invaders were going to advance, the central plain was where they were headed. Once Agesilaus made his move, the Arcadians at Asea made theirs.

And once they reached Tegea, the Arcadians had Agesilaus and his army completely surrounded. To the south were the Arcadians who had assembled at Asea, in the east and west were the mountains enclosing the central Arcadian plain, and in the north, of course, were the sizable and skilled Mantineians. "The next day Agesilaus set up camp about twenty stadia from the city of Mantinea."[78] It seems as if the Spartans had now set up camp due west of Mantineia; they were only about three to five kilometers from the city, roughly the distance across the plain. They could not have been camped along the eastern mountains because once they had settled in to their new location, "the Arcadians from Tegea—a great many hoplites—made their appearance skirting the mountains between Mantineia and Tegea."[79] Unfortunately, Xenophon does not specify a number. Two things are clear enough, though. First, this large force, numbering at least in the thousands, was moving along the eastern limit of the central Arcadian plain; second, from the invaders' perspective, the Arcadians' arrival was unexpected.

But were these hoplites the Arcadians who had originally assembled at Asea and moved to Tegea, or only a contingent? Some Arcadians presumably stayed in Tegea to maintain the strategic advantage that they had just gained. But why move in the first place? Were the Arcadians making a show of force, were they attempting to augment their numbers at Mantineia, or did they have something else in mind? According to Xenophon, "They wanted to join up with the Mantineians."[80] But how would Xenophon (or his source) have known the Arcadians' intentions?

Modern research of road networks in the mountainous eastern region of Arcadia north of Mt. Parthenion offers a different perspective. Had the Arcadians merely wanted to join up with the Mantineians as Xenophon suggests, there were a number of safer, more surreptitious, and arguably faster options open to them.[81] That the Arcadians chose to skirt the mountains along the eastern limit of the central plain means that they wanted to be seen.

"There were also Argives with them," reports Xenophon, "but not in full force."[82] The Argives had long been allies of whichever Arcadians were currently opposing Sparta, so it should not come as a surprise that they were aiding the Arcadian League here.[83] The Argives could have marched directly to Mantineia, so for them to have joined the Arcadian force marching north, they needed to assemble first at Tegea using the mountain roads just mentioned. All of this suggests that the Arcadians were orchestrating an elaborate defense that the invaders clearly did not appreciate.

In the Spartan camp, continues Xenophon, "some were trying to persuade Agesilaus to attack them before they could join the Mantineians, but he was afraid that while he was advancing against them the Mantineians would come out of the city and attack his flank and rear."[84] Evidently, the size of the Arcadian-Argive force did not deter "some" high-ranking Spartans from attacking, but Agesilaus (or someone advising Agesilaus) sensed that the Arcadians were up to something.

The Mantineians likely would have attacked from the north had the Spartans gone after the Arcadians, and little did Agesilaus know but there may have been another Arcadian attack waiting for them from the south out of Tegea. In addition, Xenophon explicitly states that the Arcadians visible to Agesilaus were hoplites. Were there light-armed Arcadians out of sight somewhere? How would Agesilaus or anyone else have known? "Agesilaus decided that the best thing to do was to allow them to join up, and if they wanted to fight, to have a conventional and open battle."[85] Put another way, Agesilaus could not discern the Arcadians' intentions, but he suspected that they were baiting him into a trap; in response, he did nothing but remain in place. He may have been willing to face the Arcadians, but only on terms that suited the strengths of his own army.

The Arcadians from Tegea continued on into Mantineia, and "now the Arcadians had all joined forces."[86] From the invaders' perspective, this could have been the entire Arcadian force or only a large contingent. The Arcadians did not appear too overwhelming in number since some of the Spartans were willing to launch an impromptu attack across the plain. This suggests that only a contingent of Arcadians had left Tegea, but it is difficult to say with certainty since there are few indications of the size of the invading army for comparison.[87]

Incidentally, Mantineia already sustained a sizable population of its own. As a result, the Mantineians needed to have some sort of system in place for accommodating thousands of additional Arcadians on short notice. They also needed provisions to support their own countryside residents who had already withdrawn into the city's fortifications.[88] This is yet another testament to the coordination of the Arcadians' defense.

Xenophon continues: "During the night the peltasts from Orchomenos and the Phliasian cavalry with them made their way past Mantineia and appeared before Agesilaus who was sacrificing before the camp at dawn."[89] The peltasts out of Orchomenos likely were the remnants of Polytropus's mercenary force. Apparently, the Orchomenians themselves offered no aid. The cavalry and peltasts would have skirted the mountains along the western limit of the central Arcadian plain. Apparently, their efforts to join Agesilaus were of little concern, since the Arcadians were not actively blocking the northern entrances into the plain. "The cavalry and peltasts caused the soldiers to rush to their stations, and Agesilaus withdrew into the camp. But when they were recognized as allies, Agesilaus obtained good omens and led out the army after breakfast."[90]

The ostensible point here is that the Spartans were not expecting reinforcements, but this passage shows that the Arcadians—by watching, waiting, and limiting their exposure—were exacting a certain psychological toll on the invaders. The Lacedaemonians were expecting an attack but had no idea when it would occur or from what direction.

Reinforced with peltasts and cavalry, Agesilaus decided it was safe to move. "In the evening, he unwittingly set up camp in the valley behind the territory of Mantineia, a rather narrow place with mountains all around."[91] Before addressing Agesilaus's decision to move his camp, we must consider what the invaders were doing during the hours of daylight between breakfast and evening in close proximity to Mantineia. Were they marching around the plain aimlessly, or ravishing the countryside to draw the Arcadians out of Mantineia? To judge from Xenophon's account, the invading army did in fact cross the plain—not that this should have taken eight hours—and ended up in a narrow valley northeast of the city of Mantineia.[92] Xenophon implies that the seasoned general made a mistake, and Agesilaus's decision raises more questions. Above all, why would Agesilaus set up camp in a narrow valley if he wanted a "conventional and open" battle with the Arcadians? Was he disoriented from meandering around all day? Agesilaus had recently visited Mantineia on an embassy and so would have been familiar with the layout of the city and perhaps even parts of the Mantineian hinterland, so this explanation is insufficient.[93] Was he trying to surprise the Arcadians somehow, perhaps by attacking the city from a more advantageous angle? Did he really think that he could move his army around Mantineia unnoticed or with impunity? If so, he was mistaken.

"The next day at dawn he was sacrificing before the camp and saw the Arcadians gathering out of Mantineia on the heights above the rear of his own army."[94] Again, according to Xenophon, Agesilaus allegedly makes the crucial observation while sacrificing before the camp. Were the Lacedaemonians that lax and oblivious so close to so many hostile Arcadians?

There are a couple of more likely possibilities. The first is that the Arcadians observed the invading army set up camp the evening prior and then, undetected, surreptitiously occupied the heights during the night to prepare for an attack at dawn.[95] Several years later, the Arcadians used a similar tactic to great effect against the Eleans near the town of Lasion.[96] It is also possible that the Arcadians were aware of the Lacedaemonians' location and disposition and organized an attack force within Mantineia to set out early the following morning. Either way, they surprised the invading army, and in particular its commander.

"Agesilaus realized that they had to get out of the valley as soon as possible, but he was afraid that if he himself led the way the Arcadians would attack the army's rear."[97] First of all, what exactly does Xenophon mean by this? Are we to believe that the Arcadians would have refrained from attacking simply because they saw Agesilaus stationed in the army's rear, or simply that the Spartans were in too vulnerable of a formation to exit the valley? This is unclear.

What is clear, though, is that the Arcadians had only shown themselves on one side of the valley—that is, the western side closest to Mantineia—and perhaps were also on the slopes of Mt. Kofinas near the northern end of the valley at the rear of the invading army. Despite having the Spartans strung out at the bottom of a valley, they apparently had no intention of leaving the heights.

Xenophon records that in response, "keeping calm, and presenting his front to the enemies, Agesilaus ordered the men at the rear to turn and move toward him behind the phalanx's frontline."[98] It seems that Agesilaus initially had everyone face to the west and then instructed those farthest from him to peel off and march behind this newly formed line of shields toward the south where they had originally entered the valley. Advancing uphill to face the Arcadians clearly was not an option. "And so, as he led them out of the narrow valley, the phalanx was becoming increasingly stronger. Once the phalanx had been doubled in depth he marched out into the plain with the same formation and then extended the line once more to nine or ten shields deep."[99] The hoplite component of Agesilaus's army managed to escape the valley with a lot of fancy footwork, but what had happened to the peltasts from Orchomenos and the Phliasian cavalry? We never hear of them again, at least not during the Defense of Arcadia. They likely did not enter the valley with the Lacedaemonian hoplites or play a role in the outcome of events as before at Orchomenos and Elymia.[100]

Yet what still demands an explanation is why Agesilaus had his army enter the valley in the first place. Was he implicitly or explicitly pressured into attacking the Arcadians? Merely sitting in the Mantineian countryside does not appear to have been an option for the Spartan commander, so there may be something to this interpretation. Then again, to dwell on Agesilaus's decisions and the activities of his army is to view the incident from only one perspective and imply, as Xenophon does, that Agesilaus somehow maintained the initiative in Arcadia. That simply was not the case.

In fact, for all that Xenophon's narrative distorts, omits, and glosses over, the analysis above points to a different explanation—namely, that it was no coincidence that Agesilaus and his hoplites one morning found themselves isolated at the bottom of a valley in Arcadia with a large force of Arcadians poised to attack them from the heights. The Arcadians would not fight in the open— they knew better than that. If the Lacedaemonians, or any other invading army, wanted to fight the Arcadians in Arcadia, they were going to have to fight on the Arcadians' terms.

According to Xenophon, "The Mantineians ceased from coming out of their city because their allies the Eleans persuaded them not to fight until the Thebans arrived."[101] Some of the Arcadians' allies persuaded them to hold back, says Xenophon. Why else would the Arcadians have failed to attack in such favorable circumstances? One explanation is that the prospects of charging down a steep slope into the bottom of a narrow mountain valley were not good: the Arcadians faced the possibility of losing control on their way down. If the Lacedaemonians did not want to fight uphill, then the Arcadians would have to fight them elsewhere—that is, assuming the Arcadians wanted to fight at all. Then again, perhaps it was the Arcadians' intention to fight but Agesilaus fled the scene so quickly and skillfully that the Arcadians never had a chance. Both are possibilities.

In either case, it is absurd to suggest that the Arcadians held back simply because the Eleans told them to wait for the Thebans, especially in light of the defenders' clear strategic and tactical advantages (and likely numerical one). It is more likely that the Spartans fled before the Arcadians could block the valley's only exit.

"The Eleans said they were quite sure that the Thebans would arrive and help because the Eleans had paid them ten talents."[102] This is one more editorial comment from Xenophon, perhaps based on credible sources and perhaps not.[103] "Hearing this, the Arcadians maintained a low profile in Mantineia."[104] Agesilaus returned to the central Arcadian plain, once again enveloped by the Arcadians based in Mantineia, those in Tegea, and the surrounding mountains—a macrocosm of the disaster he had just avoided.

Now all the Arcadians needed to do was wait, adjust the balance of their forces if necessary, and watch for another bad decision. Xenophon writes that "Agesilaus was quite anxious to lead the army away—it was the middle of the winter—but he remained three days not far from the polis of Mantineia so as not to appear eager to withdraw because he was afraid."[105] With a finite amount of provisions in the middle of winter, the Lacedaemonians could not have stayed long in any single place. Soon they would have to move, but then they would be vulnerable since the wintertime mud of the central Arcadian plain restricted large-scale movements of people and animals.[106] The Arcadians were leaving Agesilaus only one option: to leave.

Xenophon continues: "On the fourth day, after an early breakfast, he led the army away intending to encamp where he had originally camped after leaving Eutaia."[107] Agesilaus intended to return to the outskirts of Tegean territory, a movement of about five kilometers across the central plain and another fifteen kilometers south that took an entire day. This amounted to a pace of about two-and-a-half kilometers (one-and-a-half miles) an hour. Indeed, the central Arcadian plain was no place for a large conventional army during the winter.

"Since the Arcadians could not be seen, he led them to Eutaia by the quickest route possible even though it was rather late. He wanted to remove his hoplites before they saw the enemies' fires so that no one could say he withdrew in flight."[108] This passage is somewhat confusing, due in large part to Xenophon's excessive apologizing for Agesilaus's decisions. Agesilaus could not see any Arcadians—which would follow, as he was five to ten kilometers from the fortifications of Tegea—so he rushed across ten kilometers of mountainous terrain at night so no one could accuse him of fleeing?[109] What else was Agesilaus doing but fleeing Arcadia?

Evidently, Agesilaus would have felt obligated to stay in Arcadia if anyone in his army were to observe the Arcadians preparing for battle. As at Eutaia during the initial stages of the invasion, he must have been expecting some form of formal, conventional defense. But after seeing the coordination of the Arcadians' movements and surviving the encounter outside of Mantineia, perhaps he finally appreciated the full extent of his disadvantages in Arcadia. It may have even dawned on him that the Arcadians had a different view of what constituted a victory in Arcadia, especially when he was allowed to pass through Asea and Tegea, a major gateway into central Arcadia from the south.

Ever the politician, though, Agesilaus found a way to spin the incident in his favor. "In his mind, he had restored Spartan morale in that he had invaded Arcadia and ravaged the country and no one came out to fight him."[110] Here Xenophon makes an almost ridiculous claim; the point of the invasion was to punish the Mantineians for assisting in the overthrow, exile, and death of the pro-Spartan party in Tegea. In any case, the amount of agricultural destruction that the Lacedaemonians could have brought about during the middle of winter was negligible.[111]

The Arcadians did give Agesilaus a chance to attack, and they were nearly successful, but Agesilaus refused to fight the Arcadians on any terms except his own. In response, the Arcadians restricted the movement of the invading army to the central Arcadian plain and left open avenues of attack that favored the defenders. The last thing that the Arcadians were going to give Agesilaus was an open and conventional battle; there was no need to concede an advantage to the invading army and risk defeat so close to home, especially after neutralizing the threat from the north. In the end, writes Xenophon, "when Agesilaus reached Laconia he sent the Spartiates home and the *perioikoi* to their towns."[112] Agesilaus demobilized his army seemingly oblivious of the Arcadians' intentions and capabilities.

"As for the Arcadians," Xenophon writes, "after Agesilaus had departed and once they perceived that he had disbanded his army (they were still assembled), they attacked the Heraians because they had refused to join the League of the Arcadians and had taken part in an invasion of Arcadia with the Lacedaemonians."[113] Heraia was far from the central plain—no less than sixty kilometers in a straight line across the most mountainous terrain that Arcadia had to offer. Given this distance, the Arcadians must have been relying on information carried to them from across the mountains. The Eutaians are the obvious candidates, along with the Alipheirans who occupied the high ground to the south of Heraia. These Arcadians were now part of the league and would have been fully capable of observing the activities of the Heraians and relaying information.[114]

After neutralizing the threat from Orchomenos and driving off the Lacedaemonians, the Arcadians remained vigilant and quite intentionally kept the army together as they prepared for their next move: "They assaulted the Heraians, set fire to their homes, and cut down their trees."[115] There certainly was a retaliatory aspect to this attack, as Xenophon figured, but at the same time, with Heraia subdued, the western entrance into Arcadian territory was now in the hands of the Arcadian League.[116]

From there, Xenophon continues, "once the Thebans were reported to have arrived at Mantineia to help, the Arcadians left Heraia and linked up with the Thebans . . . [who] thought that things had worked out well in that they had come to the assistance of the Arcadians."[117] That is, the Thebans thought they had seized an opportunity to bolster their influence in the Peloponnese. "But not seeing a single enemy in the country, they prepared to leave."[118]

Aftermath

The Arcadians had other plans for both the Thebans and the Lacedaemonians. First, they convinced the Thebans to stay and take part in an invasion of Laconia. The Arcadians spearheaded this invasion, fighting their way through the pass at Oion while the Thebans marched through the pass at Karyai unopposed. The Karyaians actually welcomed the invasion. Together, the Arcadians and Thebans (along with the Argives and Eleans) spent the next three to four days ravaging the land, plundering homes, and in general, menacing the Spartans.[119]

Yet if the Arcadians were capable of invading Laconia in the winter of 370, it would seem that they also could have prevented the Lacedaemonians from leaving Arcadia. Furthermore, they could have fought the Lacedaemonians in Arcadia on a number of occasions, but in each instance, the Arcadians held back. This prompts a question: Why did the Arcadians refuse to pull the trigger, so to speak, when they had the Lacedaemonians surrounded in Arcadia?

Analysis

Diodorus has the impression that the Arcadians felt a "prudent respect" for the Lacedaemonians—that is, they were uneasy about fighting them without external support and so refused to engage with Agesilaus's army during the invasion.[120] Xenophon is silent on the matter, although he does lead his readers in the same direction. Diodorus's interpretation of the encounter still prevails, but there are a number of problems with his view.

First, the Arcadians already had external support during the invasion: the Argives and Eleans. The Argives and Eleans were actually the only support that the Arcadians had during the winter of 370, since the Arcadians had yet to formalize an alliance with the Thebans. Consequently, when the Lacedaemonian army made its way to Mantineia, the Arcadians had already obtained as much external support as was possible.

Furthermore, even if the Arcadians really were uneasy about fighting a Lacedaemonian army, they certainly did not hesitate to attack a Spartan-led mercenary one; recall the Mantineians' annihilation of Polytropus's mercenary force at Elymia. It is possible that the Arcadians maintained a distinction between fighting light-armed mercenaries (even Spartan-led ones) and Spartan hoplites. But if so, the Arcadians misplaced their "prudent respect" shortly before they invaded Laconia.

In addition, Xenophon relates that at an unspecified date within a year of the Defense, the Argives had called on the Arcadians for aid against the Spartans.[121]

(Evidently, the Argives were unaware of a widespread fear of Spartans among Arcadians.) The Arcadians, without the support of allies, fulfilled the request. They attacked the Spartan garrison at Asine in the southern Argolid, killed its Spartan commander, and then devastated the surrounding countryside. In sum, a fear of fighting the Spartans simply does not explain the Arcadians' refusal to fight Agesilaus's army in 370.

Instead of a direct confrontation with Agesilaus, the Arcadians enacted their version of a Fabian defensive strategy: they wore down and eventually drove off the large-scale, invading army. But why would the prizefighters of the ancient Greek world need to develop such a strategy? By the first quarter of the fourth century the Arcadians had considerable military resources at their disposal. Why not devote these resources to preventing the Spartans and their allies from entering Arcadia in the first place?

Without question, the Arcadians could have prevented a Spartan army from entering Arcadia, but only if they knew where the Lacedaemonians were going to make their entrance. The problem was that there were at least three potential entry points into Arcadia from Laconia: the mountain pass near Oresthasion that led to Eutaia, the pass at Oion, and the one at Karyai. The distance between Oresthasion and Karyai was about thirty kilometers. Furthermore, as the invasion of 370 revealed, the Arcadians were also vulnerable from the north.

Keeping the Spartans and their allies out of Arcadia was virtually impossible. The Arcadians needed a strategy for resisting the Spartans and their allies should they ever invade Arcadia, and they needed one before the invasion of 370. Their strategy was to contain and delay the invading army, neutralize whatever advantages the invaders could bring to bear, limit the army's movement to predictable routes, and maintain the threat of attack. The Arcadians achieved these goals by focusing their efforts on the central Arcadian plain. With Mantineia in the north, Tegea in the south, and the mountains to the east and west, the Arcadians could envelop a large-scale army and then attack, harass, or threaten it from any direction.[122] The ultimate aim of the Arcadians' defensive strategy was to drive off the invading army. They were prepared to fight a conventional battle, but only as a last resort.

Why a last resort? By fighting an open engagement with a large-scale army within the territorial limits of Arcadia, the Arcadians would have sacrificed nearly all of the strategic and tactical advantages they had gained. Furthermore, if the Arcadians fought such a battle and lost, the invading army could have then gained control of Mantineia or Tegea and put an end to the Arcadian koinon. In fact, disrupting widespread political unity in Arcadia is exactly what Agesilaus had in mind with the invasion of 370, as Xenophon suggests.

Outside of Arcadia, the Arcadians could afford to risk a defeat to the Spartans. They could concede whatever ground they occupied, withdraw, and then regroup back home. During their war with Elis in 366-365, the Arcadians did just that on several occasions, yet protecting their home territory from an invasion called for a different approach.[123]

In response to the two-pronged invasion of 370, most Arcadian combatants assembled at Asea to deal with the invading army to the south, but a sizable contingent remained at Mantineia. The Mantineians then dislodged and annihilated the threat from the north, thereby depriving Agesilaus of a light-armed capability. The Arcadians at Asea allowed Agesilaus to advance from Eutaia, then they moved their base of operations to Tegea. With that, the Arcadians had enveloped the invading army in the central Arcadian plain.

From there, an Arcadian-Argive contingent from Tegea enticed the Spartans to advance toward the eastern mountains of the plain. Agesilaus did not take the bait. Later, when Agesilaus attempted to move outside of the plain and attack Mantineia from a different direction, the Arcadians drove him back into the open. Since Agesilaus did not persist, the Arcadians let the invading army withdraw. Thus, they achieved the aim of their defense.

The Defense of 370 clearly was a short-term success, but it did more than merely preserve the existence of the nascent Arcadian League. By driving off the invading Lacedaemonian army, the Arcadians proved that the koinon they had formed earlier in the year was now a significant political entity in the Greek world. To what extent, then, was the League's defensive strategy rooted in the collective concerns and capabilities of pre-league Arcadians?

Throughout the fifth and early fourth centuries, the main threat to pre-league Arcadians had been a relative constant: Sparta. If the Mantineians and Tegeans ever hoped to be free of Sparta—and their rocky relationship with the Spartans during this time suggests that they did—they needed a plan for when (not if) the Spartans invaded Arcadia to suppress a revolt.

In the immediate aftermath of Leuctra, very little had changed between the Arcadians and Spartans. True, the Spartans lost the battle, but they remained the leading power of the Peloponnese. They did not capitulate to the Thebans, they could still field an army of their own, and they retained a number of key allies. From the Arcadians' perspective, a Spartan invasion was still a possibility circa 370, just as it was in previous generations. It follows, then, that the defensive strategy on display in the Defense of Arcadia had pre-league roots.

But were the Arcadians capable of ethnos-level planning before the founding of the league? The fifth-century symmachy suggests that they were, but so does the Defense of 370. Without pre-league planning, within the span of a couple of months, the Arcadians would have needed to develop a defensive strategy from scratch and form a standing army. Yet Xenophon makes no mention of the so-called *eparitoi* in his description of the Arcadian League's founding—remember, the Arkadikon repelled the invasion of 370—and his first mention of such an army is in 366-365.[124] By that time, the army of *eparitoi* had indeed become a formal institution of the Arcadian League, and the paying of its members was creating internal conflict.

If the federal army of the 360s developed from the Arkadikon of 370, as it seems it did, the Arkadikon must have represented the pre-league Arcadian army—that is, the ethnos-wide force that could mobilize and respond to external threats on short notice. The main support for this argument is the Arcadians' initial point of assembly at Asea. After all, Mantineia was the working capital of the league from 370 to 368, and along with Tegea, it offered an ideal location to assemble and house a standing army. Yet the Arcadians initially assembled in the mountains at Asea, where there had never been Spartan influence.

More to the point, unlike Mantineia and Tegea, Asea provided an ideal location to base a pre-league defense of Arcadia. Naturally protected, the mountain stronghold had access to the substantial resources and strategic advantages of the central plain, but it did not occupy a vulnerable position on the plain. With the addition of Tegea, the Arcadian League gained even more advantages over potential invaders, which the Arcadians then adapted to the working strategy of the late fifth or early fourth century.

This explains why the Arcadians were prepared for the invasion of 370, even though the traditional campaigning season had ended and the Arcadians' newly formed koinon was still in its infancy; before the founding of the league, the Arcadians already understood the consequences of the Mantineians and Tegeans declaring their full independence from Sparta. In response, they took steps to defend themselves accordingly.

Despite its promising start, the Arcadian League was short-lived. By the middle of the 360s, Arcadian federal magistrates disagreed on nearly every major issue pertaining to the league. Then, early in 363, a treaty with Elis effectively split the koinon between the Mantineians, the Tegeans, and their respective supporters.[125] The Second Battle of Mantineia soon followed, after which the koinon of the Arcadians disappears from the historical record.

As events of the 360s revealed, the koinon never solidified the loose bonds that connected pre-league Arcadia. This lack of cohesion was not fatal per se; rather, security and self-government simply were not enough for the Arcadians. Immediately after the successful defense of 370, they began to pursue other interests—namely, expansion in and hegemony over the Peloponnese.

But the Arcadians never fully agreed on how they were to attain their collective aims, and not all Arcadian communities desired to expand. Only the most powerful constituent polities embraced the difficulties inherent to the Arcadians' more active role in Greek affairs. Among smaller Arcadian polities, local traditions of autonomy and self-determination eventually prevailed over the greater interests of the league. When they did, one of the most dynamic federal states in ancient Greek history ceased to exist as a political entity.[126]

Conclusion

> Among the many objects to which a wise and free
> people find it necessary to direct their attention, that
> of providing for their *safety* seems to be the first.
>
> —John Jay, *Federalist No.3*

Variety and Unity

The defensive activities of the Phocians, Aetolians, Acarnanians, and Arcadians circa 490–362 share some basic features, but they also exhibit a wide variety. For example, although all four ethnē immediately emptied the countryside at the arrival of an invading force, the Phocians and Aetolians abandoned their settlements and then gathered en masse at Tithorea and Aigition, respectively. Both of these sites were centrally located and easily defensible. In contrast, the Acarnanians withdrew into fortified settlements that were scattered across the region, while some Arcadian civilians remained in place as the Arcadians of fighting age gathered at Asea.

In terms of tactics, the Aetolians and Acarnanians were comparatively more aggressive than the Phocians and Arcadians. The Aetolians, for instance, prepared an ambush at Aigition and then waited as the physical geography of the region gradually brought the Athenians into the kill zone. Once the Athenians entered Aigition, the Aetolians launched their ruthless attack. Similarly, the Acarnanians used their livestock as bait to set up an elaborate attack against the Spartans at the unnamed lake. In both cases, it seems that the primary aim of the defenders was to annihilate the invading army, unlike the aim of the Arcadians and Phocians.

In fact, the Phocians would have been content to let the Thessalians plunder and pass through the Kephisos River Valley and Parnassus region, but they were also prepared to fight. When the Thessalians left them with no other option, the Phocians launched the Chalk Raid, effectively ending Thessalian aggression against Phocis for the rest of the classical period. In a similar way, the Arcadians avoided large-scale engagements, although they did initiate limited-scale, highly effective attacks against contingents of the invading army. At the same time, they contained and menaced the Spartans in the central Arcadian plain and ultimately forced the invaders to withdraw.

The potential threats to each ethnos exhibit even more variety. The Phocians and Arcadians were dealing with long-standing, hostile neighbors known for their aggressive tendencies. For the Phocians, the threat was the Thessalians and their various allies in the central mainland; for the Arcadians, it was the Spartans and their allies in the Peloponnese. The threats to the Aetolians and Acarnanians were less clear. Both lacked aggressive neighbors in the western mainland, and neither ethnos was directly at odds with one of the main centers of power during the classical period. However, the Aetolians and Acarnanians understood that their regional rivals could call on the Athenians or Spartans for assistance. Both upland ethnē were also aware that their attempts to seize coastal settlements could prompt an invasion.

Finally, the amount of foreign involvement in each defense provides yet another source of variation. The Aetolians and Acarnanians had outside assistance when attacking regional rivals, but no allies came to their aid during the invasions of 426 and 389. The Phocians had no outside assistance at all, aside from a possible foreign adviser, while the Arcadians had a great deal of outside assistance for the defense of 370 and the subsequent invasion of Laconia.

Nevertheless, despite all of this variety, a common theme cuts across the four cases that reveals an underlying unity to the defense of Greek upland ethnē. The Phocians circa 490, the Aetolians circa 426, the Acarnanians circa 389, and the Arcadians circa 370 developed peculiar defensive strategies tailored to their respective geopolitical circumstances that guarded against potential invasions from the lowlands. More specifically, the Greeks of each ethnos implemented their own version of defense in depth.[1] That is, they yielded portions of their territory, exploited the physical environment to neutralize and contain invading armies, lured these armies to locations that maximized the defenders' advantages, and from there judiciously attacked. Their methods and aims may have been different, but the calculation, coordination, and sophistication on display in the Phocian Chalk Raid of the Thessalian Camp, the Aetolian Rout of the Athenians, and the Defenses of Acarnania and Arcadia show that these upland Greeks recognized the potential threats that surrounded them and had planned accordingly.

Yet this strategic capability is far from obvious in the ancient historical narratives. In fact, Herodotus, Thucydides, and Xenophon give no indication that they or their respective audiences knew anything about the defensive capabilities of upland ethnē. Furthermore, to judge from their narratives, there was no standard way of relating encounters with upland Greeks among classical writers. That is, although stereotypes of upland peoples and their way of life certainly prevailed during the time in question, Herodotus, Thucydides, and Xenophon wrote their narratives without recourse to established tropes of what ethnē do when the mighty polis armies advance into the mountains.[2] What their narratives offer instead are biased outsiders' impressions of the defensive responses of the Phocians, Aetolians, Acarnanians, and Arcadians.

But by drawing on various archaeological, topographical, and ethnographic studies, the critical readings at the heart of this book piece together the dynamics of the four defenses, recreate the experience of unconventional mountain warfare between Greeks, and thereby provide an entirely different perspective of these one-sided ancient accounts. By shedding new light on the defensive capabilities of upland ethnē, these readings stand alone as contributions in their own right, but the underlying unity that they bring to light leads to even broader insights into the character of classical upland ethnē.

A Way of War beyond the Polis

The Phocians, Aetolians, Acarnanians, and Arcadians circa 490–362 practiced a peculiar way of war that differed from that of the polis-centric realm in three key respects.[3] First, the Greeks of upland ethnē displayed little interest in fair, open, or gentlemanly fights. Instead, upland Greeks engineered the site of violent encounters to surprise and gain tactical advantages over conventional armies. They did this by harassing and baiting armies into basins and valleys, attacking at night, abandoning settlements, and feigning retreats. To spring their homicidal surprises, they often exploited the physical constraints of the natural environment, as illustrated best by the Aetolians and Acarnanians. Upland Greeks did not avoid direct confrontations but engaged in them only under particular circumstances.

Second, whereas warfare in the polis-centric realm placed a premium on territorial integrity, the Phocians, Aetolians, Acarnanians, and Arcadians readily made territorial concessions to achieve greater ends. In each case, the seemingly advantageous toeholds or bases of operations initially gained by the invaders turned out to favor the aims of the defenders. The best example of this stratagem comes from the Phocian Chalk Raid. The Thessalians probably felt quite secure at Neon shortly before the whitened Phocians descended on their camp.

Third, upland ethnē adhered to a different notion of military victory. From the polis-centric perspective, unopposed crop destruction constituted a major victory of rank and status. Agesilaus figured he had won against the Arcadians in 370 because they would not fight him after he devastated the countryside surrounding Mantineia. But victory meant something else to upland ethnē. From the defenders' perspective, it was virtually impossible to prevent a Thessalian-, Athenian-, or Spartan-led invading army from entering and occupying a portion of their respective geographical realms. However, the Phocians, Aetolians, Acarnanians, and Arcadians could still achieve victory in a very real sense by driving off such an invading army without compromising their own political integrity. To do so, they did not always have to fight, although they often did. In the end, the defenses of circa 490, 426, 389, and 370 were so successful that no lowland power ever attempted another invasion of the same ethnos. Each defense, in short, was a major victory.

Notwithstanding these differences, the way of war practiced by upland ethnē in the mountains of classical Greece was still very much in dialogue with the polis-centric way of war. The Phocians, some of the Acarnanians, and most of the Arcadians fought as hoplites. This means that three of the four ethnē had adapted the technologies of the polis-centric realm to their upland environments before the invasions on record. The Acarnanians even integrated their hoplite resources with contingents of peltasts and slingers. And even though the Aetolians lacked hoplites, they certainly were adept at containing and killing large numbers of them with seeming familiarity. In any case, all four upland ethnē systematically manipulated the conventions of their lowland invaders, and it was this way of war that preserved their ethnos-level political communities. In sum, we see a way of war shaped less by ideology and more by actual circumstances.

The Military Roots of Ancient Federal States

In a way, the experience of ethnos-level defense was analogous to the experience of citizenship within upland ethnē. That is, as in other less violent activities at the ethnos-level, defensive actions were transitory periods of relatively intense collective action. Admittedly, the exact nature of ethnos-level political communities circa 490–362 is hazy, but all four polities constituted at least loose confederacies when their respective defensive strategies came into effect, and each eventually became a formal federal state—the Arcadians shortly before the invasion of 370. Consequently, before forming federal states, the experience of defense would have been the primary experience of citizenship at the ethnos-level for most Phocians, Aetolians, Acarnanians, and possibly even the Arcadians.

Yet unlike the polis-centric realm, the relationship between the military experience and the experience of citizenship within upland ethnē defies neat categorization. The experience of hoplite warfare, for example, clearly informed and was reinforced by the civic practices and ideals of individual city-states. Similarly, in the case of Athens, the organizational and tactical development of the fleet was intimately tied to developments in Athenian democracy.[4] In the realm of upland ethnē, though, there was no analogue to the hoplite-polis or rower-democracy perspective that works so well for studying Athens, Sparta, Thebes, or any other polis-centric political community. Appreciating the full significance of the military activities of upland ethnē, then, demands an even broader perspective.

That is just what the critical readings at the heart of this book offer. As in previous work on the ancient face of battle, these studies attend to the practical realities of military encounters—how individuals dealt with the physical circumstances of campaigning and battle, the perspectives and emotions of combatants (though at all levels), the use and effects of spears, javelins, and slings—but at the same time, they show that these practical realities were rooted in a collective outlook that informed high-level planning. They also show that the defensive coordination that stemmed from this planning bore a direct relationship to the social and political structures that gave shape to classical Phocis, Aetolia, Acarnania, and Arcadia.

In short, the way of war practiced by these upland polities speaks to their way of life. By studying how the Phocians, Aetolians, Acarnanians, and Arcadians circa 490–362 organized and executed their ethnos-wide defenses, we learn about the internal character of each polity and its relationship to the classical Greek world writ large. But what exactly do we learn? The answer is twofold.

First, upland ethnē were well-organized and efficient polities that were thoroughly adapted to their respective environmental and geopolitical contexts, but their success did not depend on the existence of a central federal government. Tables 1 and 2 help to illustrate this point. Table 1 outlines the basic criteria for confederations in the classical Greek world. Table 2 outlines the basic criteria for federations. A checkmark means that there is unambiguous evidence for a particular criterion, a minus sign that there is no evidence at all, and a question mark that the evidence is only circumstantial.

Table 1   Basic confederation criteria ca. 490–362

BASIC CONFEDERATION CRITERIA	COHERENT SET OF SELF-GOVERNING STATES OR SUBREGIONS	ETHNIC IDENTITY RECOGNIZABLE TO OUTSIDERS	WIDE-SCALE CONCERTED ACTION	INVOLVEMENT IN FOREIGN AFFAIRS AS A COLLECTIVE
Phocis ca. 490	√	√	√	√
Aetolia ca. 426	√	√	√	√
Acarnania ca. 389	√	√	√	√
Arcadia ca. 370	√	√	√	√

The Phocians, Aetolians, Acarnanians, and Arcadians easily met all of the basic confederation criteria during the time in question, but less clear is the extent to which these same polities met the basic federation criteria. Aside from the Arcadian federal decree of 369, no other form of evidence attests to the existence of a standing, central government in Phocis, Aetolia, or Acarnania. Among the four polities, the Arcadians constituted the only case of an unambiguous koinon. Yet even then, chapter 4 has shown that the Defense of 370 must have been rooted in the pre-league organization of the fifth- and fourth-century ethnos.

Beyond-the-polis scholarship has often posited the existence of early koina to argue that classical ethnē were not playing catch-up with the polis-centric world—that they were in fact capable of their own complex responses to shifting political circumstances. Such scholarship has also convincingly challenged the view that later koina were nothing more than evolved ethnē, showing instead that the founding of a koinon was always a deliberate, creative act. For earlier periods, then, the existence of a koinon would seemingly provide the best evidence that the Thucydidean view of upland Greeks was incorrect.

But just as it is incorrect to think of an ethnos as the negative image or precursor of the polis, and incorrect to think of a koinon (federation) as an evolutionarily advanced ethnos (tribe), it is equally incorrect to suppose that upland ethnē required a formal federal structure for complex and creative responses to the challenges of their surroundings. The defenses of circa 490, 426, 389, and 370 did not require the direction of a central government, yet each was still complex and creative, deliberate, innovative, sensible, and brutally efficient.

The second thing we learn is that upland ethnē formed part of a connected sphere on the classical Greek mainland, but in a surprising sense. This sphere was not the product of mutual understanding, or even mutual misunderstanding à la Richard White. Rather, while the Thessalians, Athenians, and Spartans to varying degrees were arrogant, ignorant, and even dismissive toward

Table 2   Basic federation criteria ca. 490–362

BASIC FEDERATION CRITERIA (INCLUDES CRITERIA FROM TABLE 1)	CENTRAL RULING POWER AS EVIDENCED BY OFFICIAL, INTERNAL DECREES	CONSTITUTION OR FORMAL MAGISTRATES	COMMON COINAGE
Phocis ca. 490	?	–	√
Aetolia ca. 426	–	–	–
Acarnania ca. 389	?	?	–
Arcadia ca. 370	√	√	√

the collective capabilities and resolve of upland ethnē, the reverse was not the case. The Phocians, Aetolians, Acarnanians, and Arcadians misunderstood very little about the threats surrounding them. And not only were they aware of the dismissive attitudes of their aggressive and more powerful neighbors, but they exploited them to great effect.

By failing to appreciate the intricacies of the defenses they related, Herodotus, Thucydides, Xenophon, and their various sources attest to the prevalence of these lowland attitudes. The desperate Phocians owed everything to a foreign seer; the Aetolians must have known about the Athenian-led invasion from the start; the complacent Acarnanians foolishly drove their livestock into the open; and the Arcadians had to have been scared of the Spartans—why else would they have refused to fight?

But by cross-examining these accounts, this book has offered very different explanations for the successful defenses of Greek upland ethnē. Whether through religious affiliations (Phocis), smaller-scale alliances (Aetolia), earlier encounters with the expansionary tendencies of Sparta and Athens (Acarnania), or mercenary experiences from the late Archaic through the classical periods (Arcadia), the Greeks of upland ethnē knew exactly what to expect from their lowland neighbors. In light of this knowledge, they developed their own way of war that neutralized and repelled potential invasions, and ensured their survival as political communities.

Backward and Forward

The foregoing discussion opens two intriguing lines of inquiry, both of which stem from the following question: Were upland defensive strategies strictly a classical phenomenon?

Looking back to the Late Bronze Age circa 1500–1200, we see that the main powers of the Mycenaean world—that is, the centers of urbanism and economic activity on the Greek mainland—were also located in the lowlands.[5] In the Peloponnese stood the palatial centers of Mycenae, Tiryns, Sparta, and Pylos; in the central mainland were Athens, Thebes, Orchomenos, and Gla; and in Thessaly there was Dimini. Constituting the periphery of the Bronze Age mainland were those areas uncontrolled or uninfluenced by these palatial centers—in particular, the same upland regions of the northern and western mainland that formed the classical periphery.[6] In other words, the broader geopolitical context of the two periods was virtually the same.

As in the classical period, the mainland of the Late Bronze Age constituted a connected political and economic sphere. However, although there is plenty of evidence for warfare and territorial expansion among Mycenaean palatial centers, there is no record of specific campaigns directed against upland regions.[7] Nevertheless, unless the Bronze Age inhabitants of what later became classical Epirus, Acarnania, Aetolia, West Locris, Phocis, Achaea, and Arcadia were somehow oblivious to their surroundings, they too would have recognized the threat of large-scale invasions from the lowlands. It is possible, then, that these Bronze Age upland polities also developed high-level contingency plans for potential invasions.

This is not to say that classical upland ethnē somehow preserved the defensive methods of their Bronze Age ancestors; military technologies changed, and we know far too little about the social and political organization of the Mycenaean upland realm to say for sure. Then again, from a world-historical perspective, the Greek mainland circa 1500–500 is widely acknowledged as one of the most illustrative examples of the collapse and regeneration of a complex society. That is, the classical Greeks (the "second generation") transformed and expanded the political and economic structures of the Mycenaean world while retaining distorted memories of the "first generation."[8] Of course, the first generation usually amounts to the palatial centers in such scholarship, and the second generation to the classical poleis—the "citadel to city-state" view.[9] But by developing defensive strategies aimed at neutralizing lowland aggression, it is possible that the classical Phocians, Aetolians, Acarnanians, and Arcadians regenerated a sociopolitical structure of the Bronze Age, only one that prevailed beyond the palace.

Looking forward to the Hellenistic period, the lowlands no longer hosted the major centers of power in the Greek world. Macedonia and Epirus controlled most of the mainland by the end of the fourth century, and by the first quarter of the third century, the Aetolian and Achaean Leagues had emerged as significant regional powers. As for the other classical upland ethnē, Acarnania was now part of the Aetolian League. Most of Arcadia formed part of the Achaean League since the Arcadian League had dissolved by the middle of the fourth century, while the Phocian League prevailed well into the third century.

The defensive concerns of these polities did change, though not drastically. The Phocians still faced a large-scale threat from the north, only now it was from the Thessalians and Macedonians. As part of the Achaean League, the Arcadians still contended with Sparta, as it took several centuries for the Spartans to give up their expansionary interests in the Peloponnese. Finally, the Aetolians and Acarnanians still dealt with threats from the coast. In fact, the Aetolians drove off a large-scale Macedonian invasion from the north in 321, and the Aetolian League repelled attempted invasions in 280 and 208.

Furthermore, Hellenistic koina functioned as efficient federal states and in general experienced a high level of success, as illustrated best by the Aetolian and Achaean Leagues. Over the course of several centuries, these two federal polities successfully resisted Macedonia and eventually Rome while pursuing expansionary interests of their own within and beyond the Greek mainland. It would follow, then, that the Aetolians, Achaeans, and other Greek federal states developed and enacted high-level plans for maintaining security, achieving long-term aims and interests, and ensuring future prosperity. It almost seems obvious. Yet there has been virtually no scholarly interest in the strategic methods of Hellenistic federal states, to say nothing of their classical roots—a potentially promising field of inquiry.

At present, the potential strategies of Hellenistic federal states and the defensive capabilities of the Mycenaean upland realm can only be touched on as they exceed the scope of this book. However, these twin themes show that the broader implications of the defense of Greek upland ethnē circa 490–362 extend well beyond the classical period.

Taking an even broader historical perspective, we see that security—both internal and external—usually drives regional integration and the formation of federal unions. Federations also enhance economic development, increase international clout, and allow for territorial expansion. But in nearly every case, external security is a basic condition for future growth.

In addition, although federal unions do not require the existence of an external threat, defensive alliances have produced a number of successful federations—especially when such an alliance or confederation forms between smaller, independent polities sharing a common identity.[10] For example, in 1787 the Constitution of the United States of America established a standing federal government that corrected the perceived inadequacies of what had been a loose confederation.[11] But it was the loose confederation established in 1781 that initially gained independence for its constituent members and provided the conditions for a "more perfect union."

In comparison, tracing the exact process whereby the loose confederations of Greek upland ethnē became formal federal states is virtually impossible; the evidence is simply insufficient. To make matters even more difficult, ancient and modern federations share only the most basic features, so comparisons between the two tend to raise more questions than they answer.[12] Nevertheless, what initially attracted the attention of ancient writers to upland ethnē were the military achievements of the Phocians, Aetolians, Acarnanians, and Arcadians circa 490–362.

Effective yet unconventional, and certainly unexpected, the collective capabilities of these polities in the face of large-scale threats demanded an explanation. This, in part, explains why the four defenses ended up in the narratives of Herodotus, Thucydides, and Xenophon as the only ethnos-level activities detailed in a classical source. Given the nature of the sources, we cannot conclude that the federations that these ethnē eventually became were primarily military phenomena. Nevertheless, the early military successes of these polities reveal an underlying violent element to the mere political experiments that koina are often made out to be.

By way of conclusion, it is worth returning once more to the Thucydidean view of upland peoples, but in a later, more complete iteration. Writing in the second century CE, Arrian related a speech allegedly delivered by Alexander the Great to his fellow Macedonians at Opis in 324. Alexander was attempting to dissuade his kinsmen from abandoning the conqueror's cause, and he opened the speech with a reminder of how far the Macedonians had come:

> I will begin with my father Philip: he found you wandering and destitute, most of you dressed in skins, grazing a few sheep in the mountains, and pathetically fighting over them with the neighboring Triballians, Illyrians, and Thracians. He gave you cloaks to wear instead of skins, and led you down from the hills into the plains. He made you a match for the neighboring barbarians, teaching you to rely not on your mountain strongholds, but on your own innate valor. He made you city dwellers, and with laws and customs, he civilized you.[13]

By this later view, the upland people of the Greek mainland led pastoral, unsettled, lawless lives with only feeble political bonds between each other. At best, they could skirmish in the hills with their tribal enemies. In contrast, the plains allowed for an agricultural, settled, city-state way of life that led to better organization in the military sphere and greater security against external threats. With regard to classical upland ethnē, the Thessalians, Athenians, and Spartans undoubtedly would have agreed with the essential features of this view. It is essentially the same as Thucydides' view of Greeks from the western mainland.

But consider the supposed opposition between relying on mountain strongholds and relying on martial prowess. Before the invasions of circa 490, 426, 389, and 370, the Thessalians, Athenians, and Spartans probably would have agreed with this point too. After all, if the Phocians, Aetolians, Acarnanians, or Arcadians were capable of properly defending themselves, why would they disappear and flock to the mountains at the sight of a foreign army? Why would they allow the destruction of their agricultural resources if they could resist like men? Why not fight like real Greeks?

Such attitudes eventually proved to be lethal to lowland invaders. The Greeks of classical upland ethnē saw no conflict between relying on the advantages of their physical environments and relying on their own martial prowess. Indeed, they relied on both. And with their defensive strategies, they turned hills, woodlands, and rivers into allies—and invaders into quarry.

Notes

Introduction

1. All dates are BCE. Ancient authors are abbreviated according to the *Oxford Classical Dictionary* (4th ed.). All translations are my own. "Upland" refers to regions of the classical mainland where the concentration of human settlement and mixed farming resources was above 400 to 500 meters above sea level (Bintliff 1997, 1). All other terminology is dealt with below.

2. For the concept of the Greek third world, or the Third Greece (*das dritte Griechenland*), see Gehrke 1986, a relatively early attempt to discuss as a whole the various state-forms of the Greek world from the Archaic period to the Roman conquest.

3. Perlman 1996; Nielsen 1996a; Beck 1997; Daverio Rocchi 1993; Morgan 2000; Gehrke 2000.

4. For an example of this view, see Hansen's opening remarks in his eminently useful distillation of the Copenhagen Polis Centre's ongoing work: "It has often, quite rightly, been said that the *polis*, as a form of state and society, was the basis of the whole of Greek civilisation; and the implication of that is that one can only understand Greek civilisation if one understands the form of the society the Greeks lived under, i.e. the *polis*" (2006, 1; see also 56–61 for the concept of the polis as a community of citizens).

5. In a slightly less abstract version, these scholars object to an Athenocentric view of political organization and community in the Greek world (Brock and Hodkinson 2000, 4–21), especially as the Athenians undeniably constituted an anomalous polity. See also Vlassopoulos 2007.

6. The territorial limits of geographical ethnē fluctuated during the late Archaic and classical periods, though not drastically. Examples of regional studies informed by the beyond-the-polis perspective include Bommeljé and Doorn 1987 (Aetolia); Helly 1995 (Thessaly); Berktold, Schmid, and Wacker 1996 (Acarnania); McInerney 1999 (Phocis); Nielsen 2002 (Arcadia); and Borza 1990 (Macedonia). Parker (1998, 19–20) discusses the distinction between geographical ethnē—primarily a phenomenon of the mainland—and what he refers to as "dispersed" ethnē, that is, those not confined to a single geographical space. The best-known examples of the latter are the Dorians and Ionians (Alty 1982).

7. See, in particular, Funke and Haake 2013; Freitag, Funke, and Haake 2006; and Morgan 2003, especially at 107–63 on cult communities. Morgan places special emphasis on the economic roles of sanctuaries as sites for storing and consuming material goods.

8. This phenomenon is not restricted to geographical ethnē. For ethnicity in the ancient Greek world in general, see J. Hall 1997 and 2002. See also J. Hall 1998 for criticisms and Hall's response. See McInerney 2001 for ethnos and ethnicity, and for archaeological perspectives, see Morgan 2001a. See also Nielsen 1999 and McInerney 1999.

9. Thuc. 1.5–6. Thucydides mentions by name the West Locrians, Aetolians, and Acarnanians but implicates the entire northern and western mainland, and even the Arcadians at 1.2. Modern iterations of this view include Ehrenberg 1969, 3–25, and Snodgrass 1980, 26–27, 42. Although geographical and ecological conditions did favor the development of more specialized pastoralist practices in upland ethnē (Howe 2008, 71–75), notably in western Arcadia, central Phocis, and Aetolia (Bommeljé and Doorn 1991), mixed agriculture was still prevalent (Morgan 2003, 168–69). See also Bakhuizen 1996.

10. Cf. Aris. *Pol.* 1261a28, 1276a29, 1326b1–7.

11. For a critique of the polis-centric perspective in modern scholarship, see McInerney 2013, 467.

12. From this core-periphery perspective, the peripheral status of ethnē during the classical period is only part of the story. From the late fourth through the second centuries, the northern and western mainland became the core (Macedonia, Epirus, and Aetolia) and the polis-centric lowlands the periphery (Bintliff 1997).

13. This point is stressed by Purcell 1990, 58: "The *polis* in general, we might say, was a cul-de-sac, an unhelpful response to the challenges of the Mediterranean reality, if building large and relatively harmonious and inclusive societies is considered a worthwhile goal."

14. In the case of Greek ethnē, a "tribe" was a distinguishable political community that lacked an urban center. The term is not necessarily synonymous with "pre-state" (Nagy 1990, 276–93) or "pre-polis" (Forrest 2000).

15. For Macedonia and Thessaly, see Archibald 2000; for Epirus, see Davies 2000 and Cabanes 1981. Cabanes highlights the stark differences between the ethnē of Epirus and Acarnania.

16. Tausend 1992, 34–47.

17. It is worth noting, though, that this theme of variation and dynamism was not lost on earlier scholars of ancient federalism, statecraft, and representative government. Freeman (1893) was well aware that ethnos polities followed a different political trajectory, as was Busolt (1926, 1395–1575) and then Larsen (1955). However, each of these scholars was most interested in the federations of the Hellenistic period, especially their constitutions (Freeman) and formal institutions (see also Larsen 1968). They also shared a more teleological historical view in that for them the pre-league polities of Archaic and even classical ethnē were remnants of older tribal states.

18. Beck 2003; Siewert and Aigner-Foresti 2005; Mackil 2013; Beck and Funke 2015. The later volume, an up-to-date synthesis of federalism in the ancient Greek world, features contributions from thirty international scholars and is itself an example of variation in ethnos studies.

19. See, for example, Corsten 1999, Funke and Haake 2013, and Mackil 2013, expanding the chronological focus of Morgan 2003.

20. Mackil 2013, 346.

21. A particularly illustrative example is that Beck's discussion of *Bundesheere* comprises only a single paragraph of his monograph on the history and structure of federal states in the fourth century (1997, 173).

22. For the board of generals in Boeotia (Boeotarchs), see *Hell. Ox.* 16.3; and Giovannini 1971, 46–50, which concentrates on the significance of the Boeotarchs in the shaping of the early Boeotian League. For the most detailed account of the Thessalian army and its relation to the state, see Helly 1995, 193–278. For military dedications, see Morgan 2001b, 20–44, and 30–34 for Archaic Thessaly. In the case of upland ethnē, federal armies are inferred from specific figures in texts or the appearance of select forces abroad. See, for example, Rzepka 2009 on the Aetolians. The existence of early land divisions (*Distrikte*) in ethnē is foundational to Corsten's general argument about the emergence and shaping of later federal states—hence his discussion of the *Heeresorganisation* of the Acarnanian League (1999, 108–12), a partial exception to the point made immediately below, although most of Corsten's evidence comes from the Hellenistic period.

23. Pritchett 1971–1991a; Sabin, van Wees, and Whitby 2007; Campbell and Tritle 2013; Kagan and Viggiano 2013.

24. Arist. *Pol.* 1297b16–28. Much of the scholarly debate has grappled with what Aristotle posited as a matter of fact: the historicity, extent, and political ramifications of increased participation in heavy infantry combat. See, for example, Snodgrass 1965; Salmon 1977; Morris 1987, 196–201; Raaflaub 1997; van Wees 2001; and Viggiano 2013.

25. For an outline and discussion of this traditional view and the major debates therein, see Wheeler 2007a.

26. Larsen 1968, at 44 for Phocis, 55–56 for West Locris, 79 for Aetolia, 86–87 for Achaea, and 90–91 for Acarnania. Larsen did not consider Epirus or Arcadia federal states before the King's Peace of 386, and he did not treat Macedonia at all.

27. Main sources for each: Hdt. 8.27–8 (Phocian Chalk Raid); Thuc. 3.94–8 (Aetolian Rout); Xen. *Hell.* 4.6 (Defense of Acarnania); Xen. *Hell.* 6.5.10–23 (Defense of Arcadia).

28. These are Whatley's basic criteria for accurately reconstructing an ancient battle (Whatley 1964).

29. Gehrke 1986, 150–63, grouped Arcadia, Aetolia, Acarnania, and Phocis together as poor agrarian states that lacked a significant maritime element (*ärmere Agrarstaaten ohne oder mit geringfügiger maritime Komponente*) and had few large-scale urban centers.

30. This is a textual device in literary and historical writing that Barthes referred to as "the reality effect" (1986, 141–48; see also 1981).

31. Kagan 2006a.

32. Inspired by Keegan's critique of modern military history (1976), the watershed study was Hanson 1989 on the minutiae of infantry battle in the classical Greek world. Following this was Hanson 1991, whose individual contributions explored most of the issues just listed. See also the contributions in Lloyd 1996, especially Mitchell 1996 on the nature of hoplite battle. Other face-of-battle studies have investigated logistics and everyday life in ancient armies, especially those on extended campaigns (Lee 2007), the psychology of Athenian hoplites based on developments in American

military psychology (Crowley 2012), and more traditional face-of-battle topics. See, for example, the contributions in Campbell and Tritle 2013 under "The Face of Battle in the Classical World" and "Impacts and Techniques." See also Krentz 2013 and Schwartz 2013. Of course, the classical Greek battle experience was never limited to land (Strauss 2000a). For the Roman face of battle, see Goldsworthy 1996, Lee 1996, and Sabin 2000. For criticisms of the ancient face of battle, see, in particular, Wheeler 2001, 169–74; Wheeler 2007b, xix–xxiii; and Wheeler 2011, 64–75. See also Lynn 2003, 1–27.

33. White 1991 treats Indian-European relations in the Great Lakes region from the seventeenth to the nineteenth century; Scott 2009 treats modern-day Zomia or upland Southeast Asia, especially at 38–39 on "strategic adaptations" of resistance: "[We] may profitably look back to Thucydides' *Peloponnesian War*, which describes a world of peoples [ethnē], some with kings, some without, whose fickle loyalties and unreliable cohesion is a source of constant anxiety to the statesmen of each of the major antagonists: Athens, Sparta, Corinth, and Syracuse" (38). The present study calls into question the notion of "unreliable cohesion."

34. For a discussion of the nation-state as a modern phenomenon, see Giddens 1985, 83–121. See also Elazer 1987, 223–31.

35. Cohen (2000) has argued that classical Athens is best understood not as a polis but as an ethnos. He considers "the imagined community" of a modern nation-state the closest approximation of an ancient ethnos.

36. For the polyvalence of ethnos, see Bakhuizen 1989; McInerney 1999, 22–25; and Hall 2007, 88–92.

37. The exception is late-sixth- and early-fifth-century Phocis. In general, when an ancient source—literary or epigraphic—applies the term *koinon* to a state or state-level institution, this is taken as evidence of the existence of a federal or league state. See, for example, Larsen 1968, xiv–xvi; and Stanton 1982.

38. Giovannini 1971, 14–24. Giovannini argued that there were only "unitary" states—a *sympoliteia* in the singular.

39. Walbank 1976–1977. Lehmann (2001) has argued that there was no theory of federalism in antiquity, that is, in the writings of Aristotle and Polybius, although he acknowledges that federal states existed in the ancient world. For attempts at defining a Greek federal state, see, for example, Beck 1997, 9–19; Corsten 1999, 14–17; and Rzepka 2002, especially 226–40; and Siewert 2005.

40. Cf. White 1991, 413.

41. Liddell Hart 1967, 322.

42. Gray 2014, 155.

43. For the strategic aims of ancient states, see the contributions in Hanson 2010. Helpful for understanding strategy in the ancient world is Mintzberg's distinction between intended strategy and realized strategy, that is, strategy as a pattern in decision making: "When a sequence of decisions in some area exhibits a consistency over time, a strategy will be considered to have formed" (1978, 935). This, I would argue, is the general sense of strategy in Hanson 2010. Freedman (2013) has recently treated the history of strategy in all of its various guises from antiquity to the present day. However, he limits his analysis of the Greeks to strategic thought in Homer, Thucydides, and Plato (22–41). The study of Roman grand strategy begins with Lu-

ttwak 1976. See K. Kagan 2006b for a survey of past debates and suggestions for future approaches. For fifth-century Athenian strategy, see Ober 1985b; and Kagan 2010. For fourth-century Athenian strategy, see Ober 1985a.

44. "Strategy is nothing without battle, for battle is the material that it applies, the very means that it employs. Just as tactics is the employment of military forces in battle, so strategy is the employment [and threat] of battles . . . to achieve the object of war" (von Clausewitz 1979, 77). This is a narrower, operational view of strategy, one more familiar to those directly involved in the actual conduct of war (Paret 1986, 3).

1. The Phocian Chalk Raid of the Thessalian Camp Circa 490

1. For the physical geography and topography of Phocis, see Schober 1924, Fossey 1986 (eastern Phocis), and McInerney 1999, 40–85.

2. The case for an early ethnic identity rests primarily on the appearance of Phocian communities in the Catalogue of Ships (Hom. *Il.* 2.517–23): "The Catalogue reified the existence of a region identifiable as Phokis by naming nine neighboring sites all occupied by the Phokians. . . . [It] is our earliest evidence for a distinct region occupied by a group identified as Phokians" (McInerney 1999, 120). The sites named in the Catalogue span the northern and southern regions, although most are located in the more mountainous south.

3. Morgan (2003, 113–34) has detailed this process in depth.

4. On pressure from Thessaly as the main source of Phocian unification, see Larsen 1968, 43–48; Beck 1997, 109; McInerney 1999, 177. The earliest mention of a Phocian koinon is Strabo 9.3.15, which refers to Phocian activities at Delphi during the mid-fifth century. Of course, Strabo was writing approximately five centuries after the fact.

5. Evidence also exists, to a lesser extent, in the representative involvement in the Delphic Amphictyony during the sixth century (Tausend 1992, 35–47). Involvement in the Amphictyony provides clear evidence of some form of political integration in Phocis (cf. Beck 1997, 192–96). For Phocian coinage, see Williams 1972, 9–18. For the Phokikon, see McInerney 1997 and McInerney 1999, 178–81.

6. See, for example, Larsen 1968, xi–xxviii; Walbank 1976–1977, 27–51; Stanton 1982; Beck 1997, 9–19; Corsten 1999, 185–240; Siewert 2005; and the introduction to this book.

7. On the different meanings of coinage in the archaic Greek world, see Kurke 1999, especially 6–22 and 41–67. See also the contributions in Meadows and Shipton 2001.

8. Williams 1972, 11. However, Martin 1985 has questioned the notion that Greeks associated the minting of coins with freedom or independence.

9. Paus. 10.5.2. French and Vanderpool (1963) originally identified the earlier structure as the sanctuary of the hero Archegetes. McInerney then interpreted the early bouleuterion-style construction of this building as the original Phokikon, correctly noting that "religious sanctuaries regularly served as federal meeting places" (1997, 203).

10. Larsen (1968, xiv) preferred the term "confederacy" to "distinguish a true federal state from a looser organization." The latter he termed a "league" or "permanent alliance." In the case of the Phocians, my use of "confederation" is closer to Larsen's *sympolity*: "[a political] organization embracing a number of cities" (1968, xv).

11. For studies that overlook the Chalk Raid or mention it only in passing, see Larsen 1968; Giovannini 1971; and Beck 1997. For a battle compendium, see Montagu 2000. There is no discussion of methodology in Montagu's work—that is, of what counts as a battle—but Herodotus specifically refers to the incident as a *machē* at 8.27.5.

12. Williams 1972, 5. Ellinger treats the Chalk Raid as part of the Phocians' national origins myth; the historicity of the incident is less important for his purposes (1993, 21). For McInerney (1999, 177), the Chalk Raid is one of a series of "colorful stories" that illustrate the Phocians' collective resolve against the Thessalians during the time in question, and little besides.

13. Ellinger 1978, 1987, and 1993. The extreme situations include the tale of Phocian Desperation, the Phocian Chalk Raid and Amphorae Trap against the Thessalians, and Thermopylae, all ca. 510–480. Ellinger and others have pieced together the Phocians' national legend from a range of ancient sources that stretch well into the Roman period; the Phocians did not articulate a coherent national legend that scholars can study as such. For the Phocian "national saga," see Burn 1960, 204.

14. Hdt 8.27.5. For the *dekate*, or war tithe, see Pritchett 1971–1991, 1:93–100, and at 93–94 for the Chalk Raid. Dedications could consist of slaves, land, money, or spoils, and the practice was common enough that without it, in Pritchett's assessment (1971–1991, 1:100), "few of the temples and other sacred buildings of Greece would have been built."

15. Paus. 10.13.3–4. See Daux 1936, 141 and 192; and Jacquemin 1999, 52–53, for discussion of these monuments. See also Parke and Boardman 1957.

16. The Persians "plundered and set on fire" the sanctuary of Apollo at Abae (Hdt. 8.33) in the vicinity of modern-day Kalapodi, an area that has been the subject of intense archaeological research in recent decades. The sanctuary destroyed by the Persians is now associated with the south temple at Kalapodi and was left buried in ruins until the Augustan period (Felsch 2007, 13–24). The lower town of Abae was destroyed again in 371 at the hands of Jason of Pherae (Xen. *Hell.* 6.4.27) and once more in 346 by Philip II (Paus. 10.35.6). See also Fossey 1986, 77–81; and McInerney 1999, 288–89.

17. The literature on Herodotus's sources of information, methods, and reliability is enormous. Marincola (2001, 31–39) outlines the major debates and highlights the problems with the past dichotomy of viewing Herodotus as wholly reliable or wholly a liar. See also Hornblower (2002) on Herodotus's handling of sources and its relation to other forms of contemporary literary and scientific discourse.

18. On the pro-Phocian tone of Herodotus's narrative, see Bowie 2007, 123.

19. Hdt. 8.30.2. Cf. Plut. *De Her. mal.* 35, who took issue with this assessment in defense of the Phocians' loyalty to the Greek cause.

20. For a basic introduction to Polyaenus's life and work, see Krentz and Wheeler 1994, vi–xxiv. For a more in-depth treatment, see Wheeler 2010.

21. Elsewhere in the historical parts of his guide to Greece, Pausanias seems to have favored and relied heavily on Herodotus (Habicht 1985, 97). Habicht does not discuss the possible exception of the Chalk Raid. See also Bingen 1996 for various discussions of Pausanias's sources and historical methods.

22. Hdt. 8.27.2. Sordi 1953b, 252–58, and Larsen 1960, 229–37, both date the incident to ca. 498–485.

23. For Phocian-Thessalian relations and conflict ca. 510–480, see Larsen 1968, 109–11; Helly 1995, 220–23; and McInerney 1999, 173–78.

24. Hdt. 8.27.2. By "large-scale invasion," I mean to convey a mobilization of forces significantly greater than that of a smaller-scale, harassing raid. See below for the distinction between "invasion" and "raid" in Phocian-Thessalian relations.

25. Polyb. 16.32; Plut. *Mor.* 244B-D (=*Mulierum virtutes* 2); Polyaenus 8.65; Paus. 10.1.7. See also Stadter 1965, 34–41, and Ellinger 1993, 233–46.

26. Raiding on horseback was how the Thessalians contributed to the failure of the settlement at Heraclea in Trachis ca. 425 (Thuc. 3.93).

27. Hdt. 8.28; Paus. 10.1.3; Polyaenus 6.18.2. The success of the Phocians' stratagem implies that such raids occurred frequently. See Fossey 1986, 72–76.

28. Hdt. 8.29.1.

29. Hdt. 8.28.1.

30. Whatever the exact chronology of specific incidents, the Chalk Raid and Amphorae Trap both speak to the Phocians' ongoing struggle for independence from the Thessalians ca. 510–480 (cf. Larsen 1968, 111; Williams 1972, 5–8; and McInerney 1999, 177).

31. Szemler 1988, 558, and Szemler 1991, 110–11. On the Phokis-Doris Expedition, see Kase 1991. Before this archaeological investigation, scholars considered the coastal route that proceeded through the pass at Thermopylae and then through east Locrian territory as the only suitable point of access from the northern mainland into Phocian territory and the rest of the central mainland (e.g., Larsen 1960; Pritchett 1982, 123–75). On the "Pass through Trachis," see Hdt. 7.175–6, 199.

32. Paus. 10.1.11.

33. On routes and roads within Phocian territory, see McInerney 1999, 42, map 1.

34. On possible Thessalian allies, see Hdt. 7.132 and Helly 1995, 131–92.

35. The only discernible unit of division within the Phocian ethnos during the time in question was the polis or town (Beck 1997, 106–11), as opposed to the *Distrikte* of other Greek ethnē (Corsten 1999). For this reason, Corsten does not treat the Phocians in his study of early Greek league-states. See also Oulhen 2004.

36. On the geographical vulnerability of the Kephisos River Valley and the proliferation of mountain refuges, see McInerney 1999, 47–54: "The consistency of settlement pattern throughout the Kephisos valley is unmistakable. Because some of the towns of the upper Kephisos valley are renowned for their fortifications [mostly dating to the midfourth century], there has been a tendency to explain their siting in terms of the defensive strength of their position. But strong walls do not mean that the site of a town was originally chosen with defense in mind. . . . A better explanation for the regularity of the settlement pattern of the upper Kephisos valley lies in the natural environment. Each environmental unit resembled each other region in that each incorporated territory extending from the river to the foothills, so that in each one the same combination of agriculture, arboriculture, viticulture, and grazing was possible" (52–53).

37. Hdt. 8.27.3; Polyaenus 6.18.1.

38. Herodotus elsewhere depicts the Phocians as under siege at 8.28.1. See also How and Wells (1912, 243).

39. Hdt. 8.32; see also McInerney 1999, 177–80. Tithorea was also the site to which Philomelos fled and where he eventually committed suicide after the defeat of his mercenary army at Neon in 355 (Diod. 16.31, Paus. 10.24.4).

40. Likely candidates include the inhabitants of Charadra, Lilaia, and Drymaia in the northern Kephisos Valley where there were no natural barriers between Phocian and Dorian territory. In addition, Tithorea was the only naturally fortified site in the region, while Neon, the town immediately beneath the refuge, was accessible by a rudimentary road, "several miles of which were suitable for carts," says Pausanias (10.32.8). See also McInerney 1999, 46.

41. For versions available to Pausanias that were competing with Herodotus, see Habicht 1985, 97. See also Ellinger 1993, 14–22.

42. On the geology of Parnassus, see Kraft 1991, 1–2; on quarrying, see Papageorgakis and Kolaiti 1992. Ellinger devotes a lengthy discussion to the distinction between *le plâtre* (building material) and *la chaux* (loose, powdery substance), since *gypsos* and its derivatives can mean both (1993, 62–88). My interpretation strikes a middle ground between this either/or scenario. Hereafter, by "chalk" I mean the whitish, chalky residue that would have remained after the limestone paste had dried.

43. Kraft 1991, 12.

44. McInerney reaches the same conclusion regarding the location of the Chalk Raid (1999, 175–76), but while acknowledging that Pausanias diverges from Herodotus's narrative (184n88), he makes no attempt to reconcile the two accounts.

45. In Pausanias's day, Tithorea included both the mountain refuge and the polis of Neon attested to in Herodotus (Paus. 10.32.9). See also Oulhen 2004, 422–23.

46. On the topography of Tithorea, see McInerney 1999, 278–80.

47. Hdt. 8.32–33.

48. Plut. *Mor.* 244B.

49. Hdt. 8.27.3; cf. Paus 10.1.11.

50. For a comprehensive treatment of the seer in the ancient Greek world, see Flower 2008, 93, for "poetic" seers in Herodotus and 153–87 for the seer in warfare. See also Pritchett 1971–1991a, 3:47–90, for military *manteis*.

51. Paus. 10.1.3.

52. Hdt. 8.28.1. The implication here is that even in Herodotus's day there was some distinction between Thessalian infantrymen and cavalrymen, regardless of the size, quality, or status of the former, and even though the latter could dismount and fight on foot (cf. Hanson 2000, 209). For the Thessalian army, see Helly 1995, 193–278; for warfare and Thessalian society in the late Archaic and early classical periods, see Morgan 2001, 30–34.

53. Bowie 2007, 121.

54. Hom. *Il.* 10.218–579; see also Strauss 2006, 131–44.

55. Thuc. 7.44.

56. The Phocians' equipment is discussed further below.

57. "Tracers work both ways" is one of Murphy's anonymous laws of combat. A tracer is a bullet equipped with a small pyrotechnic charge that allows the shooter to follow the projectile's trajectory with the naked eye, even in daylight conditions.

58. I base this estimate on Krentz's estimation of casualties in hoplite battle at 14 percent for the defeated side in conventional circumstances and near 20 to 25 percent in unconventional ones such as the Athenian defeat at Syracuse discussed above (Krentz 1985b). The relative accuracy of 4,000 is based primarily on the size of the *dekate* that funded the monuments at Delphi and Abae and the number of shields that

the Phocians are said to have dedicated. Also, in 373, Jason of Pherae assembled an army of 8,000 cavalrymen, at least 20,000 hoplites, and an equal number of peltasts. This included allies, although most were Thessalians (Xen. *Hell.* 6.1.19; see also Helly 1995, 252–56). The estimate above amounts to approximately half of what the Thessalians and their allies could field in Jason's day.

59. Hdt. 8.27.3, Paus. 10.1.11.

60. The figure of 1,000 Phocian hoplites appears at Hdt. 7.203 and 7.217 where the Phocians assemble to protect their countryside at Thermopylae and Trachis, and at 9.17 and 9.31 where they are compelled to fight on the Persian side under the command of a preeminent Phocian named Harmocydes.

61. No source explicitly mentions the activities or involvement of noncombatants in the incident as Herodotus does at 8.32–33 during the Persian invasion.

62. Hdt. 7.216–18. Of course, no civilians were involved in this particular incident.

63. For hoplite equipment and mobility, see Anderson 1991, 15–37, and Krentz 2010, 45–50.

64. Paus. 10.1.11; Polyaenus 6.18.1.

65. "At least in pairs" hearkens back to the nighttime incursion of Diomedes and Odysseus (Hom. *Il.* 10.220–6).

66. Hdt. 8.27.3; cf. Paus. 10.1.11 and Polyaenus 6.18.1.

67. Polyaenus 6.18.1.

68. Perhaps this should come as no surprise given that Polyaenus was of Macedonian descent and so may have been favorably disposed toward the Thessalians (Schettino 1998, 191–278). It is interesting to point out, however, that with "it is said" at 10.1.11, Pausanias also distances himself from the notion that the Thessalians all fled in terror. The implication in Pausanias's account is that the whitened Phocians seemed more supernatural than anything else and to a certain extent were mistaken as auxiliaries.

69. Hdt. 8.27.3.

70. Hdt. 8.27.2; Paus. 10.1.11.

71. McInerney 1999, 44.

72. On methods of killing with hoplite equipment, see Lazenby 1991.

73. Hdt. 8.27.3; cf. Polyaenus 6.18.1.

74. Herodotus also uses this word at 8.27.1 to describe the Spartan defeat at Thermopylae.

75. Hdt. 8.27.3.

76. In 379, conspirators against the pro-Sparta party at Thebes armed themselves with spoils that were hanging in the stoas (Xen. *Hell.* 5.4.8; see also Pritchett 1971–1991a, 1:95n9).

77. Hdt. 9.17.

78. Hdt. 9.31.

79. Paus. 10.2.1.

80. Buckler 1989.

81. Xen. *Hell.* 6.4.21. In Xenophon's view, this ability is the reason that Jason of Pherae rushed through Phocian territory so quickly.

82. Hdt. 8.32.

83. Even for the rest of the fifth century, there is no evidence to suggest that the Phocians fought as anything other than hoplites. The fourth century is a different

matter, notably in the exploits of Philomelos during the Third Sacred War. These exploits involved Phocian cavalry and perhaps even Phocian peltasts (Diod. 16.30–31; see also Buckler 1989, 23–24). For pastoral conflict between Phocians and West Locrians, see Howe 2003 and Howe 2008, 72 and 85–86.

84. Larsen (1968, 44) raises the possibility of local resources available to later writers that were "lost to the main currents of Greek historiography" and so are no longer extant.

85. In addition, there is an early fourth century decree that granted Phocian citizenship to three Athenians (Giovannini 1971, 52–53). For the epigraphic record of the Phocian koinon ca. 350–280, see McInerney 1999, 236–41.

86. McInerney 1999, 181.

87. On these common features of koina, see McInerney 2013, 470–71.

88. Thuc. 1.107.

89. On the attack and seizure of Delphi, see Plut. *Cim.* 17.3; on hostilities against Thessaly, see Thuc. 1.111. The possible alliance with the Athenians is based on a fragmentary Athenian decree (McInerney 1999, 188–89).

90. See, for example, Martín-Gil et al. 2007.

2. The Aetolian Rout of the Athenians in 426

1. Hom. *Il.* 9.529, 9.549, 23.633; Pind. *Ol.* 3.10. See also Brennan 1987, 1–3, for a possible ethnic joke in Homer at the Aetolians' expense.

2. Ephorus *FGrHist* 70F122; Diod. Sic. 18.25.1; Livy 36.30.4; Strabo 10.2.3–4.

3. Hdt. 6.127.

4. Thuc. 1.5–6; see also the introduction to this book.

5. Eur. *Phoen.* 138. For the origins and legacy of the ancient topos of barbarism vis-à-vis the Aetolians, see Antonetti 1987a, especially 209–13. See also Dench 1995, 111–53, on the differences between ancient and modern preoccupations with mountain societies. For the relationship between drama and social reality in fifth- and fourth-century Athens, see E. Hall 2006.

6. Polyb. 4.3.5,, 4.62.2, 4.64.8, 4.67.3–4, 4.79.1, 18.7–9. For Polybius and the Aetolians, see Sacks 1975, Mendels 1984/1986, and Champion 2007.

7. Livy 32.24.3–4. Antonetti (1990, 43–143) has traced the devolution of these ancient attitudes toward the Aetolians from the classical through the Roman periods.

8. For Aetolian raiding as a transhistorical phenomenon, see Bakhuizen 1996. See Grainger 1999, 3–25, for the argument against the view of late classical and Hellenistic Aetolia as a pirate state.

9. On the importance of pastoralism, see Bommeljé and Doorn 1991.

10. Sebastiaan Bommeljé's observation that "from an archaeological point of view, Aetolia is still one of the most poorly researched regions of Greece" (1987a, 14) remains valid. The most recent archaeological activity in the region has concentrated on the prehistoric era (Dietz and Moschos 2006) and on areas that were not "Aetolian" during the time in question, in particular Calydon (Dietz and Stavropoulou-Gatsi 2011a and 2011b).

11. Funke 1987, Bommeljé 1987b, 21–23.

12. Bommeljé 1987a, 13.

13. On the Aetolian League, see Grainger 1999 and Scholten 2000; on the Athenian decree, see Rhodes and Osborne 2003, 168–73.

14. On the character of the early Aetolian ethnos, see Larsen 1968, 78–80.

15. For the development of the emergent Aetolian koinon, see Giovannini 1971, 60–63; Beck 1997, 43–54; Funke 1997, 152–63; Corsten 1999, 133–59; and Mackil 2013, 52–57.

16. For the embassy to Sparta, see Thuc. 3.100 (discussed further below). For the text and commentary of the fifth-century defensive alliance with Sparta, see Meiggs and Lewis 1989, 312, and Baltrusch 1994, 21–30. For conflict over Naupactus, see Jacquemin and Laroche 1982, 192–204, which discusses a Messenian monument at Delphi celebrating a victory over the Aetolians at Naupactus dated roughly to the early fifth century. See also Xen. *Hell.* 4.6.14. In 402, upwards of a thousand selected (*epilektoi*) Aetolians helped the Eleans in their conflict with the Spartans (Diod. 14.17 and see Rzepka 2009, 18–19). For defense, see below.

17. Thuc. 3.94–98.

18. See, for example, Stahl's study of recurring structural elements (*Wiederkehrende Strukturmomente des Geschehens*) and event complexes (*Ereigniskomplexe*) in 3.94–114 and 4.2–5.14 (1966, 129–57).

19. For defenses of Demosthenes against Thucydides, see Woodcock 1928 and Treu 1956. Roisman 1993 has reevaluated Demosthenes' generalship and assessed his place in the history of Greek warfare by studying Demosthenes' career as documented by Thucydides. For the study of individuals in Thucydides, see Westlake 1968, 97–121, and 261–76 for Demosthenes.

20. The central issue with Aigition—a polis in the urban sense—is whether the site also functioned as a polis in the political sense ca. 426–367, roughly from the Aetolian Rout of the Athenians until the emergence of the Aetolian koinon in the epigraphic record. Funke (1997) argues in the affirmative, but see the cautions of Hansen 1995, 39–40, 43.

21. For the incident as illustrative of general attitudes toward ethnē, see Morgan 2003, 7–8. For attitudes toward the Aetolians, see Antonetti 1990, 77–85.

22. Lazenby 2004, 61. See also Ober (1991, 178), who cites the Athenians' failure to construct a suitable escape route as a key factor in the loss of so many hoplites. This rendered the Athenians overly susceptible to pursuit.

23. Van Wees 2004, 64. On the early indication of the rise of light-armed troops, see Best 1969, 17–35, and Anderson 1970, 117.

24. "There is a note of pathos in the usually somber Thucydides when he describes the fate of a phalanx of five hundred [*sic*] of the best Athenian infantry who during the early years of the Peloponnesian War stumbled clumsily into the mountainous wilds of Aitolia only to be bled white by the javelins and arrows of lightly armed native irregulars. Nowhere was there an enemy phalanx visible to test the Athenians' spears and unbroken ranks" (Hanson 1989, 16).

25. Diodorus's summary version (12.60), if not based entirely on Thucydides, adds nothing.

26. The literature devoted to Thucydides' method—its philosophical basis, intellectual predilections, rhetorical strategies, and the role of historical truth, among other things—is immense. Major root treatments include de Romilly 1956, Stahl

1966, Hunter 1973, and Connor 1984. For the contested modern image of Thucydides as a historian, see, for example, Connor 1977 and Loraux 1980. See also Dover 1983 for the debate of Thucydides "as history" and "as literature." For the same debate in the case of battles, see Paul 1987, tempered by Hunt 2006, 388–89.

27. Thuc. 3.90. Hornblower calls this "a unique and very interesting programmatic statement by Th. of a general method—selectivity—which he in fact practises throughout his work" (1991, 498, citing his earlier treatment of this theme at 1987, 37–44). The statements also suggest a reliance on memory, elsewhere ridiculed in Thucydides' work (Meyer 2008).

28. Compare his claim to authority in detailing the plague (2.48) and his use of the third person to relate his own involvement in the Athenian defeat at Amphipolis in 424 (4.102–8).

29. For Demosthenes as Thucydides' source, see Westlake 1968, 97. The argument rests on the unusually high level of detail in incidents involving Demosthenes and, more importantly, on the personal relationship the two had as colleagues on the board of *stratēgoi* in 424/423.

30. Key archaeological and ethnographic studies include Bommeljé and Doorn 1987, and Doorn 1993. Key topographical studies include Freitag 1999 on the Gulf of Corinth, and Pritchett 1991b, 47–82 ("Demosthenes' Campaign in Southern Aitolia in 426 BC"). For the literary aspects of Thucydidean geography, see Funke and Haake 2006.

31. Thuc. 3.89–91; Diod. Sic. 12.60. For further contextual analysis, see Kagan 1974, 187–201, and Lendon 2010, 219–33. See also Westlake 1945 for the general pattern and aims of Athenian seaborne raids in Periclean strategy, and Bosworth 1992 for the Athenians' intervention in Sicily.

32. Thuc. 3.92–93; Diod. 12.59. For a brief discussion of the strategic significance of Heraclea in Trachis for the Spartans, see Andrewes 1978, 95–99. See also Malkin 1994, 219–35.

33. Thuc. 2.102, 2.28; see also Krentz and Sullivan 1987.

34. Thucydides hints at a tense equilibrium between the western Greeks (3.113): the Acarnanians preferred to contend with the defeated and subdued Ambraciots—as opposed to annihilating them—if this would prevent a permanent Athenian presence in the region. Incidentally, the Aetolians were the first to dominate this part of the Greek world, emerging as a regional power toward the end of the fourth century (Larsen 1968, 195–215; Mendels 1984; Corsten 1999, 133–59; Grainger 1999, 29–104; Arnush 2000; Scholten 2000, 14–28).

35. Thucydides is imprecise about the exact timing of the incident, but given his system of chronology (Meritt 1962, Pritchett 1986) and the scale of subsequent events, the Athenians would have arrived in the region some time between early March and early June.

36. Thuc. 3.91, 3.94.

37. On the settlement at Naupactus, see Thuc. 1.103 and Lewis 1992, 118.

38. Thuc. 3.95. For a discussion of Demosthenes' aims, see Roisman 1993, 24–25.

39. Thuc. 3.94.4.

40. For the use of *ethnos* in Thucydides, focusing on the Macedonians and Thracians, see Xydopoulos 2007.

41. Freitag, Funke, and Moustakis 2004, 382–86.

42. The territorial boundaries of the Aetolian groups mentioned by name remain unclear, even from later periods, and they likely never were clear except to the groups themselves (Antonetti 1987b and 1988).

43. For Aetolian topography and geography, Woodhouse 1897, 3–52, remains a useful reference. For a more general overview, see Deylius 1987, 32–38.

44. Thuc. 3.94.5. It is unclear whether these ethnographic observations apply to Aetolians writ large or just to the more remote Eurytanians, although the latter seems to be the case.

45. For the relationship between Homeric Aeolis and the fifth- and fourth-century Aetolian ethnos, see Bommeljé 1988.

46. An important qualification: in the Messenians' view, the warlike Aetolians were militarily feeble only in isolation of each other (cf. Lendon 2010, 478n28: "Demosthenes' attack on Aetolia was premised on the military feebleness of the Aetolians"). It was the Aetolians' ability to unite that the Messenians encouraged Demosthenes to keep in mind.

47. Thuc. 3.95.2–3; see also Gomme 1956, 404. Although the exact location of this base—the precinct of Neman Zeus—remains uncertain, Pritchett estimates approximately one kilometer as the distance from the harbor at Oineon to the site of the camp (1991b, 60). See also Lerat 1952, 195–97.

48. For the duties and responsibilities of Athenian marines, see Morrison, Coates, and Rankov 2000, 107–26. See also Rawlings (2000), who does not consider hoplite equipment to have been constraining. In general, Rawlings views hoplites as military "all-rounders" capable of performing a range of duties without significant modification of their armament (2007, 224).

49. Thuc. 3.95.3.

50. For the topography of Ozolian Locris, see Lerat 1952, especially 62–72, and Freitag 1999, 58–113, concentrating on the coast.

51. Thuc. 3.95.3. The phrase "armed in a similar fashion" suggests a preference for a light armament, but the description is vague in a military context, as is the adjective *psilos* (Lendon 2005, 412–13).

52. For a general discussion of conflict over pasture and grazing rights, see Howe 2008, 77–97. Such conflict would have been the norm between Aetolians and West Locrians, given the ecology of the region. Pritchett (1991b, 75) notes that the Locrians' failure to meet up with the Athenians and their allies later in the invasion is somewhat suspicious.

53. Thuc. 3.96.2.

54. For the identifications of these sites—Poteidania is the only one identifiable by an inscription—I am relying on Pritchett's autopsy of the region and his synthesis and criticism of previous topographical research (1991b, 47–82). I have measured all distances in my reconstruction from his 1:50,000 maps. As for the Aetolians' lack of resistance, the term for "booty" in this case refers to goods from captured towns, not from stripped enemies (Hornblower 1991, 512). See also Pritchett 1971–1991a, 1:53–84.

55. According to Thucydides, Demosthenes was envisioning a subsequent invasion of the Ophionions should they refuse to join him, but the wording of this notice in 3.96 seems to conflict with the Messenians' original advice (Gomme 1956, 404–5).

56. Thuc. 3.96.3.

57. Using known Hellenistic sites as a starting point, the archaeological team conducted the study by physically occupying 242 sites in southern and eastern Aetolia. Ultimately, the archaeologists concluded that the settlement pattern in the region "appears to form a distinct interrelated system, or better, several clusters of sites which have inter-visibility" (Bommeljé 1987a, 23).

58. Plut. *Mor.* 210.

59. Just. 24.1.

60. Livy 28.8.

61. Ober 1991, 178.

62. Thuc. 3.96.3.

63. For possible ancient transhumance routes and lines of communication based on modern ethnographic analyses in the *eparchy* of Doris (eastern Aetolia), see Doorn 1985: "In sum, the region displays some important stable spatio-ecological characteristics, such as the limitation of resources suitable for human exploitation and the restriction for the possibilities for communication" (278), all due in no small part to the severe and limiting nature of the region's terrain. See also Bommeljé and Doorn 1991, and Doorn 1993.

64. Thuc. 3.97.2. This notice makes van Wees's point regarding Thucydides' remarkable failure to acknowledge the presence of light-armed rowers all the more puzzling (cf. Hornblower 1991, 361, 513).

65. Thuc. 3.97.1. See also Gomme (1956, 405), who interprets Thucydides to mean that the Messenians gave Demosthenes better or different advice about proceeding with the invasion.

66. Thuc. 3.97.2.

67. Pritchett 1991b, 72–73. This distance assumes that the Athenians and their allies followed the most direct route feasible. The course of the modern circuitous road connecting modern-day Varna (ancient Teichion) and Strouza (ancient Aigition) would have been a less arduous but longer route.

68. On the polyvalence of "polis" from a physical location in one context to a community of citizens in another, see Hansen 2006, 56–61. See above for the debate surrounding the case of fifth-century Aigition. See Bommeljé 1981–1982, 248, for the results of a Dutch survey dedicated to the topography and historical ecology of the Strouza region and the history of ancient Aigition.

69. Thuc. 3.97.2–3. The surrounding heights—three are easily discernible—are located to the north and east of Aigition (Pritchett 1991b, 74; see also Pls. 86, 89, and 90).

70. Thuc. 3.97.3.

71. These were the exact tactics that the Aetolians employed to great effect against the Spartans in 402 at Elis (Diod. 14.17) and during the Macedonian invasion of 321 (Diod. 18.24–25).

72. Thuc. 3.97.3.

73. Thuc. 3.97.3.

74. On the weight of hoplite equipment, see Krentz 2010, 45–50.

75. The language of pursuits and tactical withdrawals draws a distinction between an active or aggressive chase and a skillful, deceptive leading on (cf. Xen. *Cyn.* 6.12). The Aetolians' presumed familiarity with hunting is based on (1) the economic and agricultural constraints throughout the region, (2) the hunting imagery (in particular, boars' heads) dominating the iconography with which the Aetolians chose to repre-

sent themselves to the rest of the Greek world in later periods (de Laix 1973)—on coinage of the Aetolian League, for example—and (3) a recent survey demonstrating that the region currently sustains the densest population of wild boars on the Balkan peninsula (Tsachalidis and Hadjisterkotis 2009). As analyses of prehistoric faunal assemblages from the region suggest, such was also the case in antiquity: "The distribution of wild animals [including boar, deer, and rabbit] does not indicate any major climate difference, as all species are all found in the area today" (Jensen 2006, 184).

76. Thuc. 3.98.1.

77. Hdt. 9.60. However, it is unclear—as is the case here—whether the archers were Athenian citizens.

78. Thuc. 4.35.

79. The distance of sixty meters is based on McLeod's estimations of the effective range of the ancient bow (1965, 1972). According to McLeod, at fifty-five to sixty meters, the Athenian archers would have been "quite accurate."

80. Thuc. 3.98.1.

81. Thuc. 3.98.1.

82. Thuc. 3.98.1.

83. Thuc. 3.98.1.

84. Thuc. 3.98.1.

85. Keegan 1993, 161. This is an irresistible comparison, but it is not without caution. Keegan primarily had in mind Eurasian steppe pastoralists, and his insights in this particular case are virtually ahistorical (see also the criticisms in Wheeler 2007b, xxv, n43). Nevertheless, Xenophon uses a similar metaphor to describe an incident that occurred in 398. Caught unaware, two hundred Greek hoplites were "cut down like cattle in a pen" by a force of armorless Bithynian raiders. The Bithynians' weapon of choice was the javelin (Xen. *Hell.* 3.8.4).

86. Throughout the history of the region, this way of life became more and more prevalent the farther one proceeded inland (Doorn 1985, 282–85).

87. Thuc. 3.98.2.

88. Gomme and Hornblower overlook this point, but it raises some interesting questions: Was Thucydides intentionally suggesting that the Aetolians, in some sense, were Homeric as opposed to backward and old-fashioned? Would this have helped to account for the Athenian disaster, or did he simply want to use a celebrated adjective to enhance his own narrative? For "swift-footed" as a natural gift, see Gomme 1956, 407.

89. Best (1969, 30) observes that Thucydides uses similar wording in a speech of Brasidas (4.126.6) to describe the fate awaiting an army of Peloponnesians should they disregard Brasidas's advice. The threat, interestingly, was a horde of Lyncestian—that is, Illyrian, or in Thucydides' words, barbarian—javelineers.

90. Thuc. 3.98.2. "The paths" calls to mind the transhumance routes and lines of communication discussed above.

91. Thuc. 3.98.3; on this being hyperbole, see Hornblower 1991, 514. Cf. Hdt. 6.79–80 for a similar burning incident from earlier in the fifth century involving Spartans and Argives.

92. Thuc. 3.98.3. The wording implies a hasty and prolonged flight. In my view, the escapees likely followed a lowland route to the east of Aigition (Ozolian Locrian territory) down to the coast and then headed west back to Oineon.

93. Thuc. 3.98.4.

94. Hornblower (1991, 514) notes the unusual nature of comments regarding the expenditure of human life in Thucydides. Gomme (1956, 407–8) makes the interesting point that these marines may have been drawn from the thetic class, a comparatively lower socioeconomic class. See also Rubincam 1991 for casualty figures in Thucydides, and Morpeth 2006 for Thucydides' use of quantification in relating war experiences. Morpeth, however, does not treat this incident in detail.

95. Thuc. 3.98.4.

96. See, for example, Wheeler 1991, and in response, Pritchett 1994, 111–44.

97. Thuc. 3.98.5.

98. "Even the relatively uncivilized Aetolians respect this traditional truce for the return of the dead" (Strassler 1996, 209, n.3.98.5a). For the identification and retrieval of battlefield dead, see Pritchett 1971–1991a, 4:94–259, and Vaughn 1991. Pritchett points out that in this instance the Athenians had to make their way back to Aigition from their base in Oineon, suggesting that "the process of collecting the bodies of those killed at Aigition and through the long fight must have consumed a considerable length of time" (189), especially if we assume that the Athenians conducted the proper rites for the dead.

99. Thuc. 3.100–102. On the new trend in Demosthenes' career, see Roisman 1993, 13.

100. The views of Rawlings (especially 2000) are apposite, as are the insights of Luraghi (2006) on the long history of hoplite mercenary service outside of the Greek world and the various demands thereof. See also chapter 3 on the performance of Spartan hoplites against the Acarnanians in 389.

101. Xen. *Hell.* 4.6.14. Also, according to Ephorus (*FGrHist* 70F122), one had to admire the Aetolians' long history of independence and inviolability.

102. Bommeljé 1988.

103. Evidently, Thucydides was impressed by how the Aetolians exploited their woodland environment, and Demosthenes seems to have borne this lesson in mind at Pylos the following year (Thuc. 4.29–30; see also Roisman 1993, 33–47, especially 37–38).

104. Cf. Snodgrass 1986, 51–52, and Hanson 2000, 209.

105. Larsen 1968, 79.

106. "Aetolia of the fifth century B.C. is the best example known of a Greek tribal state. Later it developed into a very efficient federal state on sympolitical lines, though, even then, it retained its primary assembly" (Larsen 1968, 78). Treatments of the emergent Aetolian koinon are referenced above.

107. On coinage, see de Laix 1973; on third-century epigraphic evidence, see Champion 1995.

108. For shifting tactical emphases in Greek warfare during the fourth century, and in particular the increased employment of light-armed troops, see Wheeler 2007a, 215–23, and Wheeler 2007b, xlvi–lxiv. See also van Wees 1995 and Hunt 1998, which argue that increased interest in light-armed troops in fourth-century sources does not necessarily mean that such individuals contributed little in fifth-century conflicts.

3. The Defense of Acarnania in 389

1. For a survey of the physical geography of fifth- and fourth-century Acarnania, see Schoch 1997, especially 9–66.

2. Not even Homer was aware of Acarnania—that is, he makes no mention of Acarnanians in his Catalogue of Ships. For Corinthian colonies in the territory of classical Acarnania, see Murray 1982, Domingo-Foresté 1988, and Jouan 1990.

3. The conflict between the Corcyraeans, the Corinthians, and the Athenians ca. 435–432 is the best-known example of such conflict in the region (Thuc. 1.24–55).

4. For the Acarnanian ethnos, see Ps.-Scylax 34 and Corsten 1999, 95–100.

5. On Acarnanian poleis, see Gehrke and Wirbelauer 2004, 354–78. For the mountainous interior of Acarnania as *Lebensraum*, see Gehrke 1996.

6. Klaffenbach (1957, xiv) was one of the first to make this suggestion. Subsequent treatments of this issue have tended to follow suit, especially those in favor of an early koinon. See, for example, Larsen 1968, 89–95; Giovannini 1971, 55–60; Freitag 1996; and Beck 1997, 31–36. See also Gehrke 1994–1995. For a survey of historical and archaeological research relating to the polis of Stratos, see Funke 2001.

7. Thuc. 3.105.1. For Olpae and its common court, see Schoch 1996.

8. Xen. *Hell.* 4.6.4

9. On Acarnanian coinage, see Imhoof-Blumer 1878; on Acarnanian "federal" coinage, see Head 1911, 282–83. As Dany notes (1999, 280–81), though, the use of a common Acarnanian ethnic inscription by itself does not necessarily mean that such coins were federal.

10. See, for example, Larsen 1968, 91.

11. Gomme 1956, 416–17.

12. The most famous example is a federal decree of the Acarnanian League found at Olympia dating to the last quarter of the third century (Habicht 1957). See also Corsten 1999, 67–94, for a discussion of Acarnanian inscriptions ca. 350–200. For the Hellenistic Acarnanian koinon, see Larsen 1968, 264–73, and Dany 1999.

13. See Corsten 2006, 157–67, on the existence of a regional cult connecting most of Acarnania during the time in question.

14. Thuc. 2.102–3. For the peculiarities of this passage, see Hornblower 1991, 377–78.

15. See, for example, Hamilton 1979, 287–88; Cartledge 1987, 224–26; and Cartledge 2002, 244.

16. In addition to the sources cited in the previous note, see Halladay 1982, 98.

17. Plut. *Ages.* 22; Paus. 3.10.2; Polyaenus 2.1.10. Xenophon also summarily treats the incident in his life of Agesilaus (Xen. *Ages.* 2.20).

18. For an eminently useful treatment of Xenophon's historical methods, see Cawkwell 1979, 15–46. See also Tuplin 1993 for the literary aims and composition of the *Hellenica*.

19. Tuplin 1986.

20. Cf. Whatley 1964.

21. For Xenophon's close relationship with Agesilaus, see Anderson 1974, 146–71, and 165 for Xenophon's possible involvement in the incident. However, the basis for Anderson's suggestion is dubious: "His reports of Agesilaus's campaigns round Corinth and in north-west Greece still read like those of an eye-witness" (cf. Pritchett 1991b, 99–100).

22. Xen. *Hell.* 4, *Hell. Oxy.*, Diod. 14; see also Hamilton 1979, 233–98.

23. For a detailed study of the Spartan disaster at Lechaeum, see Konecny 2001.

24. Xen. *Hell.* 4.2.17.

25. Xen. *Hell.* 4.6.1. The dating of the embassy to the late summer (between July and October) is based on the logistical constraints of the invasion and the timing of

the invading army's departure from Acarnania. Kahrstedt (1910, 194–95) also argued for this time of year based solely on the structure of Xenophon's *Hellenica*. For Achaean control of Calydon in the fourth century, see Merker 1989.

26. Xen. *Hell*. 4.6.2.

27. Xen. *Hell*. 4.6.3.

28. Xen. *Lac*. 11. Anderson estimates six hundred hoplites as the most realistic size of a *mora* during this time (1970, 225–26). Toynbee estimates 1,120 (1969, 379). I avoid the anachronistic and inaccurate convention of referring to a Spartan *mora* as a regiment.

29. For the Spartan army in the age of Xenophon, see Lazenby 1985, 3–50. For Spartan *hippeis*, see Figueira 2006.

30. At Xen. *Hell*. 4.6.4, the Acarnanians are "offered" an alliance only with the Spartans and Achaeans, suggesting the presence of very few additional allies. However, the Eleans, smaller Arcadian poleis, or even the Phocians could have supplied additional contingents.

31. Xen. *Hell*. 4.6.3

32. On divisions (*merea*), see Hdt. 1.145. For the fifth- and fourth-century Achaean ethnos, see Larsen 1968, 80–89; Beck 1997, 55–66; Corsten 1999, 160–65; and Mackil 2013, 46–52. See also Morgan 2000.

33. Xen. *Hell*. 4.6.4. The "country districts," that is, the expansive agricultural lowlands near the Acheloos River, complemented the more mountainous interior of the Acarnanian landscape. The boundaries of these districts appear to have remained relatively consistent in antiquity (Schoch 1997). On Acarnanian fortifications, see Pritchett 1992, 115–44. Presumably, the *astē* were the urban centers of the Acarnanian system of poleis that Xenophon alludes to later in his narrative.

34. Landgraf and Schmidt 1996, 112. See also Freitag 1999, 30–57, for the topography of the Acarnanian-Aetolian coast.

35. For Oiniadai as a hub of maritime activity in the region, see Mulliez 1982 and Freitag 1994.

36. Thuc. 3.106.

37. Xen. *Hell*. 4.6.4. This is the earliest mention of an Acarnanian koinon, but not necessarily the earliest evidence of a federal political structure in Acarnania (cf. Gehrke 1994–1995, 42–43).

38. Xen. *Hell*. 4.6.4.

39. Xen. *Hell*. 4.6.5.

40. For an approximate stadion conversion (1 stadion = 200 meters), see Bauslaugh 1979. For methods of agricultural devastation, see Hanson 1998, 42–76, especially 49 and 54–56.

41. Wherever the landing site was, the actual starting point of the invasion is uncontroversial, even though Xenophon does not mention the exact location (Pritchett 1991b, 91; Landgraf and Schmidt 1996, 111–12).

42. Xen. *Hell*. 4.6.5.

43. The only mention of the Acarnanians' allies comes much later in the narrative (4.6.14), when Xenophon explains that the Athenian fleet was blocking the sea passage to the Peloponnese from Oiniadai. This forced Agesilaus to cross the Gulf of Corinth elsewhere. It is unclear whether the Athenians were supporting the Acarnanians or using Oiniadai as a base of operations for their own purposes.

44. Xen. *Hell.* 4.6.6.

45. On this meandering route, see Landgraf and Schmidt 1996, 109.

46. These individuals are unnamed in the narrative, but the task of tactical reconnaissance and surveillance for Spartan armies usually fell to the Sciritai and hippeis, according to Xenophon (*Lac.* 12–13). For tactical information gathering during the fifth and fourth centuries, see Russell 1999, 10–62.

47. The sheer number of lakes in Acarnania renders Underhill's suggestion (1900, ad loc.) untenable, namely, that Xenophon's imprecise usage of "the Lake" assumed "a previous acquaintance with the facts." That is, the reader would have understood which lake Xenophon meant. As Landgraf and Schmidt point out (1996, 109n19), Xenophon (or his source) may not have even known the name of the lake. This entire issue is discussed further below.

48. Here are three examples: (1) "[Agesilaus's strategy] took the form of a day's march of forty kilometres into the interior to a position by a lake where the Akarnanians had fondly supposed their cattle, horses, other animals, and slaves would all be quite secure" (Cartledge 1987, 225). (2) "In any case, [the army's] slow pace lulled the Akarnanians into security, and they brought their cattle from the mountains to a certain lake" (Pritchett 1991b, 91). (3) "The Acarnanians . . . [from the army's slow advance and their own peltast capabilities] were given a sense of security—a false sense as events later turned out—and continued to work their holdings as long as possible" (Hanson 1998, 127–28).

49. Xen. *Hell.* 4.6.6.

50. For booty as "taken by the spear, captive, [or] prisoner of war," see Pritchett 1971–1991a, 5:169.

51. Xen. *Hell.* 4.6.6.

52. Pritchett 1991b, 91.

53. Xen. *Hell.* 4.6.7.

54. The Acarnanian peltasts presumably were from the more mountainous interior of Acarnania, itself a resource-rich environment (Gehrke 1996) that would have required protection. The peltasts' specialization is implied from the terminology of the narrative, as Xenophon for the most part distinguishes between Greek peltasts and light-armed troops (*psiloi*) in his writings (Best 1969, 45–47).

55. Cf. Hanson 1998, 127.

56. Corsten (1999, 113) suggests that the Acarnanians' larger poleis—in particular, Oiniadai and Stratos—functioned as gathering points for mobilizing the Acarnanian army later in the fourth century and into the third. See also Gernet 1982, 21–61.

57. Xen. *Hell.* 4.6.7

58. On javelins and light spears, see Best 1969, 3–16; on clay, stone, and lead sling bullets, see Pritchett 1971–1991a, 5:39–53. I use the term "javelineers" below to leave open the possibility that less-specialized Acarnanian or even non-Acarnanian (Thuc. 2.80–82) light-armed troops (*psiloi*) took part in the incident. There are no Acarnanian *psiloi* in Xenophon's narrative of the incident in the *Hellenica*; only peltasts are named explicitly. In Xenophon's summary account of the incident in his *Agesilaus* (2.20), he uses the term *psiloi* to describe the Acarnanians. On this "discrepancy," see Tuplin 1986, 44–45.

59. Xen. *Hell.* 4.6.7.

60. Xen. *Hell.* 4.6.7.

61. Customarily, after setting up a camp, "the *hippeis* were posted where they could observe someone approaching from afar" (Xen. *Lac.* 12). For Spartan encampment in general, see Anderson 1970, 59–66, and Lazenby 1985, 32–36.

62. Xen. *Hell.* 4.6.8

63. On Lake Ambracia, see Oberhummer 1887, 121–22; on the Lake of Lutraki, see Leake 1835, 3.508–9; on the Lake of Podovinissa, see Heuzey 1860, 357–58.

64. Pritchett 1991b, 90–100; Landgraf and Schmidt 1996.

65. Xen. *Hell.* 4.6.8.

66. Xen. *Hell.* 4.6.8.

67. I base this estimate on the reconstruction of an eighth-century/seventh-century Egyptian sling excavated at el-Lahun (Burgess 1958) that fired projectiles similar in weight and shape to those recovered in the Greek world.

68. Xen. *Hell.* 4.6.9.

69. The strong points were not actual fortifications but "places inaccessible to hoplites and horses" (Underhill 1900, ad loc.).

70. On the peltasts at Lechaeum, see Xen. *Hell.* 4.5.14–18. The Spartan hippeis may have been fighting on foot as hoplites at this time—evidently their usual practice (Figueira 2006, 57)—although later in the incident it is clear that some were also fighting on horseback.

71. Best 1969, 120–26.

72. Xen. *Hell.* 4.6.9.

73. On Agesilaus's generalship, see Cartledge 1987, 203–41.

74. It is a speculative point, but this may be the significance of the different "attack" verbs that Xenophon uses in 4.6.9 to describe the Acarnanians' activities on both sides of the basin. At 4.6.11, he uses yet another projectile verb that suggests the Acarnanians were throwing missiles from a distance—that is, not at close quarters (or as close as those attacking from the army's right), but not at a great distance either.

75. Xen. *Hell.* 4.6.9.

76. On the circulation of orders, see Xen. *Lac.* 11, discussed in depth by Humble 2006. For sacrifice before battle, a conventional practice in hoplite warfare, see Pritchett 1971–1991, 1:109–15, and Jameson 1991.

77. Xen. *Hell.* 4.6.10.

78. Xen. *Hell.* 4.6.10.

79. Cf. Arr. *Tact.* 27; see also Krentz 1991 for the *salpinx* in Greek warfare during the time in question.

80. On the pilos helmet, see Cartledge 1977, 14.

81. Xen. *Hell.* 4.6.11.

82. It is important to note that Agesilaus's plan would have been ineffective if the Acarnanians were attacking in uncoordinated and unpredictable waves (cf. Pritchett 1971–1991a, 5:65–66, on organized corps of stone throwers).

83. Xen. *Hell.* 4.6.11.

84. For the advantage of fighting from higher ground in hoplite engagements, see Rawlings 2007, 89.

85. Xen. *Hell.* 4.6.11.

86. For hoplites carrying two spears, throwing one and fighting with the other, see Anderson 1991, 19–21.

87. Xen. *Hell.* 4.6.11

88. This was a tactical retreat; Xenophon does not use a verb of fleeing as he usually does to depict a hasty or disordered retreat, such as in 4.6.11 (the Spartans' initial assault out of the basin). See also Xen. *Hell.* 3.4, 4.4, 4.5, 6.5, and 7.2.

89. Cf. Holladay 1982, 98, and Cartledge 1987, 225, who credit only Agesilaus's skillful and determined leadership for the Spartans' success in these circumstances.

90. Xen. *Hell.* 4.6.11

91. Xen. *Hell.* 4.6.9.

92. For the social status of slingers and stone throwers, see Pritchett 1971–1991a, 5:53–54, to which we could include unskilled light-armed troops (javelineers, *psiloi*).

93. Xen. *Hell.* 1.2, 2.4, 3.5, 4.3, 4.13, 6.2, 6.4, 7.1, 7.5. In this light, it may be worth considering Xenophon's silence on the booty that resulted from this particular engagement. Was there even any to speak of?

94. Xen. *Hell.* 4.6.12. On "trophy" as an expression of victory, see Pritchett 1971–1991a, 2:246–75.

95. Xen. *Hell.* 4.6.12.

96. For possible distinctions between *poleis* and *astē*, see Hansen 2006, 56–61. Xenophon could be using both terms as synonyms for towns; *poleis* could refer to Acarnanian settlements, with the *astē* understood as their urban center; or by "not taking a single one," Xenophon may have meant that Agesilaus was unable to win over the political community associated with a given polis (cf. Xen. *Hell.* 4.6.13). Some combination of the above explains Xenophon's wording.

97. On the logistics for a geographically constrained invasion, see van Wees 2004, 106.

98. For this reason, Phormio put an early end to his campaign in Acarnania during the winter of 429–428 (Thuc. 2.102–3).

99. Xen. *Hell.* 4.6.12.

100. Xen. *Hell.* 4.6.13.

101. Xen. *Hell.* 4.7.1, *Ages.* 2.20.

102. On their joining of the Second Athenian League, see Rhodes and Osborne 2003, 108–13 (cf. Diod. Sic. 15.36.5); on their alliance with Thebes, see Xen. *Hell.* 6.5.23.

103. Thuc. 3.109.

4. The Defense of Arcadia in 370

1. On Arcadians in the Catalogue of Ships, see Hom. *Il.* 2.603–14. For Archaic Arcadia (ca. 600–479), its geographical extent, and the emergence of its various historical communities, see Nielsen 2002, 92–97 and 159–228.

2. For Arcadia as "fundamentally a human construct," see Morgan 2003, 39.

3. For Archaic Arcadian sanctuaries, most which were located in eastern Arcadia, see Jost 1994 and Morgan 2003, 155–62.

4. Hdt. 8.73.1. For the emergence and development of an Arcadian regional or "national" identity, see Hejnic 1961, Nielsen 1999, and Scheer 2010. The essential features of this identity included a common name, a common myth of origin, a shared culture, and an association with a specific territory.

5. See Trundle (2004, 53–54), who discusses the epigraphic and literary evidence for Arcadian mercenaries.

6. The landmark study of Arcadian coinage is Williams 1965. Williams, among others, interpreted the coinage as distinctively federal in character, but a series of subsequent studies has pointed out the problems with this view (Roy 1972a, Psomi 1999, Nielsen 2002, 121–41). In short, coinage alone cannot establish the existence of a federation, and in this case, there is no additional literary or epigraphic evidence to support a "federal" interpretation for the fifth century.

7. Larsen, for instance, did not treat the Arcadians as a confederacy before the King's Peace. For the possible symmachy of the fifth century, see Nielsen 2002, 142–45.

8. Xen. Hell. 6.5.6, Diod. Sic. 15.59.1.

9. For the structure and character of the Arcadian League, see Larsen 1968, 186–89; Giovannini 1971, 43–46; Beck 1997, 75–83; Corsten 1999, 61–66; and Roy 2000b.

10. Rhodes and Osborne 2003, 156–61 (cf. Xen. Hell. 7.4.33).

11. See, for example, Cartledge 1987, 383–84; Cartledge 2002, 253; Hamilton 1991, 223; and Roy 1991, 190.

12. Both events are discussed further below.

13. For Arcadians in Xenophon's Anabasis, see Roy 1972b. See Anderson 1974, 172–73, for Xenophon's residence in Elis.

14. Xen. Hell. 6.5.10–23.

15. Diod. Sic. 15.59, 62. See Stylianou 1998, 49–50, for Diodorus's sources for the Greek and Persian narratives of books 11–16. Importantly, Xenophon does not appear to have been one of them.

16. For the King's Peace, or Peace of Antalcidas, which was renewed in 375, see Xen. Hell. 5.1.31, 6.2.1; Urban 1991; Badian 1991; and Seager 1994.

17. For a concise survey and analysis of the sources and issues surrounding Leuctra and its aftermath, see Hamilton 1991, 204–14.

18. The other major poleis were Orchomenos and Heraia.

19. Xen. Hell. 6.5.7–9.

20. Xen. Hell. 6.5.10.

21. Roy 1971b, citing the 2,400 Tegean hoplites at the River Nemea in 394. See also B. Forsén 2000, 35–55, for estimates of the entire civilian population.

22. On the size of Tegean territory, see Nielsen 2004, 531.

23. Xen. Hell. 6.5.10.

24. On post-Leuctra oaths, see Xen. Hell. 6.5.2, a reaffirmation of those sworn immediately before the battle in 371 (Xen. Hell. 6.3.18–20; see also Cawkwell 1979, 335).

25. On the strained relations between Mantineia and Sparta during the late fifth and fourth centuries, see Nielsen 1996b, 87–93.

26. Xen. Hell. 6.5.3–5.

27. Xen. Hell. 6.5.10.

28. On Agesilaus's ties with Mantineia, see Xen. Hell. 5.2.3, 6.5.4.

29. "For the first time in seven years [Agesilaus] took the field at the head of an army, and it is a fair measure of his and Sparta's desperation that he did so in the winter of late 370" (Cartledge 1987, 383–84).

30. The significance of the time of year is discussed further below.

31. Incidentally, the ancient truism of Arcadian ferocity was articulated most explicitly by Xenophon himself (Xen. Hell. 7.1.23–26).

32. Xen. *Hell.* 6.5.11.

33. See J. Forsén and B. Forsén 1997, 176, for the population estimate. For the geography, topography, and settlement history of the Asea Valley, see the contributions in Forsén and Forsén 2003.

34. On the size of Asean territory, see J. Forsén and B. Forsén 1997, 175.

35. B. Forsén 2003.

36. For the Arcadians' standing army, the *eparitoi*, see Beck 1997, 173. However, there is no evidence that the Arcadians maintained a standing army at this time, even if they had already designated the *eparitoi* who are first mentioned for the year 366 in Xen. *Hell.* 7.4.22 (cf. Larsen 1968, 188). The most suitable and consequently most likely locations for such a permanent garrison would have been Tegea or Mantineia, as at Xen. *Hell.* 7.4.33 and 7.4.36. Significantly, Asea was not the only potential mobilization point in Arcadia at this time.

37. Xen. *Hell.* 6.5.11.

38. Diodorus (15.62.1) places the size of Polytropus's force at 1,500. See also Stylianou 1998, 423–24.

39. On Mantineian territory and the border with Orchomenos, see Hodkinson and Hodkinson 1981, 242–46. The Arcadian district of Kleitor was farther north, part of the Arcadian League at this time, and had also been at odds with Orchomenos (Roy 1972c); however, there is no mention of the Kleitorians being involved in this particular incident. The Azanians were another northern Arcadian community (Nielsen and Roy 1998), but again, they are absent from Xenophon's narrative.

40. Xen. *Hell.* 6.5.11.

41. On Lepreon, see Nielsen 1997, 129–62, and Roy 1997; on Heraia, see Nielsen 2004, 513–14; see also Roy 2000a, for the frontier between Arcadia and Elis.

42. Xen. *Hell.* 6.5.12. For rites of crossing, see Jameson 1991, 202–3.

43. On Oresthasion, see Roy 2009, 206; see also Drakopoulos 1991.

44. On the pass at Oion open to Agesilaus, see Xen. *Hell.* 6.5.25–26.

45. Xen. *Hell.* 6.5.12.

46. On Eutaia, see Nielsen 1996a, 132–34, and Nielsen 1996b, 95.

47. Xen. *Hell.* 6.5.12. It is not entirely clear what Xenophon meant by *to Arkadikon*, since elsewhere he refers to the joint army of the Arcadians explicitly as the *eparitoi* (Xen. *Hell.* 7.5.3). Incidentally, the legend ARKADIKON—a variation of the ethnic proper of Arcadia (*Arkás*)—was also prevalent on fifth- and early fourth-century Arcadian coins either in full or abbreviated form. See also Corsten 1999, 62–63, n.8.

48. Xen. *Hell.* 6.5.12.

49. Xen. *Hell.* 6.5.12.

50. Pikoulas 1988, 75, associates the wall mentioned here with what appears to be a fortification wall found on a nearby hill. The lower town of Eutaia itself seems to have been unfortified. At any rate, if Agesilaus was attempting to gain an ally, he failed.

51. Xen. *Hell.* 6.5.13.

52. Cf. Xen. *Hell.* 7.4.38: Threatened by the Thebans in 365, the Mantineians called on the "cities of Arcadia" to take up arms and man the passes. In addition, the presumed mobilization order could have reached the rest of Arcadia in much the same way that summons and voting information reached the assembly of 10,000 (Larsen 1968, 186–88). See also Rhodes and Osborne 2003, 256–61, on a federal decree listing

voting members of the Arcadian assembly in 369 that attests to the geographical expanse of the League's constituents.

53. Xen. *Hell.* 6.5.13.

54. Paus. 8.13.2. For the walls of Orchomenos—2,300 meters long and enclosing a space of approximately 20 hectares—see Winter 1989, 194–95.

55. Whether there was an actual residential area within the fortification walls of Orchomenos at this time has been debated (Osborne 1987, 118), but it is difficult to say, as archaeological investigations to date have focused only on the agora, theater, and temple of Artemis (Nielsen 2004, 524). For a survey of Orchomenian territory—the two subplains in relation to the city—see Jost 1985, 113–14.

56. In 420 the Mantineians sent 1,000 hoplites to Olympia to protect the games against an expected Spartan attack (Thuc. 5.50.4). Lysias (34.7), writing in 403, points out that the Mantineians were resisting the Spartans even though there were less than 3,000 capable of doing so, suggesting a number slightly less than that. There is no record of Mantineians fighting as anything other than hoplites during the fifth and fourth centuries, but light-armed individuals likely would have accompanied the hoplites. See, for example, Hdt. 9.29.2 for a *psilos* accompanying each of the 1,500 Tegean hoplites that fought at Plataea in 479 and Xen. *Hell.* 6.5.26 for what must have been light-armed Arcadians on the attack at Oion during the invasion of Laconia in 370. Diodorus (15.62.2) claims that the entire Arcadian army advanced against Orchomenos and puts their numbers at 5,000, but as we saw, according to Xenophon—a more credible source in this particular instance—most of the Arcadians were still gathered at Asea.

57. Xen. *Hell.* 6.5.13.

58. Little else is known about Elymia aside from what can be deduced from this notice in Xenophon's narrative.

59. For hoplite methods of constructing routes and traversing mountains, see Ober 1991, 174–79.

60. Xen. *Hell.* 6.5.13.

61. According to Diodorus, Lycomedes led the attack on Orchomenos (15.62.2). Larsen (1968, 188) takes this as evidence that Lycomedes was the Arcadian League's first elected *stratēgos*—Lycomedes would be elected for certain in 366 (Diod. Sic. 15.67.2)—but Xenophon is silent on the matter (cf. Xen. *Hell.* 7.3.1 on the election of Aeneas of Stymphalus to *stratēgos* sometime between 370 and 366).

62. Xen. *Hell.* 6.5.14.

63. On the comparative advantages and disadvantages of hoplites versus peltasts during the first half of the fourth century, see Anderson 1970, 111–40.

64. The most famous example of this was the Spartans' repeated feigned retreats at Thermopylae (Hdt. 7.211). More recently, Thespian hoplites executed a similar tactic to great effect against the Thebans and their mercenary peltasts (Xen. *Hell.* 5.4.42–45), although again, in Xenophon's view, the Thespians' success was the result of desperation.

65. According to Diodorus, the Arcadians killed a total of two hundred individuals in addition to Polytropus (15.62.2), but he makes no mention of mercenaries.

66. Xen. *Hell.* 6.5.14.

67. Compare, for example, the postbattle activities of Arcadians and Spartans at Xen. *Hell.* 7.4.22–24. That said, the inclusion of such details is inconsistent across the Xenophontic corpus (Tuplin 1986, 39–41).

68. Xen. *Hell.* 6.5.15.

69. On reconnaissance and surveillance agents as part of Greek armies, see Russell 1999, 10–62. This does not prove that Agesilaus had such capabilities, but as Russell demonstrates, the practice of scouting appears to have been prevalent toward the middle of the fourth century.

70. Xen. *Hell.* 6.5.15.

71. See above on the Tegeans' potential numbers even after the departure of those loyal to Stassipus.

72. Xen. *Hell.* 6.5.15.

73. On the Mantineian territory covering most of the northern half of the central plain (also referred to as the Plain of Mantineia), see Hodkinson and Hodkinson 1981, 234.

74. Xen. *Hell.* 6.5.15. For a detailed study of the agricultural potential of the Mantineian countryside and the literary and archeological evidence of extra-urban settlements in the region, see Hodkinson and Hodkinson 1981, 261–71. Based on the results of this research, and Xenophon's silence on the matter, it seems that Agesilaus was unable or unwilling to harm the smaller Mantineian towns and villages scattered throughout the area. In addition, it is curious that Xenophon makes no explicit mention of livestock (cf. Xen. *Hell.* 7.5.15), as Mantineia was unusually rich in this respect.

75. The potential effectiveness of the Spartans' agricultural devastation is discussed further below.

76. Xen. *Hell.* 6.5.16.

77. Diodorus is the only source for this number. Pritchett (1971–1991a, 2:223) considers 5,000 too large, but given the potential numbers of individual Arcadian contingents discussed above, a combined number in the range of 3,500 to 5,000 is entirely possible. Tegea later accommodated the *eparitoi* for an extended period of time, and in 362, the city itself was the base of a substantial Boeotian garrison (Xen. *Hell.* 7.5.8).

78. Xen. *Hell.* 6.5.16.

79. Xen. *Hell.* 6.5.16.

80. Xen. *Hell.* 6.5.16.

81. On road networks of eastern Arcadia connected to Tegea, see Petronotis 2005. See also Pikoulas 1999 on the remains of extant wheel ruts in central and eastern Arcadia.

82. Xen. *Hell.* 6.5.16.

83. On Argive relations with the Arcadian League, see Piérart 1982.

84. Xen. *Hell.* 6.5.16.

85. Xen. *Hell.* 6.5.16.

86. Xen. *Hell.* 6.5.17.

87. Cartledge estimates that approximately 1,000 Spartiates remained after Leuctra (2002, 251–52), but the potential number of non-Spartans—both *perioikoi* and helots—capable of taking up arms could have reached approximately 6,000 (cf. Xen. *Hell.* 6.5.29). We would have a better sense of the invading army's size had Xenophon known or cared to detail the types and numbers of Lacedaemonian contingents entrusted to Agesilaus.

88. Based on a variety of methods—army figures in ancient authors, demographic modeling, comparisons with modern populations—estimations of the urban population of Mantineia range from 10,000 to 12,000, but the territory of Mantineia could have supported upward of 18,000 (Hodkinson and Hodkinson 1981, 274–77, 286, and

B. Forsén 2000, 42–44, 51–54). As long as the population of Mantineia was not at full capacity, and there are no indications that it was, it would have been entirely possible to accommodate the additional Arcadians for a short period of time.

89. Xen. *Hell.* 6.5.17.

90. Xen. *Hell.* 6.5.17.

91. Xen. *Hell.* 6.5.17.

92. Hodkinson and Hodkinson identify this as the Valley of Nestane (1981, 244; see also plates 46a and 46b in the same volume), a narrow 3,000-meter extension of the Nestane Plain—the so-called Untilled Plain in Pausanias's day (Paus. 8.7.1–3)—between Mt. Stavromiti (800m) and Mt. Kofinas (1,100m). The Nestane Plain itself is at approximately 615m above sea level. Except for the entrance at the south, the valley is completely enclosed by mountains.

93. Xen. *Hell.* 6.5.4.

94. Xen. *Hell.* 6.5.18.

95. An ideal location for this observation would have been from the heights of Mt. Stavromiti, also the location of a fortified tower that is unmentioned in Xenophon's narrative but appears to date to the fourth century (Lattermann 1913, 425–27).

96. Xen. *Hell.* 7.4.13.

97. Xen. *Hell.* 6.5.18.

98. Xen. *Hell.* 6.5.18.

99. Xen. *Hell.* 6.5.19. See Underhill 1900, ad loc., for a lucid grammatical exegesis of this complicated passage.

100. "The mercenaries from Orchomenos" resurface in defense of Laconia during the same winter (Xen. *Hell.* 6.5.29). Where they were in the meantime is unknown.

101. Xen. *Hell.* 6.5.19. The Eleans shared with the Arcadians a long history of resisting the Spartans (see, for example, Capreedy 2008) but their relations with the Arcadians could be strained at times (Nielsen 2002, 398).

102. Xen. *Hell.* 6.5.19.

103. According to Diodorus (15.62.3), the Athenians had rejected an alliance with the Arcadians in the late winter of 370 (hence the involvement of the Thebans), but in Xenophon's account, the Thebans were already on their way to Arcadia before this alleged offer to the Athenians would have been possible (cf. Cawkwell 1979, 341). For Boeotian involvement in Peloponnesian affairs ca. 370–362, see Roy 1971a.

104. Xen. *Hell.* 6.5.20.

105. Xen. *Hell.* 6.5.20.

106. Researchers have discovered another ancient road that led from Tegea to Mantineia that seems to have intentionally avoided the level ground of the central Arcadian plain. Based on some ethnographic comparisons, one researcher concluded that the "entire route was normally used during winter when the roads across the plains were buried in mud" (Petronotis 2005, 194).

107. Xen. *Hell.* 6.5.20.

108. Xen. *Hell.* 6.5.21.

109. Xenophon later approves of Epaminondas's decision to set up camp within the fortifications of Tegea in 362 instead of at Nemea (Xen. *Hell.* 7.5.8). He notes Epaminondas's ability to observe the activities and disposition of his enemies from a secure location that was well provisioned, and importantly, the inability of his enemies

to observe what he was doing. This means that although Agesilaus did not see any Arcadians at Tegea, the reverse was not the case. For the topography of Tegea to include the remains of the city wall and its history of urbanization, see Ødegård 2005.

110. Xen. *Hell.* 6.5.21.

111. Importantly, by the time of the invasion, the Arcadians would have been well past their olive and vine harvests, and their fields would already have been planted. For the effects and effectiveness of agricultural devastation in general, see Hanson 1998, 129–73.

112. Xen. *Hell.* 6.5.21.

113. Xen. *Hell.* 6.5.22.

114. On Alipheira in the Arcadian League, see Nielsen 1996a, 132–34.

115. Xen. *Hell.* 6.5.22.

116. Furthermore, by 367 at the latest, both Heraia and Orchomenos were part of the Arcadian League (Rhodes and Osborne 2003, 156–61).

117. Xen. *Hell.* 6.5.22–23.

118. Xen. *Hell.* 6.5.23.

119. On the invasion of Laconia, see Xen. *Hell.* 6.5.25–32; Diod. Sic. 15.63.3–65.5; Cartledge 2002, 253–55; Hamilton 1991, 220–31.

120. Diod. Sic. 15.62.3.

121. Xen. *Hell.* 7.1.25.

122. Morgan's observation (2003, 39) that Arcadia lacked a unifying geographical feature is somewhat puzzling in this light.

123. Xen. *Hell.* 7.4.13–40.

124. Xen. *Hell.* 7.4.22, 33–34.

125. Xen. *Hell.* 7.4.35–9, 7.5.1–5.

126. Cf. Larsen 1968, 186.

Conclusion

1. For defense in depth (or elastic defense) in the ancient world, see Ober 1985a, 80.

2. In comparison, Roman writers did have access to such tropes. See, for example, Dench 1995, 111–53, on Roman accounts of mountain peoples from the Central Apennines.

3. For a survey of the basic conventions and shape of warfare in the polis-centric realm, see Krentz 2002 and Hanson 2000.

4. Strauss 1996 and 2000b.

5. I thank Sturt Manning for bringing my attention to the similarity between the Mycenaean and classical periphery of the Greek mainland.

6. For a brief survey of the Mycenaean periphery and its relation to some of the main centers of power, see Tartaron 2010, 161–83.

7. See, for example, Davis and Bennet 1999.

8. Morris 2006. This is the collapse-depression-regeneration model originally put forth in Snodgrass 1971.

9. Thomas and Conant 1999.

10. See M. Burgess 2006, 81–97, for a historical survey of the motives of federal union.

11. In addition, as is commonly acknowledged in present-day studies of federalism, "the passage from the American Articles of Confederation of 1781 to the innovative Constitution of 1787 is the critical event that led to the now conventional distinction between confederation and federation" (Karmis and Norman 2005, 5).

12. Giovannini 2003.

13. Arr. *Anab.* 7.9.2.

References

Alty, John. 1982. "Dorians and Ionians." *Journal of Hellenic Studies* 102:1–14.

Anderson, J. K. 1970. *Military Theory and Practice in the Age of Xenophon*. Berkeley: University of California Press.

Anderson, J. K. 1974. *Xenophon*. New York: Charles Scribner's Sons.

Anderson, J. K. 1991. "Hoplite Weapons and Offensive Arms." In *Hoplites: The Classical Greek Battle Experience*, edited by Victor Davis Hanson, 15–37. London and New York: Routledge.

Andrewes, Antony. 1978. "Spartan Imperialism?" In *Imperialism in the Ancient World*, edited by Peter Garnsey and C. R. Whittaker, 91–102. Cambridge: Cambridge University Press.

Antonetti, Claudia. 1987a. "Agraioi et agrioi, montagnards et bergers: Un prototype diachronique de sauvagerie." *Dialogues d'histoire ancienne* 13:199–236.

Antonetti, Claudia. 1987b. "Le popolazione settentrionali dell'Etolia." In *L'Illyrie méridionale et l'Epire dans l'antiquité*, edited by Pierre Cabanes, 95–113. Clermont-Ferrand: Editions Adosa.

Antonetti, Claudia. 1988. "Problemi di geografia storica del territorio etolo-acarnano: Appunti sulla base di nuove testimonianze epigrafiche." In *Geographia: Atti del secondo convegno maceratese su geografia e cartografia antica*, 11–38. Rome: Università degli Studi di Macerata.

Antonetti, Claudia. 1990. *Les Étoliens: Image et religion*. Paris: Les Belles Lettres.

Archibald, Zofia. 2000. "Space, Hierarchy, and Community in Archaic and Classical Macedonia, Thessaly, and Thrace." In *Alternatives to Athens: Varieties of Political Organization and Community in Ancient Greece*, edited by Roger Brock and Stephen Hodkinson, 212–33. Oxford: Oxford University Press.

Arnush, Michael. 2000. "Argead and Aetolian Relations with the Delphic Polis in the Late Fourth Century BC." In *Alternatives to Athens: Varieties of Political Organization and Community in Ancient Greece*, edited by Roger Brock and Stephen Hodkinson, 293–307. Oxford: Oxford University Press.

Badian, Ernst. 1991. "The King's Peace." In *Georgica: Greek Studies in Honour of George Cawkwell*, edited by Michael Flower and Mark Toher, 25–48. London: University of London, Institute of Classical Studies.

Bakhuizen, Simon. 1989. "The *Ethnos* of the Boeotians." In *BOIOTIKA: Vorträge vom 5. internationalen Böoten-Kolloquium*, edited by Hartmut Beister and John Buckler, 65–72. Munich: Editio Maris.

Bakhuizen, Simon. 1996. "Men of the Mountains. Observations on Aitolian Raiding." In *Stuttgarter Kolloquium zur historischen Geographie des Altertums 5*, edited by Eckart Olshausen and Holger Sonnabend, 223–34. Amsterdam: Hakkert.

Baltrusch, Ernst. 1994. *Symmachie und Spondai: Untersuchungen zum griechischen Völkerrecht der archaischen und klassischen Zeit (8.–5. Jahrhundert v. Chr.).* Berlin: Walter de Gruyter.

Barthes, Roland. 1981. "The Discourse of History." Translated by Stephen Bann. *Comparative Criticism* 3:7–20.

Barthes, Roland. 1986. *The Rustle of Language.* Translated by Richard Howard. New York: Hill and Wang.

Bauslaugh, Robert. 1979. "The Text of Thucydides IV 8.6 and the South Channel at Pylos." *Journal of Hellenic Studies* 99:1–6.

Beck, Hans. 1997. *Polis und Koinon: Untersuchungen zur Geschichte und Struktur der griechischen Bundesstaaten im 4. Jahrhundert v. Chr.* Stuttgart: Franz Steiner.

Beck, Hans. 2003. "New Approaches to Federalism in Ancient Greece: Perceptions and Perspectives." In *The Idea of European Community in History*, vol. 2, edited by Kostas Buraselis and Kleanthis Zoumboulakis, 177–90. Athens: National and Capodistrian University of Athens.

Beck, Hans, and Peter Funke, eds. 2015. *Federalism in Greek Antiquity.* Cambridge: Cambridge University Press.

Berktold, Percy, Jürgen Schmid, and Christian Wacker, eds. 1996. *Akarnanien: Eine Landschaft im antiken Griechenland.* Würzburg: Ergon.

Best, Jan. 1969. *Thracian Peltasts and Their Influence on Greek Warfare.* Groningen: Wolters-Noordhoff.

Bingen, Jean, ed. 1996. *Pausanias historien: Huit exposés suivis de discussions.* Geneva: Foundation Hardt.

Bintliff, John. 1997. "Regional Survey, Demography, and the Rise of Complex Societies in the Ancient Aegean: Core-Periphery, Neo-Malthusian, and Other Interpretive Models." *Journal of Field Archaeology* 24:1–38.

Bommeljé, Sebastiaan. 1981–1982. "Strouza (Aigition): A Historical-Topographical Fieldwork." *Archaeologicon Deltion* 36:236–48.

Bommeljé, Sebastiaan. 1987a. "The Aetolians: A Greek Ethnos." In *Aetolia and the Aetolians: Towards the Interdisciplinary Study of a Greek Region*, edited by Sebastiaan Bommeljé and Peter Doorn, 13–17. Utrecht: Parnassus Press.

Bommeljé, Sebastiaan. 1987b. "The Aetolian Studies Project: The First Two Years (1985–6)." In *Aetolia and the Aetolians: Towards the Interdisciplinary Study of a Greek Region*, edited by Sebastiaan Bommeljé and Peter Doorn, 18–26. Utrecht: Parnassus Press.

Bommeljé, Sebastiaan. 1988. "Aeolis in Aetolia: Thuc. 3.102.5 and the Origins of the Aetolian Ethnos." *Historia* 37:297–316.

Bommeljé, Sebastiaan, and Peter Doorn, eds. 1987. *Aetolia and the Aetolians: Towards the Interdisciplinary Study of a Greek Region.* Utrecht: Parnassus Press.

Bommeljé, Sebastiaan, and Peter Doorn. 1991. "Transhumance in Aetolia, Central Greece: A Mountain Economy Caught between Storage and Mobility." *Rivista di Studi Liguri* 56:81–97.

Borza, Eugene. 1990. *In the Shadow of Olympus: The Emergence of Macedon.* Princeton, NJ: Princeton University Press.

Bosworth, Brian. 1992. "Athens' First Intervention in Sicily: Thucydides and the Sicilian Tradition." *Classical Quarterly* 42:46–55.

Bowie, Angus, ed. 2007. *Herodotus.* Histories Book 8. Cambridge: Cambridge University Press.

Brennan, T. Corey. 1987. "An Ethnic Joke in Homer?" *Harvard Studies in Classical Philology* 91:1–3.

Brock, Roger, and Stephen Hodkinson, eds. 2000. *Alternatives to Athens: Varieties of Political Organization and Community in Ancient Greece.* Oxford: Oxford University Press.

Buckler, John. 1989. *Philip II and the Sacred War.* Leiden: Brill.

Burgess, E. Martin. 1958. "An Ancient Egyptian Sling Reconstructed." *Journal of the Arms and Armour Society* 10:226–30.

Burgess, Michael. 2006. *Comparative Federalism: Theory and Practice.* London and New York: Routledge.

Burn, Andrew. 1960. *The Lyric Age of Greece.* New York: St. Martin's Press.

Busolt, Georg. 1926. *Griechische Staatskunde II.* 3rd ed. Munich: Beck.

Cabanes, Pierre. 1981. "Les états fédéraux de Grèce du nord-ouest. Pouvoirs locaux et pouvoirs fédéraux." In *Actes de IVe colloque international d'Histoire du Droit grec et hellénistique*, edited by Panayotis Dimakis, 99–111. Athens: Faculté autonome des sciences politiques.

Campbell, Brian, and Lawrence Tritle, eds. 2013. *The Oxford Handbook of Warfare in the Classical World.* Oxford: Oxford University Press.

Capreedy, Jim. 2008. "A League within a League: The Preservation of the Elean Symmachy." *Classical World* 101:485–503.

Cartledge, Paul. 1977. "Hoplites and Heroes: Sparta's Contribution to the Technique of Ancient Warfare." *Journal of Hellenic Studies* 97:11–27.

Cartledge, Paul. 1987. *Agesilaos and the Crisis of Sparta.* Baltimore: Johns Hopkins University Press.

Cartledge, Paul. 2002. *Sparta and Lakonia: A Regional History 1300–362 BC.* 2nd ed.. London: Routledge.

Cawkwell, George, ed. 1979. *Xenophon: A History of My Times.* Translated by Rex Warner. London: Penguin Books.

Champion, Craige. 1995. "The Soteria at Delphi: Aetolian Propaganda in the Epigraphical Record." *American Journal of Philology* 116:213–20.

Champion, Craige. 2007. "Polybius and Aetolia: A Historiographical Approach." In *A Companion to Greek and Roman Historiography*, vol. 2, edited by John Marincola, 356–62. Malden, MA: Wiley-Blackwell.

Cohen, Edward. 2000. *The Athenian Nation.* Princeton, NJ: Princeton University Press.

Connor, W. Robert. 1977. "A Post Modernist Thucydides?" *Classical Journal* 72:289–98.

Connor, W. Robert. 1984. *Thucydides.* Princeton, NJ: Princeton University Press.

Corsten, Thomas. 1999. *Vom Stamm zum Bund: Gründung und territoriale Organisation griechischer Bundesstaaten.* Munich: Oberhummer Gesellschaft.

Corsten, Thomas. 2006. "Stammes- und Bundeskulte in Akarnanien." In *Kult—Politik—Ethnos: Überregionale Heiligtümer im Spannungsfeld von Kult und Politik*, edited by Klaus Freitag, Peter Funke, and Matthias Haake, 157–67. Stuttgart: Franz Steiner.

Crowley, Jason. 2012. *The Psychology of the Athenian Hoplite: The Culture of Combat in Classical Athens*. Cambridge: Cambridge University Press.

Dany, Oliver. 1999. *Akarnanien im Hellenismus: Geschichte und Völkerrecht in Nordwestgriechenland*. Munich: C. H. Beck.

Daux, Georges. 1936. *Pausanias à Delphes*. Paris: Picard.

Daverio Rocchi, Giovanna. 1993. *Città-stato e stati federali della Grecia classica*. Milan: LED.

Davies, J. K. 2000. "A Wholly Non-Aristotelian Universe: The Molossians as Ethnos." In *Alternatives to Athens: Varieties of Political Organization and Community in Ancient Greece*, edited by Roger Brock and Stephen Hodkinson, 234–59. Oxford: Oxford University Press.

Davis, Jack, and John Bennet. 1999. "Making Mycenaeans: Warfare, Territorial Expansion, and Representations of the Other in the Pylian Kingdom." In *Polemos: le contexte guerrier en Egée à l'âge du Bronze*, edited by Robert Laffineur, 105–20. Liège: Université de Liège.

de Laix, Roger. 1973. "The Silver Coinage of the Aetolian League." *California Studies in Classical Antiquity* 6:47–75.

Dench, Emma. 1995. *From Barbarians to New Men: Greek, Roman, and Modern Perceptions of Peoples from the Central Apennines*. Oxford: Oxford University Press.

de Romilly, Jacqueline. 1956. *Histoire et Raison chez Thucydide*. Paris: Les Belles Lettres.

Deylius, Michiel. 1987. "The Aetolian Landscape: A Physical-Geographical Perspective." In *Aetolia and the Aetolians: Towards the Interdisciplinary Study of a Greek Region*, edited by Sebastiaan Bommeljé and Peter Doorn, 32–38. Utrecht: Parnassus Press.

Dietz, Søren, and Ioannis Moschos, eds. 2006. *Chalcis Aitolias I: The Prehistoric Periods*. Athens: Danish Institute at Athens.

Dietz, Søren, and Maria Stavropoulou-Gatsi, eds. 2011a. *Kalydon in Aitolia I: Reports and Studies, Danish/Greek Field Work 2001–2005*. Athens: Danish Institute at Athens.

Dietz, Søren, and Maria Stavropoulou-Gatsi, eds. 2011b. *Kalydon in Aitolia II: Catalogues, Danish/Greek Field Work 2001–2005*. Athens: Danish Institute at Athens.

Domingo-Foresté, Douglas. 1988. "A History of Northern Coastal Acarnania to 167 BC: Alyzeia, Leukas, Anaktorion and Argos Amphilochikon." Diss., University of California, Santa Barbara.

Doorn, Peter. 1985. "Geographical Analysis of Early Modern Data in Ancient Historical Research: The Example of the Stroúza Region Project in Central Greece." *Transactions of the Institute of British Geographers* 10:275–91.

Doorn, Peter. 1993. "Geographical Location and Interaction Models and the Reconstruction of Historical Settlement and Communication: The Example of Aetolia, Central Greece." *Historical Social Research* 67:35–71.

Dover, Kenneth J. 1983. "Thucydides 'As History' and 'As Literature.'" *History and Theory* 22:54–63.

Drakopoulos, Eleftherios. 1991. "Orestheum or Oresthasion in Arcadia." *L'Antiquité Classique* 60:29–41.

Ehrenberg, Victor. 1969. *The Greek State*. 2nd ed. London: Methuen.

Elazer, Daniel. 1987. *Exploring Federalism*. Tuscaloosa: University of Alabama Press.

Ellinger, Pierre. 1978. "Le gypse et la boue I. Sur les mythes de la guerre d'anéantissement." *Quaderni Urbinati di Cultura Classica* 29:7–35.

Ellinger, Pierre. 1987. "Hyampolis et le sanctuaire d'Artemis Elaphébolos dans l'histoire, la légende et l'espace de la Phocide." *Archäologischer Anzeiger* 1:88–99.

Ellinger, Pierre. 1993. *La légende nationale phocidienne: Artémis, les situations extremes et les récits de guerre d'anéantissement*. Paris: Bocard.

Felsch, Rainer, ed. 2007. *Kalapodi II. Ergebnisse der Ausgrabungen im Heiligtum der Artemis und des Apollon von Hyampolis in der antiken Phokis*. Mainz am Rhein: Verlag Philipp von Zabern.

Figueira, Thomas. 2006. "The Spartan *Hippeis*." In *Sparta and War*, edited by Stephen Hodkinson and Anton Powell, 57–84. Swansea: Classical Press of Wales.

Flower, Michael. 2008. *The Seer in Ancient Greece*. Berkeley: University of California Press.

Forrest, William G. 2000. "The Pre-Polis Polis." In *Alternatives to Athens: Varieties of Political Organization and Community in Ancient Greece*, edited by Roger Brock and Stephen Hodkinson, 280–92. Cambridge: Cambridge University Press.

Forsén, Björn. 2000. "Population and Political Strength of Some Southeastern Arkadian Poleis." In *Further Studies in the Ancient Greek* Polis, edited by Pernille Flensted-Jensen, 35–55. Stuttgart: Franz Steiner.

Forsén, Björn. 2003. "The Road Network of the Valley." In *The Asea Valley Survey: An Arcadian Mountain Valley from the Palaeolithic Period until Modern Times*, 63–75. Stockholm: Svenska Institutet i Athen.

Forsén, Jeannette, and Björn Forsén. 1997. "The Polis of Asea: A Case Study of How Archaeology Can Expand Our Knowledge of the History of a Polis." In *Yet More Studies in the Ancient Greek Polis*, edited by Thomas Nielsen, 163–76. Stuttgart: Franz Steiner.

Forsén, Jeannette, and Björn Forsén, eds. 2003. *The Asea Valley Survey: An Arcadian Mountain Valley from the Palaeolithic Period until Modern Times*. Stockholm: Svenska Institutet i Athen.

Fossey, John. 1986. *The Ancient Topography of Eastern Phocis*. Amsterdam: Gieben.

Freedman, Lawrence. 2013. *Strategy: A History*. Oxford: Oxford University Press.

Freeman, Edward. 1893. *History of Federal Government in Greece and Italy*. 2nd ed. London: Macmillan.

Freitag, Klaus. 1994. "Oiniadai als Hafenstadt: einige historisch-topographische Überlegungen." *Klio* 76:212–38.

Freitag, Klaus. 1996. "Der Akarnanische Bund im 5. Jh. V. Chr." In *Akarnanien: Ein Landschaft im antiken Griechenland*, edited by Percy Berktold, Jürgen Schmid, and Christian Wacker, 75–86. Würzburg: Ergon.

Freitag, Klaus. 1999. *Der Golf von Korinth: Historisch-topographische Untersuchungen von der Archaik bis in das 1. Jh. v. Chr.* Münster: tuduv-Verlagsgesellschaft.

Freitag, Klaus, Peter Funke, and Matthias Haake, eds. 2006. *Kult—Politik—Ethnos: Überregionale Heiligtümer im Spannungsfeld von Kult und Politik*. Stuttgart: Franz Steiner.

Freitag, Klaus, Peter Funke, and Nikola Moustakis. 2004. "Aitolia." In *An Inventory of Archaic and Classical Poleis*, edited by Mogens H. Hansen and Thomas Nielsen, 379–90. Oxford: Oxford University Press.

French, Edward, and Eugene Vanderpool. 1963. "The Phokikon." *Hesperia* 32:213–25.

Funke, Peter. 1987. "Zur Datierung befestigten Stadtanlagen in Aitolien: Historisch-Philologische Anmerkungen zu einem Wechselverhältnis zwischen Siedlungstruktur und politischer Organisation." *Boreas* 10:87–96.

Funke, Peter. 1997. "Polisgenese und Urbanisierung in Aitolien im 5. und 4. Jh. v. Chr." In *The Polis as an Urban Centre and as a Political Community*, edited by Mogens H. Hansen, 145–88. Copenhagen: Royal Danish Academy of Sciences and Letters.

Funke, Peter. 2001. "Acheloos' Homeland: New Historical-Archaeological Research on the Ancient Polis Stratos." In *Foundation and Destruction, Nikopolis and Northwestern Greece: The Archaeological Evidence for the City Destructions, the Foundation of Nikopolis and the Synoecism*, edited by Jacob Isager, 189–203. Athens: Aarhus University Press.

Funke, Peter, and Matthias Haake. 2006. "Theatres of War: Thucydidean Topography." In *Brill's Companion to Thucydides*, edited by Antonios Rengakos and Antonis Tsakmakis, 369–84. Leiden: Brill.

Funke, Peter, and Matthias Haake, eds. 2013. *Greek Federal States and Their Sanctuaries: Identity and Integration*. Stuttgart: Franz Steiner.

Gehrke, Hans-Joachim. 1986. *Jenseits von Athen und Sparta: Das Dritte Griechenland und seine Staatenwelt*. Munich: C. H. Beck.

Gehrke, Hans-Joachim. 1994–1995. "Die kulturelle und politische Entwicklung Akarnanienns vom 6. bis zum 4. Jahrhundert v. Chr." *Geographia Antiqua* 3–4:41–48.

Gehrke, Hans-Joachim. 1996. "Bergland als Wirtschaftsraum. Das Beispiel Akarnaniens." In *Gebirgsland als Lebensraum. Stuttgarter Kolloquium zur Historischen Geographie des alterums Altertums, 5, 1993*, edited by Eckart Olshausen and Holger Sonnabend, 71–78. Amsterdam: Hakkert.

Gehrke, Hans-Joachim. 2000. "Ethnos, Phyle, Polis: Gemäßigt unorthodoxe Vermutungen." In *Polis and Politics: Studies in Ancient Greek History*, edited by P. Flensted-Jensen, Thomas Nielsen, and Lene Rubinstein, 159–76. Copenhagen: Museum Tusculanum Press.

Gehrke, Hans-Joachim, and Eckhard Wirbelauer. 2004. "Akarnania and Adjacent Areas." In *An Inventory of Archaic and Classical Poleis*, edited by Mogens H. Hansen and Thomas Nielsen, 351–78. Oxford: Oxford University Press.

Gernet, Louis. 1982. *Anthropologie de la Grèce antique*. Paris: Champs-Flammarion.

Giddens, Anthony. 1985. *The Nation-State and Violence*. Vol. 2 of *A Contemporary Critique of Historical Materialism*. Berkeley: University of California Press.

Giovannini, Adalberto. 1971. *Untersuchungen über die Natur und die Anfänge der bundesstaatlichen Sympolitie in Griechenland*. Gottingen: Vandenhoeck & Ruprecht.

Giovannini, Adalberto. 2003. "Genèse et accomplissement de l'état fédéral de la Grèce antique à la constitution américanine de 1787–1789." In *The Idea of European Community in History: Conference Proceedings*, vol. 2, edited by Kostas Buraselis and Kleanthis Zoumboulakis, 143–76. Athens: Greek Ministry of Education and Religious Affairs.

Goldsworthy, Adrian. 1996. *The Roman Army at War 100 BC—AD 200*. Oxford: Oxford University Press.

Gomme, Arnold W. 1956. *A Historical Commentary on Thucydides II*. Oxford: Clarendon Press.

Grainger, John. 1999. *The League of the Aitolians*. Leiden: Brill.

Gray, Colin. 2014. *Strategy and Defence Planning: Meeting the Challenge of Uncertainty*. Oxford: Oxford University Press.

Habicht, Christian. 1957. "Ein Urkunde des Akarnanischen Bundes." *Hermes* 85:86–122.

Habicht, Christian. 1985. *Pausanias' Guide to Ancient Greece*. Berkeley: University of California Press.

Hall, Edith. 2006. *The Theatrical Cast of Athens: Interaction between Ancient Greek Drama and Society*. Oxford: Oxford Universiy Press.

Hall, Jonathan. 1997. *Ethnic Identity in Greek Antiquity*. Cambridge: Cambridge University Press.

Hall, Jonathan. 1998. "Ethnic Identity in Greek Antiquity." *Cambridge Archaeological Journal* 8:265–83.

Hall, Jonathan. 2002. *Hellenicity: Between Ethnicity and Culture*. Chicago: University of Chicago Press.

Hall, Jonathan. 2007. *A History of the Archaic Greek World ca. 1200–479 BCE*. Malden, MA: Wiley-Blackwell.

Halladay, A. J. 1982. "Hoplites and Heresies." *Journal of Hellenic Studies* 102:94–103.

Hamilton, Charles. 1979. *Sparta's Bitter Victories: Politics and Diplomacy in the Corinthian War*. Ithaca, NY: Cornell University Press.

Hamilton, Charles. 1991. *Agesilaus and the Failure of Spartan Hegemony*. Ithaca, NY: Cornell University Press.

Hansen, Mogens H. 1995. "Boiotian Poleis—a Test Case." In *Sources for the Ancient Greek City-State*, edited by Mogens H. Hansen, 13–63. Copenhagen: Royal Danish Academy of Sciences and Letters.

Hansen, Mogens H. 2006. *Polis: An Introduction to the Ancient Greek City-State*. Oxford: Oxford University Press.

Hanson, Victor Davis. 1989. *The Western Way of War: Infantry Battle in Classical Greece*. Berkeley: University of California Press.

Hanson, Victor Davis, ed. 1991. *Hoplites: The Classical Greek Battle Experience*. London and New York: Routledge.

Hanson, Victor Davis. 1998. *Warfare and Agriculture in Classical Greece*. 2nd ed. Berkeley: University of California Press.

Hanson, Victor Davis. 2000. "Hoplite Battle as Ancient Greek Warfare: When, Where, and Why?" in *War and Violence in Ancient Greece*, edited by Hans van Wees, 201–32. Swansea: Classical Press of Wales.

Hanson, Victor Davis, ed. 2010. *Makers of Ancient Strategy: From the Persian Wars to the Fall of Rome*. Princeton, NJ: Princeton University Press.

Head, Barclay. 1911. *Historia Numorum: A Manual of Greek Numismatics*. 2nd ed. Oxford: Clarendon Press.

Hejnic, Josef. 1961. *Pausanias the Perieget and the Archaic History of Arcadia*. Prague: Czeckoslovakian Academy of Sciences.

Helly, Bruno. 1995. *L'état thessalien: Aleuas le Roux, les tétrades et les Tagoi*. Lyon: Maison de l'Orient Méditerranéen.

Heuzey, León. 1860. *Le Mont Olympe et l'Acarnanie*. Paris: Firmin Didot Fréres.

Hodkinson, Stephen, and Hilary Hodkinson. 1981. "Mantineia and the Mantinike: Settlement and Society in a Greek Polis." *Annual of the British School at Athens* 76:239–96.

Holladay, A. James. 1982. "Hoplites and Heresies." *Journal of Hellenic Studies* 102:94–103.

Hornblower, Simon. 1987. *Thucydides*. Baltimore: Johns Hopkins University Press.

Hornblower, Simon. 1991. *A Commentary on Thucydides*. Vol. 1, *Books I–III*. Oxford: Clarendon Press.

Hornblower, Simon. 2002. "Herodotus and His Sources of Information." In *Brill's Companion to Herodotus*, edited by Egbert Bakker, Irene de Jong, and Hans van Wees, 373–86. Leiden: Brill.

How, Walter W., and Joseph Wells. 1912. *A Commentary on Herodotus*. Vol. 2. Oxford: Oxford University Press.

Howe, Timothy. 2003. "Pastoralism, the Delphic Amphiktyony and the First Sacred War: The Creation of Apollo's Sacred Pastures." *Historia* 52:129–46.

Howe, Timothy. 2008. *Pastoral Politics: Animals, Agriculture, and Society in Ancient Greece*. Claremont, CA: Regina Books.

Humble, Noreen. 2006. "Why the Spartans Fight So Well . . . Even in Disorder—Xenophon's View." In *Sparta and War*, edited by Stephen Hodkinson and Anton Powell, 219–34. Swansea: Classical Press of Wales.

Hunt, Peter. 1998. *Slaves, Warfare, and Ideology in the Greek Historians*. Cambridge: Cambridge University Press.

Hunt, Peter. 2006. "Warfare." In *Brill's Companion to Thucydides*, edited by Antonios Rengakos and Antonis Tsakmakis, 385–413. Leiden: Brill.

Hunter, Virginia. 1973. *Thucydides: The Artful Reporter*. Toronto: Hakkert.

Imhoof-Blumer, Friedrich. 1878. "Die Münzen Akarnaniens." *Numismatische Zeitschrift* 10:1–180.

Jacquemin, Anne. 1999. *Offrandes monumentales à Delphes*. Athens: École française d'Athènes.

Jacquemin, Anne, and Didier Laroche. 1982. "Notes sur trois piliers Delphiques." *Bulletin de correspondance hellénique* 106:191–218.

Jameson, Michael. 1991. "Sacrifice before Battle." In *Hoplites: The Classical Greek Battle Experience*, edited by Victor Davis Hanson, 197–227. London and New York: Routledge.

Jensen, Pernille. 2006. "The Animal Bones from Pangali" and "The Animal Bones from Aghia Triada." In *Chalcis Aitolias I: The Prehistoric Periods*, edited by Søren Dietz and Ioannis Moschos, 162–70, 178–95. Athens: Danish Institute at Athens.

Jost, Madeleine. 1985. *Sanctuaires et cultes d'Arcadie*. Paris: Librairie philosophique J. Vrin.

Jost, Madeleine. 1994. "The Distribution of Sanctuaries in Civic Space in Arkadia." In *Placing the Gods: Sanctuaries and Sacred Space in Ancient Greece*, edited by Susan Alcock and Robin Osborne, 217–30. Oxford: Clarendon Presss.

Jouan, François. 1990. "Le Corinthiens en Acarnanie et leur prédécesseurs mythiques." In *Mythe et politique: Actes du Colloque de Liege, 14–16 septembre 1989*, edited by François Jouan and André Motte, 155–66. Paris: Les Belles Lettres.

Kagan, Donald. 1974. *The Archidamian War*. Ithaca, NY: Cornell University Press.

Kagan, Donald. 2010. "Pericles, Thucydides, and the Defense of Empire." In *Makers of Ancient Strategy: From the Persian Wars to the Fall of Rome*, edited by Victor Davis Hanson, 31–57. Princeton, NJ: Princeton University Press.

Kagan, Donald, and Gregory Viggiano, eds. 2013. *Men of Bronze: Hoplite Warfare in Ancient Greece*. Princeton, NJ: Princeton University Press.

Kagan, Kimberly. 2006a. *The Eye of Command*. Ann Arbor: University of Michigan Press.

Kagan, Kimberly. 2006b. "Redefining Roman Grand Strategy." *The Journal of Military History* 70:333–62.

Kahrstedt, Ulrich. 1910. *Forschungen zur Geschichte des ausgehenden fünften und des vierten Jahrhundert*. Berlin: Weidmannsche Buehhandlung.

Karmis, Dimitrios, and Wayne Norman, eds. 2005. *Theories of Federalism: A Reader*. New York: Palgrave Macmillan.

Kase, Edward, ed. 1991. *The Great Isthmus Corridor Route: Explorations of the Phokis-Doris Expedition*. Vol. 1. Dubuque, IA: Kendall Hunt.

Keegan, John. 1976. *The Face of Battle*. New York: Viking.

Keegan, John. 1993. *A History of Warfare*. New York: Random House.

Klaffenbach, Günther, ed. 1957. *Inscriptiones Graecae IX, 1.2*. 2nd ed. Berlin: German Academy of Sciences.

Konecny, Andreas. 2001. "Katekopsen ten moran Iphikrates: Das Gefecht bei Lechaion im Frühsommer 390 v. Chr." *Chiron* 31:79–127.

Kraft, John. 1991. "Geology of the Great Isthmus Corridor." In *The Great Isthmus Corridor Route: Explorations of the Phokis-Doris Expedition*, vol. 1, edited by Edward Kase, 1–16. Dubuque, IA: Kendall Hunt.

Krentz, Peter. 1985a. "The Nature of Hoplite Battle." *Classical Antiquity* 4:50–61.

Krentz, Peter. 1985b. "Casualties in Hoplite Battles." *Greek Roman and Byzantine Studies* 26:13–20.

Krentz, Peter. 1991. "The *Salpinx* in Greek Battle." In *Hoplites: The Classical Greek Battle Experience*, edited by Victor Davis Hanson, 110–20. London and New York: Routledge.

Krentz, Peter. 2002. "Fighting by the Rules: The Invention of the Hoplite Agōn." *Hesperia* 71:23–39.

Krentz, Peter. 2010. *The Battle of Marathon*. New Haven, CT: Yale University Press.

Krentz, Peter. 2013. "Hoplite Hell: How Hoplites Fought." In *Men of Bronze: Hoplite Warfare in Ancient Greece*, edited by Donald Kagan and Gregory Viggiano, 134–56. Princeton, NJ: Princeton University Press.

Krentz, Peter, and C. Sullivan. 1987. "The Date of Phormio's First Expedition to Akarnania." *Historia* 37:241–43.

Krentz, Peter, and Everett Wheeler, eds. 1994. *Polyaenus: Stratagems of War*. Vol. 1. Chicago: Ares.

Kurke, Leslie. 1999. *Coins, Bodies, Games, and Gold: The Politics of Meaning in Archaic Greece*. Princeton, NJ: Princeton University Press.

Landgraf, Regine, and Gudrun Schmidt. 1996. "Der Feldzug des Agesilaos im korinthischen Krieg." In *Akarnanien: Eine Landschaft im antiken Griechenland*, edited by Percy Berktold, Jürgen Schmid, and Christian Wacker, 105–12. Würzburg: Ergon.

Larsen, Jakob A. O. 1955. *Representative Government in Greek and Roman History*. Berkeley: University of California Press.

Larsen, Jakob A. O. 1960. "A New Interpretation of the Thessalian Confederacy." *Classical Philology* 55:229–48.

Larsen, Jakob A. O. 1968. *Greek Federal States: Their Institutions and History*. Oxford: Clarendon Press.

Lattermann, Heinrich. 1913. "Nestane und das Argon Pedion." *Archäologischer Anzeiger* 28:395–428.

Lazenby, John. 1985. *The Spartan Army*. Warminster: Aris & Phillips.

Lazenby, John. 1991. "The Killing Zone." In *Hoplites: The Classical Greek Battle Experience*, edited by Victor Davis Hanson, 87–109. London and New York: Routledge.

Lazenby, John. 2004. *The Peloponnesian War: A Military Study*. London and New York: Routledge.

Leake, William. 1835. *Travels in Northern Greece III*. London: J. Rodwell.

Lee, A. D. 1996. "Morale and the Roman Experience of Battle." In *Battle in Antiquity*, edited by Alan Lloyd, 199–217. Swansea: Classical Press of Wales.

Lee, John. 2007. *A Greek Army on the March: Soldiers and Survival in Xenophon's Anabasis*. Cambridge: Cambridge University Press.

Lehmann, Gustav. 2001. *Ansätze zu einer Theorie des griechischen Bundesstaates bei Aristoteles und Polybios*. Göttingen: Vandenhoeck & Ruprecht.

Lendon, Jon E. 2005. *Soldiers and Ghosts: A History of Battle in Classical Antiquity*. New Haven, CT: Yale University Press.

Lendon, Jon E. 2010. *Song of Wrath: The Peloponnesian War Begins*. New York: Basic Books.

Lerat, Lucien. 1952. *Les Locriens de l'Ouest I: Topographie et ruines*. Paris: Editions de Boccard.

Lewis, David. 1992. "Mainland Greece, 479–451 BC." In *The Cambridge Ancient History*, vol. 5, *Fifth Century BC*, 2nd ed., edited by David Lewis, John Boardman, J. K. Davies, and Martin Ostwald, 96–120. Cambridge: Cambridge University Press.

Liddell Hart, Basil. 1967. *Strategy*. 2nd ed. London: Faber & Faber.

Lloyd, Alan, ed. 1996. *Battle in Antiquity*. Swansea: Classical Press of Wales.

Loraux, Nicole. 1980. "Thucydide n'est pas un collègue." *Quademi di Storia* 12:55–81.

Luraghi, Nino. 2006. "Traders, Pirates, Warriors: The Proto-History of Greek Mercenary Soldiers in the Eastern Mediterranean." *Phoenix* 60:21–47.

Luttwak, Edward. 1976. *The Grand Strategy of the Roman Empire: From the First Century A.D. to the Third*. Baltimore: Johns Hopkins University Press.

Lynn, John. 2003. *Battle: A History of Combat and Culture*. Boulder: Westview Press.

Mackil, Emily. 2013. *Creating a Common Polity: Religion, Economy, and Politics in the Making of the Greek Koinon*. Berkeley: University of California Press.

Malkin, Irad. 1994. *Myth and Territory in the Spartan Mediterranean*. Cambridge: Cambridge University Press.

Marincola, John. 2001. *Greek Historians*. Oxford: Oxford University Press.

Martín-Gil, Jesús, Gonzalo Palacios-Leblé, Pablo Martín Ramos, and Francisco Martín-Gil. 2007. "Analysis of a Celtiberian Protective Paste and Its Possible Use by Arevaci Warriors." *Journal of Interdisciplinary Celtic Studies* 5:63–76.

Martin, Thomas. 1985. *Sovereignty and Coinage in Classical Greece*. Princeton, NJ: Princeton University Press.

McInerney, Jeremy. 1997. "The Phokikon and the Hero Archegetes." *Hesperia* 66:193–207.

McInerney, Jeremy. 1999. *The Folds of Parnassos: Land and Ethnicity in Ancient Phokis*. Austin: University of Texas Press.

McInerney, Jeremy. 2001. "Ethnos and Ethnicity in Early Greece." In *Ancient Perceptions of Greek Ethnicity*, edited by Irad Malkin, 51–73. Cambridge, MA: Harvard University Press.

McInerney, Jeremy. 2013. "*Polis* and *koinon*: Federal Government in Greece." In *A Companion to Ancient Greek Government*, edited by Hans Beck, 466–79. Malden, MA: Wiley-Blackwell.

McLeod, Wallace. 1965. "The Range of the Ancient Bow." *Phoenix* 19:1–14.

McLeod, Wallace. 1972. "The Range of the Ancient Bow: Addenda." *Phoenix* 26:78–82.

Meadows, Andrew, and Kirsty Shipton, eds. 2001. *Money and Its Uses in the Ancient Greek World*. Oxford: Oxford University Press.

Meiggs, Russel, and David Lewis. 1989. *A Selection of Greek Historical Inscriptions*. 2nd ed. Oxford: Clarendon Press.

Mendels, Doron. 1984. "Aetolia 331–301: Frustration, Political Power, and Survival." *Historia* 33:129–80.

Mendels, Doron. 1984/1986. "Did Polybius Have 'Another' View of the Aetolian League?" *Ancient Society* 15/17:63–73.

Meritt, Benjamin. 1962. "The Seasons in Thucydides." *Historia* 11:436–46.

Merker, Irwin. 1989. "The Achaians in Naupaktos and Kalydon in the Fourth Century." *Hesperia* 58:303–11.

Meyer, Elizabeth. 2008. "Thucydides on Harmodius and Aristogeiton, Tyranny, and History." *Classical Quarterly* 58:13–34.

Mintzberg, Henry. 1978. "Patterns in Strategy Formation." *Management Science* 24:934–48.

Mitchell, Stephen. 1996. "Hoplite Warfare in Ancient Greece." In *Battle in Antiquity*, edited by Alan Lloyd, 87–106. Swansea: Classical Press of Wales.

Montagu, John. 2000. *Battles of the Greek and Roman Worlds: A Chronological Compendium of 667 Battles to 31 BC, from the Historians of the Ancient World*. London: Greenhill Books.

Morgan, Catherine. 2000. "Politics without the Polis: Cities and the Achaean Ethnos, c. 800–500." In *Alternatives to Athens: Varieties of Political Organization and Community in Ancient Greece*, edited by Roger Brock and Stephen Hodkinson, 189–211. Oxford: Oxford University Press.

Morgan, Catherine. 2001a. "Ethne, Ethnicity, and Early Greek States, ca. 1200–480: An Archaeological Perspective." In *Ancient Perceptions of Greek Ethnicity*, edited by Irad Malkin, 75–112. Cambridge, MA: Harvard University Press.

Morgan, Catherine. 2001b. "Symbolic and Pragmatic Aspects of Warfare in the Greek World of the 8th to 6th Centuries BC." In *War as a Cultural and Social Force: Essays on Warfare in Antiquity*, edited by Tønnes Bekker-Nielsen and Lise Hannestad, 20–44. Copenhagen: Royal Danish Academy of Sciences and Letters.

Morgan, Catherine. 2003. *Early Greek States beyond the Polis*. London and New York: Routledge.

Morpeth, Neil. 2006. *Thucydides' War: Accounting for the Faces of Conflict*. Hildesheim: Georg Olms.

Morris, Ian. 1987. *Burial and Ancient Society: The Rise of the Greek City-State*. Cambridge: Cambridge University Press.

Morris, Ian. 2006. "The Collapse and Regeneration of Complex Society in Greece, 1500–500 BC." In *After Collapse: The Regeneration of Complex Societies*, edited by Glenn Schwartz and John Nichols, 72–84. Tucson: University of Arizona Press.

Morrison, John, John Coates, and N. Boris Rankov. 2000. *The Athenian Trireme: The History and Reconstruction of an Ancient Warship*. 2nd ed. Cambridge: Cambridge University Press.

Mulliez, Dominique. 1982. "Notes sur le transport du bois." *Bulletin de correspondance hellénique* 106:107–18.

Murray, William. 1982. "The Coastal Sites of Western Akarnania: A Topographical-Historical Survey." Diss., University of Pennsylvania.

Nagy, Gregory. 1990. *Greek Mythology and Poetics*. Ithaca, NY: Cornell University Press.

Nielsen, Thomas. 1996a. "Arkadia: City-Ethnics and Tribalism." In *Introduction to an Inventory of Poleis*, edited by Mogens H. Hansen, 117–63. Copenhagen: Munksgaard.

Nielsen, Thomas. 1996b. "A Survey of Dependent Poleis in Classical Arkadia." In *More Studies in the Ancient Greek Polis*, edited by Mogens H. Hansen, 63–106. Stuttgart: Franz Steiner.

Nielsen, Thomas. 1997. "*Tryphilia*: An Experiment in Ethnic Construction and Political Organisation." In *Yet More Studies in the Ancient Greek Polis*, edited by Thomas Nielsen, 129–62. Stuttgart: Franz Steiner.

Nielsen, Thomas. 1999. "The Concept of Arkadia—The People, Their Land, and Their Organisation." In *Defining Ancient Arkadia*, edited by Thomas Nielsen and James Roy, 16–79. Copenhagen: Royal Danish Academy of Sciences and Letters.

Nielsen, Thomas. 2002. *Arkadia and Its Poleis in the Archaic and Classical Periods*. Göttingen: Vandenhoeck & Ruprecht.

Nielsen, Thomas. 2004. "Arkadia." In *An Inventory of Archaic and Classical Poleis*, edited by Mogens H. Hansen and Thomas Nielsen, 505–39. Oxford: Oxford University Press.

Nielsen, Thomas, and James Roy. 1998. "The Azanians of Northern Arkadia." *Classica et Mediaevalia* 49:5–44.

Ober, Josiah. 1985a. *Fortress Attica: Defense of the Athenian Land Frontier 404-322 B.C.* Leiden: Brill.

Ober, Josiah. 1985b. "Thucydides, Pericles, and the Strategy of Defense." In *The Craft of the Ancient Historian: Essays in Honor of Chester G. Starr*, edited by John Eadie and Josiah Ober, 171–88. Lanham, MD: University Press of America.

Ober, Josiah. 1991. "Hoplites and Obstacles." In *Hoplites: The Classical Greek Battle Experience*, edited by Victor Davis Hanson, 173–96. London and New York: Routledge.

Oberhummer, Eugen. 1887. *Akarnanien, Ambrakia, Amphilochia, Leukas im Altertum*. Munich: Theodor Ackermann.

Ødegård, Knut. 2005. "The Topography of Ancient Tegea: New Discoveries and Old Problems." In *Ancient Arcadia*, edited by Erik Østby, 209–21. Athens: Norwegian Institute at Athens.

Osborne, Robin. 1987. *Classical Landscapes with Figures: The Ancient Greek City and Its Countryside*. London: George Philip.

Oulhen, Jacques. 2004. "Phokis." In *An Inventory of Archaic and Classical Poleis*, edited by Mogens H. Hansen and Thomas Nielsen, 388–430. Oxford: Oxford University Press.

Papageorgakis, J., and E. Kolaiti. 1992. "The Ancient Limestone Quarries of Profitis Elias near Delphi (Greece)." In *Ancient Stones: Quarrying, Trade, and Provenance: Interdisciplinary Studies on Stones and Stone Technology in Europe and the Near East from the Prehistoric to the Early Christian Period*, edited by Marc Waelkens, Norman Herz, and Luc Moens, 37–42. Leuven: Leuven University Press.

Paret, Peter, ed. 1986. *Makers of Modern Strategy: From Machiavelli to the Nuclear Age*. Princeton, NJ: Princeton University Press.

Parke, H. W., and John Boardman. 1957. "The Struggle for the Tripod and the First Sacred War." *Journal of Hellenic Studies* 77:276–82.

Parker, Robert. 1998. *Cleomenes on the Acropolis*. Oxford: Clarendon Press.

Paul, G. M. 1987. "Two Battles in Thucydides." *Classical Views* 31:307–12.

Perlman, Paula. 1996. "*Polis Upēkoos*: The Dependant Polis and Crete." In *Introduction to an Inventory of Poleis*, edited by Mogens H. Hansen, 233–87. Copenhagen: Munksgaard.

Petronotis, Argyres. 2005. "E ta malista leophoros (Pausanias 8.54.5) in Arkadia." In *Ancient Arcadia*, edited by Erik Østby, 185–96. Athens: Norwegian Institute at Athens.

Piérart, Marcel. 1982. "Argos, Cleonai et le Koinon des Arcadiens." *Bulletin de Correspondance Hellénique* 106:119–38.

Pikoulas, Yiannis. 1988. "I notia Megalopolitiki chora apo ton 8 o. os ton 4 o. m. Ch. aiona." Diss., University of Ioannina, Athens.

Pikoulas, Yiannis. 1999. "The Road Network of Arcadia." In *Defining Ancient Arkadia*, edited by Thomas Nielsen and James Roy, 248–319. Copenhagen: Royal Danish Academy of Sciences and Letters.

Pritchett, W. Kendrick. 1971–1991a. *The Greek State at War*. 5 vols. Berkeley: University of California Press.

Pritchett, W. Kendrick. 1982. *Studies in Ancient Greek Topography*. Part 4, *Passes*. Berkeley: University of California Press.

Pritchett, W. Kendrick. 1986. "Thucydides' Statement on His Chronology." *Zeitschrift für Papyrologie und Epigraphik* 62:205–11.

Pritchett, W. Kendrick. 1991b. *Studies in Ancient Greek Topography*. Part 7. Amsterdam: Brill.

Pritchett, W. Kendrick. 1992. *Studies in Ancient Greek Topography*. Part 8. Amsterdam: Brill.

Pritchett, W. Kendrick. 1994. *Essays in Greek History*. Amsterdam: Brill.

Psomi, S. 1999. "Arkadikon." *Horos* 13:81–96.

Purcell, Nicholas. 1990. "Mobility and the Polis." In *The Greek City from Homer to Alexander*, edited by Oswyn Murray and Simon Price, 29–58. Oxford: Clarendon Press.

Raaflaub, Kurt. 1997. "Soldiers, Citizens, and the Evolution of the Early Greek Polis." In *The Development of the Polis in Archaic Greece*, edited by Lynette Mitchell and P. J. Rhodes, 49–59. London and New York: Routledge.

Rawlings, Louis. 2000. "Alternative Agonies: Hoplite Martial and Combat Experiences." In *War and Violence in Ancient Greece*, edited by Hans van Wees, 233–60. Swansea: Classical Press of Wales.

Rawlings, Louis. 2007. *The Ancient Greeks at War*. Manchester: Manchester University Press.

Rhodes, P. J., and Robin Osborne. 2003. *Greek Historical Inscriptions 404–323 BC*. Oxford: Oxford University Press.

Roisman, Joseph. 1993. *The General Demosthenes and His Use of Military Surprise*. Stuttgart: Franz Steiner.

Roy, James. 1971a. "Arcadia and Boeotia in Peloponnesian Affairs, 370–362 BC." *Historia* 20:569–99.

Roy, James. 1971b. "Tegeans at the Battle near the River Nemea in 394 BC." *Parola del Passato* 91:439–41.

Roy, James. 1972a. "An Arcadian League in the Earlier Fifth Century BC?" *Phoenix* 26:334–41.

Roy, James. 1972b. "Arcadian Nationality as Seen in Xenophon's *Anabasis*." *Mnemosyne* 25:129–36.

Roy, James. 1972c. "Orchomenus and Clitor." *Classical Quarterly* 22:78–80.

Roy, James. 1991. "Thebes in the 360s BC." In *The Cambridge Ancient History*. Vol. 6, *The Fourth Century BC*, 2nd ed., edited by David Lewis, John Boardman, Simon Hornblower, and Martin Ostwald, 187–208. Cambridge: Cambridge University Press.

Roy, James. 1997. "The *Perioikoi* of Elis." In *The Polis as an Urban Centre and as a Political Community*, edited by Mogens H. Hansen, 282–320. Copenhagen: Danish Academy of Sciences and Letters.

Roy, James. 2000a. "The Frontier between Arkadia and Elis in Classical Antiquity." In *Polis and Politics: Studies in Ancient Greek History*, edited by P. Flensted-Jensen, Thomas Nielsen, and Lene Rubinstein, 133–56. Copenhagen: Museum Tusculanum Press.

Roy, James. 2000b. "Problems of Democracy in the Arcadian Confederacy, 370–362 BC." In *Alternatives to Athens: Varieties of Political Organization and Community in Ancient Greece*, edited by Roger Brock and Stephen Hodkinson, 308–26. Oxford: Oxford University Press.

Roy, James. 2009. "Finding the Limits of Laconia: Defining and Redefining Communities on the Spartan-Arkadian Frontier." *British School at Athens Studies* 16:205–11.

Rubincam, Catherine. 1991. "Casualty Figures in the Battle Descriptions of Thucydides." *Transactions of the American Philological Association* 121:181–98.

Russell, Frank. 1999. *Information Gathering in Ancient Greece*. Ann Arbor: University of Michigan Press.

Rzepka, Jacek. 2002. "*Ethnos, Koinon, Sympoliteia*, and Greek Federal States." In *Euergesias Charin: Studies Presented to Ewa Wipszycka and Benedetto Bravo by Their Disciples*, edited by Tomasz Derda, Jakhub Urbanik, and Marek Wecowski, 225–47. Warsaw: Journal of Juristic Papyrology Supplements.

Rzepka, Jacek. 2009. "The Aetolian Elite Warriors and Fifth-Century Roots of the Hellenistic Confederacy." *AKME* 4:3–34.

Sabin, Philip. 2000. "The Face of Roman Battle." *Journal of Roman Studies* 90:1–17.

Sabin, Philip. 2007. "Battle, A. Land Battles." In *The Cambridge History of Greek and Roman Warfare*, vol. 1, edited by Philip Sabin, Hans van Wees, and Michael Whitby, 399–433. Cambridge: Cambridge University Press.

Sabin, Philip, Hans van Wees, and Michael Whitby, eds. 2007. *The Cambridge History of Greek and Roman Warfare*. Vol. 1. Cambridge: Cambridge University Press.

Sacks, Kenneth. 1975. "Polybius' Other View of Aetolia." *Journal of Hellenic Studies* 95:92–106.

Salmon, John. 1977. "Political Hoplites?" *Journal of Hellenic Studies* 97:84–101.

Scheer, Tanja. 2010. "Ways of Becoming Arcadian: Arcadian Foundation Myths in the Mediterranean." In *Cultural Identity in the Ancient Mediterranean: Issues and Debates*, edited by Erich Gruen, 11–25. Los Angeles: Getty Research Institute.

Schettino, Maria. 1998. *Introduzione a Polieno*. Pisa: ETS.

Schober, Friedrich. 1924. "Phokis." Diss., University of Jena.

Schoch, Marcel. 1996. "Die Schiedsstätte Olpai." In *Akarnanien: Ein Landschaft im antiken Griechenland*, edited by Percy Berktold, Jürgen Schmid, and Christian Wacker, 87–90. Würzburg: Ergon.

Schoch, Marcel. 1997. *Beiträge zur Topographie Akarnaniens in klassischer und hellenistischer Zeit*. Würzburg: Ergon.

Scholten, Joseph. 2000. *The Politics of Plunder: Aitolians and Their Koinon in the Early Hellenistic Era, 279–217 BC*. Berkeley: University of California Press.

Schwartz, Adam. 2013. "Large Weapons, Small Greeks: The Practical Limitations of Hoplite Weapons and Equipment." In *Men of Bronze: Hoplite Warfare in Ancient Greece*, edited by Donald Kagan and Gregory Viggiano, 157–75. Princeton, NJ: Princeton University Press.

Scott, James. 2009. *The Art of Not Being Governed: An Anarchist History of Upland Southeast Asia*. New Haven, CT: Yale University Press.

Seager, Robin. 1994. "The King's Peace and the Second Athenian Confederacy." In *The Cambridge Ancient History*, vol. 6, *The Fourth Century BC*, 2nd ed., edited by David Lewis, John Boardman, Simon Hornblower, and Martin Ostwald, 156–86. Cambridge: Cambridge University Press.

Siewert, Peter. 2005. "Föderalismus in der griechischen Welt bis 338 v. Chr." In *Föderalismus in der griechischen und römischen Antike*, edited by Peter Siewert and Luciana Aigner-Foresti, 17–42. Munich: Franz Steiner.

Siewert, Peter, and Luciana Aigner-Foresti, eds. 2005. *Föderalismus in der griechischen und römischen Antike*. Munich: Franz Steiner.

Snodgrass, Anthony. 1965. "Hoplite Reform and History." *Journal of Hellenic Studies* 85:110–22.

Snodgrass, Anthony. 1971. *The Dark Age of Greece: An Archaeological Survey of the Eleventh to the Eight Centuries BC*. Edinburgh: Edinburgh University Press.

Snodgrass, Anthony. 1980. *Archaic Greece: The Age of Experiment*. Berkeley: University of California Press.

Snodgrass, Anthony. 1986. "Interaction by Design: The Greek City-State." In *Peer Polity Interaction and Socio-Political Change*, edited by Colin Renfrew and John Cherry, 47–58. Cambridge: Cambridge University Press.

Sordi, Marta. 1953a. "Le origini del koinon etolico." *AKME* 6:419–45.

Sordi, Marta. 1953b. "La guerra tessalo-focese del V secolo." *Rivista di Filologia* 81:235–58.

Stadter, Philip. 1965. *Plutarch's Historical Methods: An Analysis of the Mulierum Virtutes*. Cambridge, MA: Harvard University Press.

Stahl, Hans-Peter. 1966. *Thukydides: Die Stellung des Menschen im geschichtlichen Prozess*. Munich: C. H. Beck.

Stanton, Gregory. 1982. "Federalism in the Greek World: An Introduction." In *Hellenika: Essays on Greek Politics and History*, edited by G. H. R. Horsley, 183–90. North Ryde, Australia: Macquarie Ancient History Association.

Strassler, Robert, ed. 1996. *The Landmark Thucydides: A Comprehensive Guide to the Peloponnesian War*. New York: Free Press.

Strauss, Barry. 1996. "The Athenian Trireme, School of Democracy." In *Dēmokratia: A Conversation on Democracies, Ancient and Modern*, edited by Josiah Ober and Charles Hedrick, 313–25. Princeton, NJ: Princeton University Press.

Strauss, Barry. 2000a. "Perspectives on the Death of Fifth-Century Athenian Seamen." In *War and Violence in Ancient Greece*, edited by Hans van Wees, 261–83. Swansea: Classical Press of Wales.

Strauss, Barry. 2000b. "Democracy, Kimon, and the Evolution of Athenian Naval Tactics in the Fifth Century BC." In *Polis and Politics: Studies in Ancient Greek History*, edited by P. Flensted-Jensen, Thomas Nielsen, and Lene Rubinstein, 315–26. Copenhagen: Museum Tusculanum Press.

Strauss, Barry. 2006. *The Trojan War: A New History*. New York: Simon & Schuster.

Stylianou, P. J. 1998. *A Historical Commentary on Diodorus Siculus Book 15*. Oxford: Clarendon Press.

Szemler, G. J. 1988. "The Great Isthmus Corridor, Delphi, Thermopylae: Centers of Resistance against Great Powers in North-Central Greece." In *Forms of Control and Subordination in Antiquity*, edited by Toru Yuge and Masaoki Doi, 553–66. Leiden: Brill.

Szemler, G. J. 1991. "From the Fifth Century to the Roman Epoch." In *The Great Isthmus Corridor Route: Explorations of the Phokis-Doris Expedition*, vol. 1, edited by Edward Kase, 105–15. Dubuque, IA: Kendall Hunt.

Tartaron, Thomas. 2010. "Between and Beyond: Political Economy in Non-palatial Mycenaean Worlds." In *Political Economies of the Aegean Bronze Age*, edited by Daniel Pullen, 161–83. Oxford: Oxbow Books.

Tausend, Klaus. 1992. *Amphiktyonie und Symmachie: Formen zwischenstaatlicher Beziehungen im archaischen Griechenland*. Stuttgart: Franz Steiner.

Thomas, Carol, and Craig Conant. 1999. *Citadel to City-State: The Transformation of Greece, 1200–700 BCE*. Bloomington: Indiana University Press.

Toynbee, Arnold. 1969. *Some Problems of Greek History*. Oxford: Oxford University Press.

Treu, Max. 1956. "Der Stratege Demosthenes." *Historia* 5:420–47.

Trundle, Matthew. 2004. *Greek Mercenaries: From the Late Archaic Period to Alexander*. London and New York: Routledge.

Tsachalidis, Efstathios, and Eleftherios Hadjisterkotis. 2009. "Current Distribution and Population Status of Wild Boar (Sus scrofa L.) in Greece." *Acta Silvatica et Lignaria Hungarica* 5:153–57.

Tuplin, Christopher. 1986. "Military Engagements in Xenophon's *Hellenica*." In *Past Perspectives: Studies in Greek and Roman Historical Writing*, edited by I. S. Moxon, J. D. Smart, and A. J. Woodman, 37–66. Cambridge: Cambridge University Press.

Tuplin, Christopher. 1993. *The Failings of Empire: A Reading of Xenophon* Hellenica *2.3.11–7.5.27*. Stuttgart: Franz Steiner.

Underhill, George. 1900. *A Commentary with Introduction and Appendices on the* Hellenica *of Xenophon*. Oxford: Clarendon Press.

Urban, Ralf. 1991. *Der Königsfrieden von 387/86 v. Chr.: Vorgeschichte, Zustandekommen, Ergebnis und politische Umsetzung*. Stuttgart: Franz Steiner.

van Wees, Hans. 1995. "Politics and the Battlefield: Ideology in Greek Warfare." In *The Greek World*, edited by Anton Powell, 153–78. London and New York: Routledge.

van Wees, Hans. 2001. "The Myth of the Middle-Class Army: Military and Social Status in Ancient Athens." In *War as a Cultural and Social Force: Essays on Warfare in Antiquity*, edited by Tønnes Bekker-Nielsen and Lise Hannestad, 45–71. Copenhagen: Danish Academy of Sciences and Letters.

van Wees, Hans. 2004. *Greek Warfare: Myths and Realities*. London: Bristol Classical Press.

Vaughn, Pamela. 1991. "The Identification and Retrieval of the Hoplite Battle-Dead." In *Hoplites: The Classical Greek Battle Experience*, edited by Victor Davis Hanson, 38–62. London and New York: Routledge.

Viggiano, Gregory. 2013. "The Hoplite Revolution and the Rise of the Polis." In *Men of Bronze: Hoplite Warfare in Ancient Greece*, edited by Donald Kagan and Gregory Viggiano, 112–33. Princeton, NJ: Princeton University Press.

Vlassopoulos, Kostas. 2007. *Unthinking the Greek Polis: Ancient Greek History beyond Eurocentrism*. Cambridge: Cambridge University Press.

von Clausewitz, Carl. 1979. *Verstreute kleine Schriften*, edited by Werner Hahlweg. Osnabrück: Biblio.

Walbank, Frank. 1976–1977. "Were There Greek Federal States?" *Scripta Classica Israelica* 3:27–51.

Westlake, H. D. 1945. "Seaborne Raids in Periclean Strategy." *Classical Quarterly* 39:75–84.

Westlake, H. D. 1968. *Individuals in Thucydides*. Cambridge: Cambridge University Press.

Whatley, Noah. 1964. "On Reconstructing Marathon and Other Ancient Battles." *Journal of Hellenic Studies* 84:119–39.

Wheeler, Everett. 1991. "The General as Hoplite." In *Hoplites: The Classical Greek Battle Experience*, edited by Victor Davis Hanson, 121–70. London and New York: Routledge.

Wheeler, Everett. 2001. "Fire Power: Missile Weapons and 'The Face of Battle.'" *Electrum* 5:169–84.

Wheeler, Everett. 2007a. "Land Battles." In *The Cambridge History of Greek and Roman Warfare*, vol. 1, edited by Philip Sabin, Hans van Wees, and Michael Whitby, 186–223. Cambridge: Cambridge University Press.

Wheeler, Everett, ed. 2007b. *The Armies of Classical Greece*. Aldershot: Ashgate Publishing.

Wheeler, Everett. 2010. "Polyaenus: *Scriptor Militaris*." In *Polyainos: Neue Studien— Polyaenus: New Studies*, edited by Kai Brodersen, 7–54. Berlin: Verlag Antike.

Wheeler, Everett. 2011. "Greece: Mad Hatters and March Hares." In *Recent Directions in the Military History of the Ancient World*, edited by Lee Brice and Jennifer Roberts, 53–104. Claremont, CA: Regina Books.

White, Richard. 1991. *The Middle Ground: Indians, Empires, and Republics in the Great Lakes Region, 1650–1815*. Cambridge: Cambridge University Press.

Williams, Roderick. 1965. *The Confederate Coinage of the Arcadians in the Fifth Century BC*. New York: American Numismatic Society.

Williams, Roderick. 1972. *The Silver Coinage of the Phocians*. London: Royal Numismatic Society.

Winter, Frederick. 1989. "Arkadian Notes I: Identification of the Agora Buildings at Orchomemos and Mantinea." *Echos du Monde Classique* 31:235–46.

Woodcock, Eric. 1928. "Demosthenes, Son of Alcisthenes." *Harvard Studies in Classical Philology* 39:93–108.

Woodhouse, William. 1897. *Aetolia: Its Geography, Topography, and Antiquities*. Oxford: Clarendon Press.

Xydopoulos, Ioannis. 2007. "The Concept and Representation of Northern Communities in Ancient Greek Historiography: The Case of Thucydides." In *Communities in European History: Representations, Jurisdictions, Conflict*, edited by Juan Pan-Montojo and Frederick Pederson, 1–22. Pisa: Pisa University Press.

INDEX

Abae, 11, 23, 112n16
Acarnania, Acarnanians: alliance with, 67; Athenian interactions with, 33–36, 44, 50–52, 54, 56–57, 67; congress of, 55; defensive activities of, 55–65; ethnos of, 1, 3, 50–52, 70–72; Hellenistic state of, 51, 103–4; territorial aggression of, 54; territory of, 50, 60
Achaea, Achaeans, 3, 54–56, 65–66
Acheloos River, 50, 52, 55, 57
Aetolia, Aetolians: defensive activities of, 36–44, 46–49; diplomatic activities of, 44, 46; ethnos of, 1, 3, 30–31, 34, 47–48; Hellenistic league of, 30, 49, 103–4; political organization of, 34, 46; stereotypes of, 29–30, 34; territorial aggression of, 44; territory of, 34; tribal groups of, 34
Agesilaus, 38; in Acarnania, 54–65; in Arcadia, 77–90; Xenophon and, 53–54, 75
agricultural destruction, 56–57, 65–66, 83, 89–90
Aigition, 31, 39–44, 46
Arcadia, Arcadians: defensive activities of, 77–90; ethnos of, 1, 3, 73, 93–94; league of, 74–77, 93–95; military reputation of, 73, 78; Spartan conflict with, 91–92; territory of, 73, 90
archaeological research, 6, 15, 30, 32, 38, 54
archers, 40–42, 45
Argos, Argives, 85, 91–92
Asea, 78, 80–81, 84, 93–94
Athens, Athenians, 2, 7, 30–32; Spartan conflict with, 33–34, 55; strategic aims of, 8; territorial aggression of, 33–44

beyond-the-polis scholarship, 1–5, 29–30, 101
Boeotia, Boeotians, 3–4, 16, 23, 34, 54
booty, 36, 58
Bronze Age, 9, 103–4

Calydon, Calydonians, 54–55, 67, 70
cavalry, 14, 18, 55, 61–64, 82, 86

central Arcadian plain, 73, 83, 88–89
civilians: involvement in defense, 20, 39, 48, 75, 80
coinage, 5, 9–10, 26, 48, 51, 73, 128n6
concession of territory, 18–24, 36, 55–56, 70, 83, 98–99
confederation, 8, 10, 26–27, 30, 49, 51, 99–105

Daphnos River, 34, 46
deception, 25–26, 60, 69–70, 82, 85
defensive strategies, 24–28, 46–49, 68–70, 92–93; comparisons between, 96–98
Delphi, 11, 23, 44
Delphic Amphictyony, 4, 111n5
Demosthenes: in Aetolia, 33–43, 45; later successes of, 44; Thucydides and, 31–32
Diodorus, 74–76

East (Opuntian) Locris, 9, 16
epibatai. See marines
ethnic identity, 3, 9, 26, 73, 111n2
ethnographic studies, 6, 32, 38–39, 132n106
ethnos, ethnē, 10, 30, 34, 50, 73–74; as geographical space, 3–4, 107n6; meaning of, 1, 7; military studies of, 4–5, 31; Thucydidean view of, 3, 27, 34, 71–72, 101–2, 105
Eutaia, Eutaians, 80–84, 89–90
eye of command, 6

face of battle, 7, 100, 109n32
federal army, 94
federal state, 4, 26–27, 48, 51–52, 71–74; criteria for, 10, 101–2; definition of, 7–8; formation of, 104–5. See also koinon
fortifications, 77, 82, 86, 89, 113n36

grand strategy, 8
Gulf of Corinth, 9, 36, 38, 54

Herodotus, 6, 11–13, 18, 55, 101–2
hippeis. See cavalry

Homer, 18, 29, 34, 42
hoplites, 19–21, 55, 61–64, 81, 84; arms and armor of, 20–22, 40, 62; mobility of, 40, 62, 87–88, 119n48; traditional views of, 31; versatility of, 45; vulnerability of, 39
Hyampolis, 14, 23

inscriptions, 30, 48, 51, 74

javelins, 40–43, 59–63

Kephisos River, 9, 14–16, 25
koinon, koina, 9, 26–27, 30, 48, 56, 71–74, 101; meaning of, 4, 7–8, 51–52, 110n37. See also federal state

land routes, 15, 38–39, 46–47, 78, 81, 84–85, 113n31
Larsen, Jakob, 5, 48–49
league state. See koinon
light-armed troops, 31, 35–36, 40–43; against hoplites, 40–43, 58–65; lack of, 26, 36, 39, 41, 61
livestock, 55, 57–58, 60, 66–69

Macedonia, Macedonians, 4–5, 30, 38, 103–4
Mantineia, Mantineians, 73, 76–78, 81–89
marines, 34–35, 40–43, 45. See also hoplites
mercenaries, 5, 73, 78, 80–82
Messenians of Naupactus, 33–36, 39, 42, 45, 48
mobilization points, 24, 39, 55, 59, 70, 78, 94
mountain refuges, 16, 20
Mt. Parnassus, 9, 16, 24, 28; as base of operations, 23; as source of chalk, 17

Naupactus, 33, 44, 48
Neon, 17, 22
nighttime operations, 18–23, 59, 84, 86, 89

observation, 37–39, 55, 58–59, 84, 90
Oineon, 35, 36, 38–39, 43, 46
Orchomenos, Orchomenians, 78, 80–82

pastoralism, 3, 29, 42
Pausanias, 10, 12–13, 53; Herodotus and, 16–17, 19
peltasts, 54, 58–65, 81–2, 86. See also light-armed troops
phalanx, 35, 61, 63, 87
Phocis, Phocians: defensive activities of, 18–23; ethnos of, 1, 3, 10, 16, 23, 26–27; Iron Age unification of, 9–10; national legend of, 11, 23–24; as network of poleis, 3, 10, 26; in the Persian Wars, 12, 16,

23–24; territorial aggression of, 27; territory of, 9; Thessalian conflict with, 9–10, 14, 25
Phokikon, 9–10
Plutarch, 26, 53
polis, poleis, 31, 34, 39, 55, 65, 78; significance of, 2–3, 107n4; warfare and, 4–5, 100
Polyaenus, 12–13, 53; Thessaly and, 21
Procles, 32–33; death of, 44

raids: on horseback, 14; at night, 18–23
retreat, 22–23, 42–43, 64–65

sacrifice, 57, 62, 79, 86
salpinx, 62
sanctuaries, 3–4, 9, 73; military dedications at, 23
sentries, 21–22, 59
slingers, 59–65
Sparta, Spartans, 2, 30–32, 44; allies of, 79; Argive conflict with, 91–92; army of, 54–55; in the Corinthian War, 54; hostilities of, 54–65, 77–90; Theban conflict with, 76, 93
spears, 20, 63–64
Stratos, 51, 55, 57
surprise, 21, 40, 79, 82, 87

technology, 6, 26, 99
Tegea, Tegeans, 73, 76–78, 83–85
Tellias of Elis, 18
Thebes, Thebans, 75, 88, 90–91
Thermopylae, 20, 23
Thessaly, Thessalians, 33; allies of, 16; cavalry of, 14, 18; ethnos of, 3–4; hostilities of, 13–18; as threat to Phocis, 9–12
Thucydides, 6, 18–19, 101–2; as historian, 31–32, 42
Tithorea, 16–20, 24–25
topographical studies, 6, 32, 52, 54, 60
towns, 55, 127n96
Trachis, Heraclea in Trachis, 15–16, 33, 44
treatment of dead, 22–23, 44, 65, 68
trophies, 65, 68

upland ethnē, 1, 5–7, 98–99; comparisons between, 99–102. See also Acarnania, Acarnanians; Aetolia, Aetolians; Arcadia, Arcadians; Phocis, Phocians

West (Ozolian) Locris, 34–39

Xenophon, 6, 45, 101–2; as historian, 53–54, 74–75

CPSIA information can be obtained
at www.ICGtesting.com
Printed in the USA
BVHW030015030320
573903BV00005B/21/J